Bringing Up Baby

Bringing Up Baby

Howard Hawks,
director

Gerald Mast, editor

Rutgers University Press

New Brunswick, New Jersey

Second printing, 1994

**Library of Congress Cataloging-in-
Publication Data**

Bringing up baby.

(Rutgers films in print ; v. 10)
Filmography: p.
Bibliography: p.
1. Bringing up baby (Motion picture)
I. Hawks, Howard, 1896–
II. Mast, Gerald, 1940–1990. III. Bringing up
baby (Motion picture) IV. Series.
PN1997.B746 1988   791.43′72   88-6438
ISBN 0-8135-1340-5
ISBN 0-8135-1341-3 (pbk.)

Acknowledgments

I want to thank Candace Mirza and her staff at the University of Chicago Film Library and Study Center for the hundreds of times they were required to wind and rewind reels of film, as I picked over the pieces of *Bringing Up Baby*. John Hall and his staff at the RKO archive in Los Angeles provided access to the film's production files, which were of inestimable value to this project. Mary Corliss at the Museum of Modern Art Film Stills archive, as always, served this scholar efficiently and courteously. My University of Chicago graduate student, A. L. Knight, helped me tidy up some scholarly details. Finally, both Leslie Mitchner and Christina Blake of the Rutgers University Press helped me over the rough spots of preparing the final manuscript. For all your help I am extremely grateful.

Contents

Introduction

"Everything's Gonna Be All Right":
The Making of *Bringing Up Baby*
Gerald Mast

When *Bringing Up Baby* opened at the Radio City Music Hall in March 1938, Frank S. Nugent, film reviewer for the *New York Times* (always a barometer of literate American taste), casually dismissed it as a fatiguing collection of Hollywood clichés: "If you've never been to the movies, *Bringing Up Baby* will be all new to you."[1] In 1981, the Harvard philosopher Stanley Cavell fit *Bringing Up Baby* into a rich tradition of romantic comedy that stretched from Rome to Shakespeare to Hollywood, "invoking Kant's characterization of the aesthetic experience . . . as providing an access to the . . . play of childhood."[2] The four decades between the two responses indicate not only a reversal in the reputation of a specific film but also a general change in thinking about the products of American popular culture. Apparently ordinary Hollywood genre films—westerns, musicals, screwball comedies—prove to be extraordinary mixtures of cultural observation, psychological insight, visual dexterity, and collaborative skill. Balancing formula and innovation, expectation and surprise, many Hollywood studio films bridge our preconceptions of the extraordinary original work and ordinary formula entertainment.

Bringing Up Baby straddles originality and formula as blithely, cheerfully, and rewardingly as any Hollywood studio film ever did. It is a truly extraordinary

---

1. The *New York Times*, March 4, 1938. Nugent's review is reprinted in this book.
2. *Pursuits of Happiness: The Hollywood Comedy of Remarriage* (Cambridge, Mass.: Harvard University Press, 1981), p. 113. Cavell's chapter on *Bringing Up Baby* has also been reprinted in this volume.

ordinary film. Its balance between the ordinary and the extraordinary begins with the earliest stages of its production. The film grew from modest program comedy to big-budget comic special, not by plan but organically, almost by itself. Commentaries in a later section of this volume, including my own, discuss the organic results: the power of structural symmetry—two leopards, two car thefts, two cages; the theme of vision, of sight and insight, that propels so many classic comedies; the effects of spending a night in a magical forest on midsummer eve; the interpenetration of the human and natural worlds—lovers, leopards, dogs, and dead bones. In contrast, my introduction concentrates not on the film's comic accomplishment but on its creative process, the way it grew into itself.

Bringing Up Baby began with two seemingly unrelated but almost simultaneous events. On March 8, 1937, after over six months of complicated negotiations, Howard Hawks signed a two-year contract with RKO pictures at $130,000 per year, for a total of up to six films, with a $260,000 guarantee.[3] On April 10, 1937, *Collier's* magazine published "Bringing Up Baby," a short story by a virtually unknown Hagar Wilde, about a tame panther who gets loose in the Connecticut countryside.[4] RKO, which had been hoping to sign Hawks as early as 1934, did not propose to assign its new prestige director to an unassuming crazy comedy. Hawks's first RKO project was to be the epic *Gunga Din,* on which he had been doing preparatory work in the fall of 1936, even before signing the RKO contract. In April 1937, when RKO was unable to borrow Clark Cable, Spencer Tracy, and Franchot Tone from MGM for *Gunga Din,* the film was postponed. (George Stevens, not Hawks, would eventually shoot it.) RKO asked Hawks to select some other project while he was waiting for *Gunga Din.* Out of the pile of stories, scripts, and treatments that RKO had optioned, Hawks picked Hagar Wilde's "Bringing Up Baby." The RKO management was receptive since they needed a film for Katharine Hepburn, ending a five-year contract that had proven disappointing for both the star and the studio.

The transformation of "Bringing Up Baby" into *Bringing Up Baby* reveals the way the collaborative Hollywood studio system could, at its best, make a silk purse out of, not a sow's ear perhaps, but out of very few and very tiny scraps of silk. At the core of Wilde's story was the film's central situation. There is a panther (not a leopard) named Baby and a dog named George. There is brother

3. All production and contractual details come directly from the production files of *Bringing Up Baby* in the RKO archives in Los Angeles.
4. The original story is reprinted in this volume.

Mark in Brazil and Aunt Elizabeth in Connecticut. Baby responds to the song with his (her? its?) name in the title—"I Can't Give You Anything but Love, Baby." Even some of the film's best lines are in the story: Susan's confusion about whether Baby's liking dogs means that he "eats dogs or is fond of them"; Aunt Elizabeth's describing George as a "perfect little fiend and you know it." On the other hand, David and Susan are already engaged in Wilde's story; the escaped animal is not the means of bringing them together but the threat that pulls them apart. David is not a scientist in the story and his last name is not Huxley. There is no museum, no Swallow, no brontosaurus, no intercostal clavicle, no golf course, no series of adventures on the road to Connecticut, no constable, no drunken gardener, no big-game hunter, and no jail. The story ends with the recapture of Baby in the Connecticut woods.

On June 11, 1937, RKO bought the rights to "Bringing Up Baby" from Hagar Wilde for $1,000. They also brought her to Hollywood to work with veteran scriptwriter Dudley Nichols on the script, at a salary of $10,725 (Nichols was paid $18,958.33). Both the scripting and the shooting of *Bringing Up Baby* were marked by a felicitous combination of happy accident and careful planning that marks so many of the best Hollywood studio films. For Nichols and Wilde, writing *Bringing Up Baby* became a literal labor of love. The two began the romantic affair that carried them through *Bringing Up Baby* and into the writing of *Carefree* for Fred Astaire and Ginger Rogers.[5] The screwball romance of Susan and David on screen was mirrored by the romance of the writers off-screen. If there was love in their collaborative teamwork, there was also fun. That fun comes through successive generations of scripts (dated June 14, June 26, July 22, August 16, and September 16, 1937), where the writers plant ironic comments that indicate they are having a terrific time. In the June 14 tentative outline, they have already named the gardener Barry Fitzgerald. They describe the serenade of Baby on the roof as "a little off-key perhaps, but a pretty good quartet." In the August 16 script they describe Major Horace Applegate as "Victor Moore, Frank Morgan, Robert Benchley, Charles Butterworth, Reginald Owen, Charles Ruggles, or Mary Boland." In the same script they confess a continuity problem: "The off-stage noise you hear is two authors being slightly sick because they don't know what Susan and David have been doing until sunset." And they conclude the July 22 script with a final clinch between Susan and

5. For the information about the Wilde-Nichols affair I am indebted to Vernon Harbin, who has worked in the RKO archives for over fifty years.

David: "We suppose we have to have him kiss her once—he hasn't kissed her for ten thousand feet—so as he kisses her we FADE OUT."

The script took shape by cutting away peripheral incidents and characters to concentrate on the screwball love affair at its center. From the beginning, the writers and director saw the film as a descendant of slapstick silent comedy. Not only did Hawks explicitly refer to this tradition in interviews,[6] but early drafts of the script contain a lengthy scene in a diner that culminates in a mammoth Mack Sennett pie fight between the two lovers. (The pies had been cut by August 16.) The film's clearest Laurel-and-Hardy moment is David's motionless stare at Susan as he silently points to the butterfly net over his head (shot 433), then, in a possible echo of Buster Keaton in *The General,* he lunges at her in a comic gesture of strangulation. The authors also felt the need for bizarrely comic character players, like an Arab bearer named Ali who spoke no English, to accompany Major Applegate (originally named Horatio Pim). Described by the writers as "Mischa Auer, Mischa Auer, or Mischa Auer," Ali served no function in the script except as taster of Applegate's food. Ali did not disappear until the script of September 16, replaced by Gogarty as Applegate's comic companion. Assuring the audience that the film was a love story, not merely a crazy comedy, was a more ticklish problem for the writers. They solved this problem as writers do— with explicit dialogue scenes in which the lovers (especially Susan) confess their feelings for one another. Hawks even shot several of these scenes,[7] then cut them all, realizing that the underlying attraction of the central pair did not require verbal confirmation.

Bringing Up Baby was scheduled to begin shooting on September 1 and finish on October 31. Unfortunately, there were still loose ends in September. RKO had only recently concluded an agreement, for $1,000, with Dorothy Fields and Jimmy McHugh, writers of "I Can't Give You Anything but Love, Baby," for rights to the song. It had not yet concluded an agreement with King Features Syndicate, publishers of a cartoon strip called "Professor Dinglehoofer und His Dog" by Knerr, for the rights to bury a dinosaur bone. The intercostal clavicle came late, midway through the script of August 16, from gagwriter Robert McGowan, who had been hired (at a salary of $7,733.33) to add gags. McGowan recalled March episodes of the Dingelhoofer strip in which the professor's dog had stolen a rare dinosaur bone and buried it. RKO signed an agreement with

---

6. See the McBride interview in this collection.
7. For examples of such scenes see the script variations 6, 16, and 47 in this volume.

King Features to use the idea, for $1,000, on September 21, two days before shooting began.

Even in mid-September casting was incomplete. Only one of the two animal stars had been signed. George would be barked by "Skippy," already familiar to film fans as Asta in *The Thin Man* and Mr. Smith in *The Awful Truth*. But when they couldn't find a suitable panther, they settled on a leopard, "Nissa," recent mother of three cubs and eight-year-old veteran of a dozen films, mostly B-picture jungle adventures. Even Hawks's animal players were established movie veterans. Baby switched from panther to leopard on page 56 of the September 16 script. Neither the script nor the film ever decided on a pronoun to assign to him/her/it.

But who would play opposite Hepburn? From the beginning RKO worried about an "expensive" leading man: "You couldn't even break even if a Hepburn show cost eight hundred grand."[8] RKO floated several inexpensive names for Hawks's consideration: Leslie Howard, Ray Milland, Fredric March. The name of Cary Grant does not appear once in the studio files before he signed his RKO contract on September 14. Where did Grant come from and why did RKO agree to such an expensive leading man? There are two possible answers. One is *The Awful Truth,* which established Grant as a powerful comic performer. *Bringing Up Baby* even refers to *The Awful Truth* when Susan gives Grant his nickname from the earlier film, "Jerry the Nipper." Although not released until November, industry insiders may have heard rumors of its comic power, and Hawks, a close friend of Leo McCarey, may well have seen rushes or a rough cut. A second possibility is that Hawks knew he was going to use Grant all along; he simply kept the name back until the appropriate moment to spring it on the RKO management. With shooting scheduled to begin in just over a week, RKO was in no position to veto such an attractive box-office choice.

Bringing Up Baby was budgeted for fifty-one days of shooting at a cost of $767,676.07, just under the "eight hundred grand" that worried RKO management about a Hepburn show. The film actually took ninety-one shooting days at a cost of $1,096,796.23. Shooting began on September 23 with the scenes in Susan's apartment. The company moved to the Bel Air Country Club for the golf sequence in early October, then to the Random country home (actually the Arthur Ranch) for both indoor and outdoor, daytime and nighttime sequences. It was at the Random home that Hawks's shooting methods of improvisation,

8. Memorandum from Lou Lusty to Sam Briskin, August 10, 1937.

setting up complicated shots, and evolving additional dialogue and business began to stretch the film's schedule and budget. After only a month of shooting, Hawks was seven days behind schedule. In an October 22 memorandum from the film's assistant director, Edward Donahue, to RKO executive Lou Lusty, Donahue confesses: "It is hard to judge the actual number of pages in our script, because Mr. Hawks works from four different treatments, and besides, every scene is rewritten before shooting it." Virtually no line in the film is identical to the one called for in any script, and many are not even remotely similar. While scenes in the Westlake jail were scheduled for five shooting days, Hawks took twelve. Even before shooting began, Lou Lusty informed studio head Sam Briskin: "Hawks is determined in his own quiet, reserved, soft-spoken manner to have his way about the making of this picture." [9]

What then was Hawks's way? Why did the shooting of the film take so much more time than anticipated? One might begin with the specific lines of dialogue and pieces of physical business that do not come from any script and were obviously improvised on the set. In the script there is no comic "Who are you" interchange between Huxley and Aunt Elizabeth at the front door, and, of course, no reference to his going "gay all of a sudden." Applegate does not enter by checking his watch against Susan's inaccurate reports, and he never climbs atop the upper half of a Dutch door, where he, like the phone, is "hung up." There are no references to David's wearing glasses, or taking them off, or breaking them. There are no references to the box David carries perpetually under his arm on the trip to Susan's apartment and Connecticut, nor to the dinner napkin and spoon he carries whenever he leaves the dinner table to pursue George like "Hamlet's ghost," nor to the dinner napkin Susan similarly carries later in the same scene. There is no "Swingin'-Door Susie," no Mickey-the-Mouse and Donald-the-Duck, and no reference to Rodin's *Thinker,* which dominates the opening and closing scenes in the Brontosaurus Hall.

The improvisation that dominates the playing and shooting of *Bringing Up Baby* could only have been accomplished by an attuned group of professionals exercising their craft and trusting one another to return every surprising serve they send in each other's direction. Improvisation means taking chances and taking time; ideas may erupt spontaneously but they then require refinement, polishing, development, selection, and, perhaps, even rejection. Hawks en-

9. Ibid. In the same memorandum Lusty refers to Hawks, somewhat contemptuously, as "that gentleman-director."

couraged Grant and Hepburn to pop in whatever wisecracks that might fit, while Walter Catlett (Slocum) added more yups and throat clearings and Charles Ruggles (Applegate) more stuttering ers and ums than could have been envisioned by any scriptwriter. In this improvisatory circus, Hawks was the ringmaster who kept performers from going over the edge or over the line, keeping them from stepping on each other's ideas. This stream of breathlessly rapid chatter not only gives the film's dialogue a spontaneous energy; it also converts articulate patterns of human speech into the pure physicality of sound, a kind of verbal music. Except for background music at the Ritz-Plaza and the occasional singing or playing of Baby's theme song, including its brief orchestral reprise to end the film, *Bringing Up Baby* has no musical score whatever. (The film's musical director, Roy Webb, had very little to do.) Its music is the breathless chatter of human speech.

Uniquely Hawksian about the film is its physicality, whether the physicality of sound and gesture or the building of scenes around concrete props and objects, easily overlooked but as important as the dialogue: the dinosaur skeleton and all the petrified artifacts of zoological life in the Brontosaurus Hall; David's top hat, which begins and ends the scene in the Ritz-Plaza; the golf clubs, pin, and ball; the box, the bone, the boots in Susan's garden; David's toasted sock, Susan's broken heel, Slocum's two-fer cigar, Lehman's cigarette case, even the croquet mallet and butterfly net (which provides an explanation of David's lunatic behavior for the circus drivers), even the chair with which David prods the "bad" leopard (also played by Nissa) into a cell, and upon which David leans for relief after his heroism. For Hawks, this contact with concrete physical objects anchors a wildly improbable farcical tale in the solid stuff of physical reality.

Hawks's shooting style works similarly. Although any number of shots in the film are conventional, functional Hollywood two-shots or group shots, others are extraordinary in their complicated choreography of movement, space, and time. Hawks sets up certain shots, usually the climactic ones that deliver the payoff for an entire comic sequence, in complicated, difficult, and demanding ways that could have been accomplished far more simply if far less effectively. Perhaps the best example is shot 93, in which David tries to protect Susan's exposed backside when she tries to escape his clutches. The shot begins with Susan's rushing away from him, assuming he merely wants to scold her for tearing his coat. He pursues her avidly, knowing that the train of her dress has been torn away. He backs her against a pillar, protecting her rear end from view. She resolutely stalks away from him into the middle of the dining room. He follows her closely and claps his

top hat over her backside with his right hand. When she turns in the other direction to avoid him, he switches the top hat to his left hand and claps it over her
backside once again. As they talk in the center of the dining room, he uses both
hands to keep the top hat over her rear end. When she turns, he twirls behind her
to maneuver her back to the pillar once again. When Susan refuses to listen, the
exasperated David gives up and lets Susan walk away, abandoning her to her
fate. As she prepares to flounce off in triumph, she sweeps her right arm behind
her to lift her train, only to discover she has no train to flounce with. This time
she herself scampers back against the pillar and asks David for his help. Only
then does the shot end.

The shot is a complete little story, with a beginning, middle, and end, from
David's strategy for protecting Susan to her discovering her need for his help. It
is also a kind of dance that pivots around a pillar, the two partners moving
backward and forward, right and left, turning and twirling, a parody of the kind
of tango the patrons of this very restaurant might perform. Finally, it allows the
two performers to demonstrate their perfect timing and physical skills, a reference perhaps to Grant's own training on the vaudeville stage. There is no way to
shoot this scene more effectively or more demandingly for the two performers.

A similar principle marks shot 232, in which Susan steals Lehman's car. As she backs out of the parking place in Lehman's limousine, David rushes into the frame, his box under one arm and the package of Baby's meat under the other. Susan tells David to jump aboard while the car is moving. He tosses his packages into the car through the window and jumps on the running board of the moving vehicle, like a classic movie gangster, the second time in the film David has hopped aboard the running board of a "wrong car" that Susan is driving. While the shot could have ended with their departure, Hawks prolongs it until Lehman and Slocum rush into the vacated parking space, in effect taking the place formerly occupied by Lehman's car. Only after Lehman has informed Slocum of the theft does the shot end. Once again, a single shot tells a complete little story— from the theft of the car to the report of the theft in the same space where the theft occurred.

In shot 445 Hawks's two stars actually swim a river. The shot begins with Susan and David midstream, after discovering that the stream was deeper than Susan promised. The shot follows the two swimmers as they return to the riverbank they just left. After a brief argument, David dives back into the river to reach the other side. Susan and the camera follow. Only after they reach the other bank, where Susan and David pull themselves from the stream, does the shot end. Like so many Hawks shots, it emphasizes both the physicality of the action and the dexterity of the players. So does shot 40, in which Hepburn not only sinks a twenty-five-foot putt in a continuous long shot, but Grant runs after the ball to scoop it out of the cup as soon as it drops. In the same way, Hawks depicts David's lifting of Susan, dangling in midair above the crumbled dinosaur (shot 670), out of the air and onto the safety of the scaffolding in an extended shot that both exploits their physicality and reveals the connection of the business to vaudeville and the circus. The film's innumerable pratfalls reveal the same physicality of space and dexterity of the performers. Susan and David take pratfalls through, into, and out of the frame, sliding on olives, tripping over branches, disappearing through car windows. The different relation of Hawks's camera to each pratfall simultaneously produces comic surprise and droll understatement.

Similarly understated is the lengthy shot 528 in Slocum's jail. As Slocum interrogates Susan off-frame, David stands alone in his cell, muttering. He discovers that the cell door is unlocked. He pushes it open, walks over to Susan's cell, and taps Slocum on the shoulder (as he repeatedly taps others on the shoulder to get their attention throughout the film). Only after David's repeated taps does Slocum turn his attention away from the chattering Susan. To get Slocum's full attention, David takes the constable by the arm and conducts him to a place of supposed quiet and privacy, his own cell. Slocum accompanies David into the cell, only to realize where he is. He panics and rushes out of the cell, criticizing Elmer for improperly locking up a dangerous criminal. When Slocum leaves the keys in the lock, David points out that the cell is still not locked. Only when Slocum locks the cell door securely does the shot end. Call this shot a little story that begins with an unlocked jail cell and ends with its secure locking.

Even Hawks's most banally functional shots demonstrate the subtle wisdom of certain setups. Conveying the presence of a second, bad leopard in Connecticut is a necessary part of the plot, which Hawks imparts in a single shot (456) that is simultaneously economical and interesting. While circus employees discuss taking the "bad cat" to Bridgeport, Hawks flanks the frame with two visual attractions. On the far left of the frame is the silhouette of a hoochy-coochy dancer, performing her bumps and grinds in a circus sideshow. To the far right of the frame is the bad leopard in a cage, observing the people center frame. The balanced cooch dancer and leopard provide visual diversion (indeed both are circus attractions) in a painfully necessary exposition scene. The balanced fig-ures on either side of the frame also continue the film's paralleling of female sexuality and feline sensuality, which begins with Baby's entrance in shot 134 as Susan talks to David on the telephone.

Hawks also uses his frames to imply intimate revelations. The first close-up in the film is shot 101, in Susan's apartment, when she hears David is to marry Miss Swallow the next day. Hawks simply breaks off Susan's chatter and cuts to her response to the information, a pause or caesura of both sight and sound, then returns to her chatter in middle-distance shots. Because there are very few close-ups in the film, their spare but deliberate use allowed Hawks to eliminate all of the scripted scenes in which Susan confesses her fondness for David. A close-up is confession enough. Perhaps no clearer examples of the difference between the way writers and directors think about conveying narrative information can be found by comparing Hawks's shot 101 and the Wilde-Nichols's dialogue scene of a "romantic spot beside a stream" (script variation 16) or the brief breakup scene between David and Miss Swallow in the film (shot 627) and the lengthy one Wilde and Nichols wrote (script variation 70).

Shooting finally ended on January 6, 1938, with the scenes outside Peabody's house—a bit frosty for June, with faint puffs of breath visible under the dia-logue. The goal in editing was to tighten a film that everyone agreed was too long without removing its essential comic business and spirit. The first cut of the film ran 10,150 feet, which RKO sent to the Production Code Administration, the industry's self-censorship board, for approval in January. The PCA's only concern was Katharine Hepburn's ripped dress: "borderline business . . . which might be deleted by a number of censor boards." The PCA also worried about the reference to living political figures—Al Smith and Jim Farley—which the film amended to Mickey-the-Mouse and Donald-the-Duck. The PCA paid no attention whatever to the film's two most outrageous moments: Cary Grant's proclamation of going gay and Katharine Hepburn's reference to George's bodily functions. In shot 305 David asks Susan where George is apt to go; she responds that he's apt to "go" anywhere, which Hepburn follows with a giggle to underline the double entendre. Either members of the PCA did not hear or did not understand these suggestions. *Bringing Up Baby* was awarded PCA seal #3752 in February 1938.

By February 18 the film had been cut to its final 9,204 feet and readied for shipment to New York. RKO had tried an even tighter cut, to 9,050 feet, and Pandro S. Berman, who had replaced Sam Briskin as RKO studio head, wanted to eliminate five minutes more. Hawks, Cary Grant (who played an important advisory role in cutting the film), and associate producer Cliff Reid disagreed with Berman. In the end Berman relented: he didn't want to be wrong "where a million dollars is involved." [10] The trimming of the film's footage followed the same principle as the building of the script. Peripheral scenes for the character players were removed (particularly Gogarty and Applegate—see script variation 33), reaction shots of amazement were deleted from the jail scene (as were reaction shots of Alice Swallow on the telephone), and lesser comic scenes were either trimmed (the confrontation of the circus truck drivers with David, "This guy ain't got all his buttons") or cut altogether (the arrival of the zoo keepers at the Random house, who come to a similar conclusion about Aunt Elizabeth's buttons).

Perhaps the most significant deletions were three explicit love scenes for Susan and David (variations 6, 16, and 47), which Hawks's cinema style had made unnecessary, and a lengthy parody of psychoanalysis for Susan and Lehman (variations 48 and 49), which may not have been very funny or which may simply have been inessential. Some of the cuts may have left explanatory holes in the plot: for example, whatever happened to Baby's thirty pounds of raw meat? Whatever happened to the zoo keepers who responded to David's telephone call? The compelling rhythm of the film carried it over these holes in the logical

10. Memorandum from Pandro S. Berman, February 1, 1938.

narrative. Hawks frequently patched shots together that did not quite match or whose dialogue did not connect. Overlapping dialogue, from both on- and off-frame, eased the connection and erased any sense of discontinuity in either the film's action or editing.

The figure of a million dollars had become a target for the film as it was for David's museum. In going forty days over schedule, the film also went almost $330,000 over budget. Most of the excess can be attributed to the additional shooting time. While sets and props for the film went only $5,000 over budget, all of the players, including Skippy, Nissa, and their trainers, had to be paid almost double their contractual salaries. Hepburn and Grant, contracted at $72,500 and $75,000 respectively, were paid $121,680.50 and $123,437.50 for their work on the film. But the biggest single budgetary expense was Hawks himself. His salary, budgeted against the film at $88,046.25, approximately one-third his $260,000 contractual guarantee, was finally charged as $202,500. The reason is that *Bringing Up Baby,* by agreement of Hawks and RKO, would be the only film he would make under his RKO contract. Hawks was also paid an additional $40,000 to confirm the termination. In effect, Hawks received $242,500 for making *Bringing Up Baby,* all but $40,000 of it charged against the film's costs, while RKO "saved" $17,500 on Hawks's contract. The termination agreement was concluded amicably for both parties on March 21, 1938.

In bringing the production to such an amicable conclusion, *Bringing Up Baby* confirmed that it was a thoroughly amicable film—from start to finish, from scripting, through playing and shooting, to final budgetary resolution. Even at $1,096,796 the film showed a modest profit.[11] In its initial run, domestic revenues were $715,000 and foreign revenues $394,000, for a total of $1,109,000—just over its cost. In a 1940–41 reissue, domestic revenues were $95,000 and foreign revenues $55,000, for an additional $150,000. The total revenues of $1,259,000 meant a final profit of $163,000 when RKO closed its books on the film.[12] Both inside the film and outside it in the studio offices, the production displayed a spirit of amicability that took its cue from the film's running gag: Susan's assurance that "everything's gonna be all right."

11. I disagree with Richard B. Jewell, "How Howard Hawks Brought Baby Up," *Journal of Popular Film and Television,* 11, no. 4 (Winter 1984), pp. 158–165. Jewell seems to have considered only the film's initial domestic revenues in reaching his different conclusion.

12. These figures were certified in a final RKO audit on June 15, 1953. The question had been raised of whether Hawks was entitled to additional payment as a percentage of the film's profits. According to Hawks's contract with RKO, he would not participate in a percentage of profits until the film's revenues reached $1,875,000.

This amicability differs strikingly from the familiar Hollywood myths about the conflict of artistic temperament and commercial forces. One might call the two dominant myths "The Embattled Genius" and "The Out-of-Control Egomaniac." The embattled genius struggles mightily against the stupidities of studio policy, either producing a masterpiece in spite of the studio (say Orson Welles with *Citizen Kane*) or suffering the disastrous consequences of studio contamination (say Orson Welles with the ending of *The Magnificent Ambersons*). It is interesting that Welles, the classic embattled genius, fought his battles at the very studio where Hawks made *Bringing Up Baby*, against some of the very executives with whom Hawks worked things out so peacefully. The out-of-control egomaniac suggests the myth of talent run amok, beyond the bounds of either artistic judgment or commercial possibility (a myth that stretches from *Intolerance* to *Heaven's Gate*). In contrast, *Bringing Up Baby* suggests a myth of Amicable Collaboration—a confidence of the writers, players, production personnel, and studio executives in one another and, especially, in the director.

Why did RKO management allow Hawks to run 50 percent over budget and 80 percent over schedule on the film? Why did they confirm their satisfaction with such an advantageous contract termination for the director? One reason may be incompetent management at RKO, interloper among the major studios (with the coming of synchronized sound), organized by a mix of radio and vaudeville people, not experienced movie people like the other major studios. RKO studio management was in perpetual chaos from the company's beginning (like the switch from Briskin to Berman during the shooting of *Bringing Up Baby*). The signing of Hawks, like the signing of Orson Welles two years later, reflected the studio's belief in the commercial power of prestige. RKO was apparently willing to let the prestigious Hawks play the game in "his own quiet, reserved, soft-spoken manner," and Hawks used that gentlemanly manner to get his way with both production and management personnel.

Perhaps Hawks's greatest general value to the film industry was his way with stars—he could make stars or remake them or reconfirm their power. Katharine Hepburn emerged from *Bringing Up Baby* as a much brighter and lighter comic actor than anyone previously expected,[13] while Cary Grant confirmed his comedic ability to play against his own suave persona. Both stars emerged from the film as more valuable commodities—especially Hepburn, whose problem in five years at RKO had been that audiences perceived her as cold, lofty, and

13. Many of the film's original reviews refer to Hepburn's surprising ability at low comedy. *Life* magazine called her "the surprise of the picture" in the "Movie of the Week," February 28, 1938.

contemptuous; an Actress, not a person. To increase the value of a star was a potential future benefit for RKO. The amicable settlement with Hawks can also be attributed to the same kind of future consideration. RKO might someday want to hire Hawks again. In point of fact, Hawks would make three films for RKO in the decade between 1941 and 1952.[14] In contrast, when Hawks's MGM contract ended in a bitter fight with Louis B. Mayer in 1933, Hawks vowed never to work for MGM again. And he never did. Evidence indicates that RKO was unwilling to lose Hawks's good will—and they didn't even need to lose money to keep it.

Its amicable spirit of collaboration and confidence make *Bringing Up Baby* the special film it is, a very ordinary Hollywood comedy raised to an extraordinary level of accomplishment by attuned writers, performers, and artisans, supported by the confidence of the studio in the project. More than anything else, the confidence, the judgment, and the integrity of Howard Hawks kept the project bubbling along, skating brilliantly over the surface of ordinary probability and narrative logic. It was Hawks who knew all along that everything was gonna be all right. On *Bringing Up Baby* he turned out to be as correct as Susan Vance.

14. Hawks's RKO future was not without its bumpy moments—particularly a disagreement with Howard Hughes, Hawks's sometime friend, who bought RKO in 1941, over interference on *The Outlaw*. When Hughes sold RKO in 1959 he kept the rights to six RKO films—*The Lost Patrol, Kitty Foyle, The Last Days of Pompeii, Stage Door, My Favorite Wife,* and *Bringing Up Baby*. Although Hughes's reasons for wanting these films is unclear, his fondness for *Bringing Up Baby* may have rested on the presence of Katharine Hepburn, with whom Hughes was having an affair in 1938. Hughes finally sold the six films to Twentieth Century–Fox in 1961.

Howard Hawks
A Biographical Sketch

Howard Winchester Hawks (May 30, 1896–December 26, 1977) was born in Goshen, Indiana. A child of the American Midwest, like Thomas Edison, in the era of America's romance with inventors and inventions, Hawks would travel on his love of machines to the art of machines, the motion picture. The son of a wealthy paper manufacturer and grandson of a wealthy lumberman, Hawks moved West with his family in 1906, where the warmer and drier air was kinder to his mother's asthma. The movies themselves traveled West at about the same time. The young Hawks moved between East and West for his education— prep school at Phillips Exeter, graduation from Pasadena High School, and a degree in engineering from Cornell University. He began to spend his free time with the new movie companies that were turning Hollywood into a company town. In 1917 he worked as a prop boy for Famous Players–Lasky, assisting Marshall Neilan on Mary Pickford films. Later that year he joined the U.S. Army Corps as a flying instructor. He would combine his two loves—for flying and filming—in many later movies.

In the early 1920s, Hawks shared a Hollywood house with several young men on the threshold of movie distinction—Allan Dwan and Irving Thalberg among them. Thalberg recommended Hawks to Jesse Lasky, who in 1924 was looking for a bright young man to run the story department of Famous Players. For two

From an encyclopedia entry by Gerald Mast for *World Film Directors*, published by the H. W. Wilson Company in 1988.

years Hawks supervised the development and writing of every script for the company that would become Paramount, the most powerful studio in 1920s Hollywood. William Fox invited Hawks to his company in 1926, offering him a chance to direct the scripts he had developed. *The Road to Glory* was the first of eight films Hawks directed at Fox in the next three years, all of them silent except *The Air Circus* (1928) and *Trent's Last Case* (1929), part-talkies in the years of Hollywood transition between silence and sound.

Of the Fox silents, only *Fig Leaves* (1926) and *A Girl in Every Port* (1928) survive. The former is a comedy of gender, tracing domestic warfare from Adam and Eve to their modern descendants. *A Girl in Every Port* is "a love story between two men," in Hawks's words, about two brawling sailor buddies who fall for the same woman. The motif of two friends who share the same love would recur in many Hawks sound films, particularly in the 1930s (*Tiger Shark, Today We Live, Barbary Coast, The Road to Glory*). The motif of two wandering pals, enjoying the sexual benefits of travel, returns with a gender reversal in *Gentlemen Prefer Blondes*—when Marilyn Monroe and Jane Russell play the two traveling buddies.

It was the coming of synchronized sound that allowed Hawks to become an independent film stylist. *The Dawn Patrol* (1930) was a remarkable early sound film in many respects. Its pacifism mirrored the reaction against the First World War in a period that produced such antiwar films as *What Price Glory?, The Big Parade,* and *All Quiet on the Western Front*. The flying sequences in *The Dawn Patrol* were as photographically brilliant as they were aeronautically accurate. Flying and filming had never before been so beautifully mated. Even more than his flying sequences, Hawks's flavorful dialogue sounded as if uttered by human beings, not orating actors. The affected, stilted diction that marked the talk in so many early talkies was entirely missing from Hawks's film. The dialogue proceeded spontaneously, casually, as if improvised on the spot. Dialogue in Hawks's films would always suggest the feel and flavor of improvised conversation rather than scripted lines. One reason, of course, is that Hawks not only permitted his players to improvise but hired players who would and could.

Scarface (1930–32) brought this spontaneous improvisation down from the wartime skies to the urban streets. *Scarface* remains simultaneously one of the most brutal and funniest of gangster films: gangster destruction mirrors the childish glee of having "fun," one of the most important words in Hawks's critical lexicon. Hawks's gangster hero, a fanciful portrait of Al Capone sketched by Paul Muni, is not only a spiteful kid; he nurses an inarticulate and repressed sexual attraction to his own sister and guns down the best friend (George Raft) who invades this Freudian turf. Hawks's recurrent piece of physical business for Raft—the flipping of a coin—has survived ever after as the quintessential definition of a gangster. It introduced the familiar Hawks method of deflecting psychological revelation from explicit dialogue to the subtle handling of physical objects.

Scarface also introduced Hawks to two important professional associates: Howard Hughes, who produced the film and would run through Hawks's entire career as both ally and enemy; and Ben Hecht, the hard-drinking, wisecracking writer who, like Hawks, wanted to make films that were "fun." Hecht and Hawks were kindred cynics who would work together for twenty years. Hughes, however, had his own war to win. A lifetime foe of industry censorship boards, Hughes resisted attempts to soften *Scarface*. He finally relented, not by toning down its brutal humor but by inserting a drab lecture on the social responsibility of voters. He also concluded the film with the fallen mobster's whining cowardice to take the glamour out of his defiance. Hughes was so enraged by the emendations that he withdrew the film from circulation for four decades. Only his death returned it to American audiences.

Hawks traveled to other studios and genres in the 1930s. At Columbia, *The Criminal Code* (1931) gave him a prison picture. *The Crowd Roars* (1932) at Warner Bros. was his first racecar picture. Auto racing was another Hawks hobby, who designed the automobile that won the 1936 Indianapolis 500. *Tiger Shark* (1932) for Warners' subsidiary, First National, took Hawks to sea with Edward G. Robinson and the fishing fleet. Hawks depicted the professional business of tuna fishing in this film with the same documentary accuracy and detail that he devoted to flying in *The Dawn Patrol* or driving in *The Crowd Roars*. Hawks returned to wartime professionals in *Today We Live* (1933) and *The Road to Glory* (1936). The former of the two films, adapted from "Turn About," a story by William Faulkner, began Hawks's personal and professional association with Faulkner. Like Hawks, Faulkner loved flying and, like Hawks, had lost a brother in an air crash. Like Hawks, Faulkner also liked drinking and storytelling. Hawks and Faulkner would drink, fly, and tell stories together over the next twenty years. *Today We Live*, made at MGM, began another Hawks pattern— walking off the set when studio bosses interfered with his filming. *Today We Live* was the only film Hawks completed under a three-picture agreement with MGM.

Perhaps Hawks's most interesting genre films in the 1930s were screwball comedies. Hawks was a master of the genre that has come to represent one of the period's most revealing glimpses of American aspirations. While Hawks always added comic touches to serious stories—from *Scarface* in 1930 to *El Dorado* in 1967—the pure comedy provided even broader comic possibilities. Since love and friendship had always been closely intertwined in Hawks films, and since Hawks friends fight as much as they talk, fight because they are friends, each convinced of his own rightness, it was a very short step from male friends to male-female lovers. Hawks's screwball comedies are distinctive in that the two lovers are as much friends as lovers and as much fighting opponents as spiritual kin, comedies of ego in which two strong personalities fight because they love.

The first of Hawks's screwball comedies, *Twentieth Century* (1934), was adapted from a stage play by Ben Hecht and Charles MacArthur. Along with Frank Capra's *It Happened One Night* of the same year and at the same studio, Columbia, *Twentieth Century* was one of the films that defined the screwball genre. The two warring egos of *Twentieth Century* are monomaniacal Oscar Jaffe (played by the monomaniacal ham, John Barrymore) and his actress Galatea, Lily Garland (played by Hawks's own cousin, Carole Lombard, in her first major comic role). The film demonstrated several Hawks traits: a breathless dialogue pace that refused to soften or sentimentalize the combat; the deflection of internal psychological motivations onto concrete external objects—the tangible, photographic means of making clear inner feelings that his characters never verbally express. The film also set the two essential Hawks patterns with movie stars: making a familiar star into a comic parody of his own persona (as Hawks would later do with Cary Grant, Humphrey Bogart, John Wayne, and Marilyn Monroe); establishing the persona of a total unknown (future Hawks Galateas included Frances Farmer, Rita Hayworth, Jane Russell, Lauren Bacall, Montgomery Clift, Joan Collins, and Angie Dickinson).

Bringing Up Baby (1938), at RKO, was the first of four Hawks screwball comedies with Cary Grant. In these films, the smooth Grant not only becomes the alter ego of the icily smooth Howard Hawks behind the camera; he also becomes the butt of jokes that the world longs to inflict on the icily smooth. Hawks mercilessly humiliates Grant with degrading attacks on his handsome masculinity, usually by removing his masculine guise and putting him in a dress. In *His Girl Friday*, adapted from *The Front Page,* another Hecht-MacArthur stage hit, Hawks changes the gender of the original newspaper reporter from male to female (Rosalind Russell), initiating a contest with her editor (Grant) that is both love and war. In the end, she recovers her eyesight to discover love in their combative friendship.

In *I Was a Male War Bride* (1949), Grant and Hawks travel to postwar Germany for another love story that begins as egotistic war (with Ann Sheridan). But in *Monkey Business* (1952) Grant returns to domestic normalcy, discovering that placid married life (with Ginger Rogers) may be more appropriate to middle-age than to dynamic youth (with Marilyn Monroe). In this Darwinian comedy of youth and age, Hawks realizes that both he and his colleagues (star Grant and writer Hecht) are a generation older than they were at the dawn of screwball comedy. Despite its careful symmetrical patterning, the spirit of screwball comedy has itself grown old in *Monkey Business*. Hawks would make only one more comedy, *Man's Favorite Sport?* (1964), which seemed to prove how old both the genre and the director had become. Because Grant himself felt too old for the role, Hawks tried to dress Rock Hudson as the young Cary Grant. Grant made only one film for Hawks that was not a comedy, *Only Angels Have Wings* (1939), a return to the professional world of flyers and the struggle among vocation, love, and friendship. As usual, the Hawks hero finds both a testing ground and meeting place for his professional commitment, personal integrity, and human feeling.

Hawks spent the early 1940s with two personalities less slick, cool, and distant than Grant. Gary Cooper made only two films for Hawks, both in 1941, softer and warmer reflections of the war years. *Sergeant York,* produced at Warners by Jesse Lasky, Hawks's first boss, features Cooper as the homespun pacifist who became a World War I hero. Hawks most honored film in his lifetime, *Sergeant York* brought him his only Academy Award nomination for best director. *Ball of Fire* takes Cooper into a den of isolated academics, where the lair of seven emotional dwarfs is invaded by a Snow White stripper (Barbara Stanwyck).

If Cooper became one wartime alternative to Grant, Bogart became another. The Bogart quality Hawks exploited, quite the opposite of Cooper's open warmth, was hiding his heart behind the mask of moral indifference and emotional taciturnity. Since Hawks had always liked characters who did and felt more than they said, Bogart became an especially effective partner for Hawks's newest find, Lauren Bacall. Hawks changed Bacall's name, hairstyle, vocal register—much as Oscar Jaffe did Lily Garland's in *Twentieth Century*—and mated Bogart and Bacall in two films at Warners.

For *To Have and Have Not* (1944), Hawks bet his friend Ernest Hemingway that he could make a good movie out of his "worst novel." Hawks, Faulkner, and frequent collaborator Jules Furthman set the adventures of a Hawks trio, Bogart, Bacall, and quirky best friend Walter Brennan, against a background of wartime espionage in the Caribbean. Like *Casablanca,* Warners' wartime hit of 1942, *To Have and Have Not* brings the loner Bogart to a patriotic affirmation; unlike *Casablanca,* the affirmation comes not from a romantic renunciation but a reconciliation of love, friendship, and vocation—as is typical of Hawks. *The Big Sleep* (1946), a wittily sexy adaptation of the Raymond Chandler novel, plunged the combatative lovers into a labyrinthine maze of plot that Hawks deliberately refused to elucidate. In Bogart and Bacall, Hawks had found a matched pair who contrasted warm interiors with cool exteriors, powerful feelings with protective reticence. His on-screen team generated even more interest with their off-screen romance and marriage.

If the decade and a half from 1938 to 1952 marked Hawks's Cary Grant period, split by the war years, the final two decades of Hawks's creative career marked his John Wayne period. *Red River* (1948) was both Hawks's first Wayne film and his first western. Although he began a Billy the Kid film for Howard Hughes in 1941, *The Outlaw,* Hawks quit when the two egos clashed. Hughes's resentment had considerable impact on *Red River,* for he demanded that Hawks delete footage resembling scenes in *The Outlaw* or face a lawsuit. *Red River* was Hawks's most epic film, the story of a cattle drive from Texas to Kansas, in which the wanderers travel thousands of miles, facing both the external challenge of the physical universe and the internal struggle against their own psychological defects. Wayne played the older rancher, Thomas Dunson, the man whose will, determination, and courage had built a cattle empire; Montgomery Clift, in his first film role, played his young partner, Matthew Garth—Dunson's adopted son, friend, and "lover." When Dunson's unswerving commitment to his own power, view, and values threatens the success of the drive, Matthew usurps Dunson's command in a western *Mutiny on the Bounty.* Dunson swears to track Matthew down and kill him. He tracks him down, but as father faces son, friend faces friend, and two men who love each other face one another in the final showdown, Dunson learns that the words of a vow spoken in haste and anger are not worth defending. In *Red River* Hawks shaped the essential John Wayne pattern—the inflexible man of honor, will, and determination who can respond flexibly to human trials.

After *Red River* Hawks and Wayne took three more trips to the Old West—in *Rio Bravo* (1959), *El Dorado* (1967), and *Rio Lobo* (1970). They also traveled to the wilds of Africa in *Hatari!* (1962), where Hawks's extended sequences of tracking wild animals provide another exquisite film document of courageous and knowledgeable professionals performing an exotically difficult job. As both Wayne and Hawks grow older, their films together express their age while defying it, settling into a comfortable social landscape with comfortable friends to perform jobs that would even be difficult for much younger men.

Those late Hawks films that do not saunter with Wayne explore other genre trails. *The Big Sky* (1952) and *Land of the Pharaohs* (1955) follow the paths of history sketched by *Red River*—the former into the American past of Lewis and Clark, the latter into ancient Egypt, Hawks's last collaboration with William Faulkner before the novelist's death. *The Thing* (1950), produced by Hawks but directed by his editor, Christian Nyby, was Hawks's only dip into the popular postwar genre of science fiction—confronting the cosmic unknown in a new era of nuclear bombs and space travel. *Red Line 7000* (1965) was Hawks's return to the racecar world of *The Crowd Roars*.

The final fifteen years of Hawks's life brought him wider public recognition than he had ever known in his busiest years of studio activity. Respected within the industry as one of Hollywood's sturdiest directors of top stars in taut stories, Hawks acquired little fame outside it until the appearance of the *auteur* theory in France, England, and America between 1953 and 1962. To some extent, it was the *auteur* theory that made Hawks a household name and Hawks that made the *auteur* theory a household idea. In an attack against both European "art films" and film adaptations of literary classics, proponents of the *auteur* view— François Truffaut, Jacques Rivette, Peter Wollen, V. S. Perkins, Ian Cameron, Andrew Sarris, John Belton, William Paul—looked for directors of ordinary Hollywood genre films whose work displayed both consistent visual style and consistent narrative motifs.

Hawks was the model of such a director. He spent fifteen years in interviews denying any serious aspirations, claiming that all he wanted to do was tell a story. But a Hawks story had an unmistakable look, feel, and focus. His visual style, though apparently unobtrusive, had always been built on consistent visual conventions: a careful attention to the sources and qualities of light (the lamps that always hang in a Hawks frame); the counterpoint of on-frame action and off-frame sound; the improvisationally casual sound of a Hawks conversation; the refusal of characters to articulate their inner feelings; the transference of emotional material from dialogue to physical objects; symmetrically balanced frames that produce a dialectic between opposite halves of the frame. So, too, Hawks's films, no matter what the genre, handled consistent plot motifs: a small band of professionals committed to doing their jobs as well as they could; pairs of friends who were also lovers and rivals; reversals of conventional gender expectations about manly men and womanly women. Dressed as familiar Hollywood genre pictures, Hawks's films were psychological studies of people in action, simultaneously trying to be true to themselves and faithful to the group. In his classic conflict of love and honor, Hawks was the American movie descendant of Corneille.

He died at the age of eighty-one in Palm Springs, California, from complications arising from a broken hip when he tripped over one of his dogs. Even as he grew older he continued to ride his motorcycle and raise his martini glass. He had married three times, seeking perpetually young and beautiful women as he grew steadily older. He had four children, two of whom work in the film industry. His primary legacies are his films and his professional persona as the modest tinkerer in a bombastic business, a man who could make the structures and strictures of that business work for him, so he could tell the stories he wanted to tell in the way he wanted to tell them.

Bringing Up Baby

Bringing Up Baby

This verbal transcription of *Bringing Up Baby* is based on a comparison of the actual 102-minute release version of the film and the studio's official continuity script of March 23, 1938, which remains the authoritative legal version. After a Hollywood film was shot and assembled, a studio assigned a staff writer to produce a continuity script, an accurate literary transcription of the finished film. This continuity script served as a legal representation of the film's content for copyright purposes. In that era of film history and copyright law (1912–1942), films were copyrighted as literary properties, not as films. Given its primarily legal purpose, the studio's continuity script was frequently longer than the final release version of the film, containing scenes that were subsequently cut, since it made legal sense to protect as much material as possible. The continuity script's legal purpose, however, made certain accuracies of dialogue, shots, and scenes unimportant.

As a result, the official studio version of *Bringing Up Baby*'s script has little relationship to the film. Many sequences that were shot were later deleted—whether whole scenes or brief exchanges. I have indicated the location of these deletions with footnote numbers in my transcription, and the deleted passages can be found in the section of "Script Variations" following the transcription of the film.

In addition to deleted passages or scenes, there are major differences between the studio's script and my transcription, which reflects the actual film. There is no correlation between claims about the number and plan of shots in the studio continuity and the actual shot and scene breakdown of the film. There is a very low correlation between lines of dialogue noted in the studio script and the actual lines uttered (or muttered) in the film. This low correlation indicates that the staff writer on this project, M. Kent, took the lines of dialogue from successive generations of scripts rather than from listening to the film itself. Indeed, the title page of the studio script indicates that it was assembled from the cutter's continuity script, not the film. Trying to hear the actual words, half-words, grunts, groans, and ahems is an extremely laborious task. As accurately as I have tried to note what I was able to hear, with repeated journeys of the film across the sound heads of a Moviola in slow motion, there are still sounds that escaped me and remain an auditory blur. This fact is a reminder of the sheer impossibility of turning a film into a book, no matter how conscientious the effort or how close the approximation.

Another major difference between the studio's continuity script and this one is that Kent felt obligated to indicate the emotions and intentions of characters in parentheses (hopefully, disappointedly, expectantly, etc.), fearing that the dramatic significance of lines and actions might be unclear without them. Many passages that were deleted from the film and appear in the section of "Script Variations" provide examples of these descriptions. I have removed these assignments of emotion—some were too simple, others simply inaccurate, and most were unnecessary—to let the lines, actions, and images speak for themselves. I have tried to confine myself in this transcription to facts—visual and vocal—rather than interpretations. The difference between the two indicates yet another difficulty of turning films into books.

More interpretive and less factual has been my use of the terminology of shots on which all film scholars depend. ECU (extreme close-up), CU (close-up), MCU (medium close-up), MS (medium shot), MLS (medium long shot), and LS (long shot) indicate approximate descriptions of codified perceptions, not empirical facts. This film scholar will confess that as confident as I am in the accuracy of the notation of shots and dialogue in this transcription, my indications of the distances of shots represent something between a guess, a hope, and a judgment.

Credits

Director
Howard Hawks

Producer
Howard Hawks

Associate Producer
Cliff Reid

Screenplay
Dudley Nichols and Hagar Wilde, based on the short story, "Bringing Up Baby," by Hagar Wilde; additional dialogue by Robert McGowan and Gertrude Purcell (both uncredited)

Cinematographer
Russell Metty

Art Director
Van Nest Polglase

Associate Art Director
Perry Ferguson

Set Dresser
Darrell Silvera

Gowns
Howard Greer

Musical Director
Roy Webb

Sound Recording
John L. Cass

Editor
George Hively

Special Effects
Vernon C. Walker

Assistant Director
Edward Donahue

Locations
RKO studios in Hollywood, California; the Bel Air Country Club; the Arthur Ranch in the San Francisco Valley; Twentieth Century–Fox backlot (Westlake street)

Shooting Schedule
September 23, 1937–January 6, 1938

Process
Black and White

Release Date
March 3, 1938

Length
102 minutes

Cast

David Huxley	**Hannah Gogarty**
Cary Grant	Leona Roberts
Susan Vance	**Peabody**
Katharine Hepburn	George Irving
Major Applegate	**Alice Swallow**
Charles Ruggles	Virginia Walker
Aunt Elizabeth	**Elmer**
May Robson	John Kelly
Constable Slocum	**Professor La Touche, Caddies,**
Walter Catlett	**Louis, Patron, Joe (Bartender),**
Dr. Lehman	**Clerk, Hat-Check Girl, Delivery**
Fritz Feld	**Man, Joe (Circus Driver), Mac,**
	Circus Manager, Man at the
Mrs. Lehman	**Circus, Motorcycle Cops**
Tala Birrell	Not Credited in the RKO Files
Gogarty	
Barry Fitzgerald	

The associate producer's function was to serve as official liaison between RKO and Hawks. The film was officially designated a "Howard Hawks production." According to contractual agreement, no RKO employee could be listed as full producer of a Hawks film, with two possible exceptions: Pandro S. Berman (RKO's top producer) and Edward Small (a longtime friend of Hawks).

Van Nest Polglase, as head of the RKO art department, received design credit for every RKO film, even when the film was designed by one of his assistants. Polglase, for example, receives credit for the stylish Astaire-Rogers films, which were actually the work of assistant Carroll Clark. Perry Ferguson, the credited associate art director, served as *Bringing Up Baby*'s actual designer (as he served on *Citizen Kane*). Indeed, there are certain vague similarities in the vast space of

David's Brontosaurus Hall and Kane's Xanadu. Hawks would work with Ferguson again on *Ball of Fire*, *A Song Is Born*, and *The Big Sky*.

Virginia Walker was under personal contract to Hawks. Unlike Carole Lombard, Frances Farmer, Lauren Bacall, and Angie Dickinson, Walker would never bloom into one of Hawks's star "discoveries."

The Continuity Script

Fade in

1. LS: *an imposing institutional building, surrounded by lawn, trees, and hedges, in the sunlight.*

2. CU: *a metal plaque reading: "Stuyvesant Museum of Natural History."*

Dissolve

The Brontosaurus Hall, day

3. LS: *the Brontosaurus Hall, Alice Swallow in the foreground, examining a large open packing box. David Huxley is seated on a high platform, studying the skeleton of a brontosaurus that fills the length of the hall, surrounded by zoological specimens in glass cases and hanging on wall plaques. Professor La Touche crosses toward Alice.*

LA TOUCHE: Good morning, Miss Swallow . . . I . . .
ALICE *(raising her hand)*: Sh-h-h.

4. MS: *La Touche and Miss Swallow, framed by the legs of the brontosaurus.*

LA TOUCHE *(lowering his voice)*: What's the matter?
ALICE: Sh-h-h. Dr. Huxley's thinking.

La Touche turns and looks toward David. The camera's movement follows his gaze.

5. MLS: *David, seated high on a construction platform in the pose of Rodin's* Thinker, *his chin on his right fist. Camera cranes toward him as he looks at the bone in his left hand.*

DAVID *(shaking his head)*: Alice, I think this one must belong in the tail.

6. MS: *Alice and La Touche.*

   ALICE: Nonsense. You tried it in the tail yesterday and it didn't fit.

7. MS: *David.*

   DAVID: Oh, yes. That's right. I did, didn't I?

8. MLS: *Alice and La Touche. Alice looks at a telegram La Touche carried in with him.*

   ALICE: Oh, David! It's a telegram for you from Utah. It's from the expedition!

9. MLS: *David.*

DAVID: Oh, oh, the expedition! Open it. I'll be right down. Gee whiz
. . . *(He almost bumps his head on the skeleton's jaw.)*

10. LS: *David descends the ladder to the platform while Alice and La Touche
stand in the foreground. Sound of an envelope opening.*

ALICE: David! They've found it. They've found it, David!

*She and La Touche hurry toward David, who meets them at the feet of the
brontosaurus.*

DAVID: Not the intercostal clavicle!

11. MLS: *Alice between La Touche and David.*

  ALICE: It's on its way here!
  DAVID: Let me see. *(He takes the telegram.)*
  ALICE: It'll be here tomorrow.

12. MS: *Alice, La Touche, and David.*

  DAVID: Oh, oh, just think of it, professor. The last bone we needed to
  complete the brontosaurus. The very last bone. The intercostal clavicle
  is arriving tomorrow. After four years' hard work.
  LA TOUCHE: Congratulations, my boy.
  DAVID: Oh, isn't it great. I can hardly believe it. Oh, Alice . . . *(He
  embraces Alice and kisses her cheek. She resists.)*

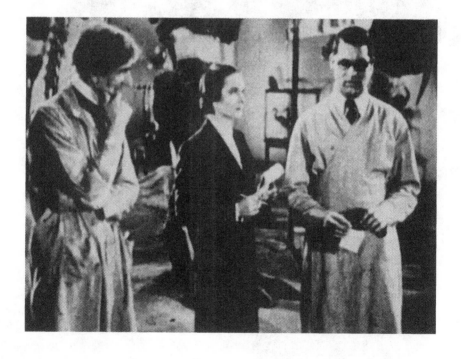

ALICE: Stop it! Really, David, there's a time and a place for everything. What will Professor La Touche think?

13. CU: *La Touche.*

LA TOUCHE: After all, my dear, you're getting married tomorrow.

14. MCU: *Alice and David.*

ALICE: Yes, I know we are . . .
DAVID: Oh, yes, that's right. We're getting married tomorrow. Isn't that odd? Two such important things happening on the same day!

15. CU: *La Touche.*

LA TOUCHE: I think the occasion calls for a celebration.

16. MCU: *Alice and David.*

DAVID: Oh, don't you worry, professor. We're going to celebrate. We're gonna go away directly we've been married.

17. MS: *Alice, La Touche, and David.*

ALICE: Going away? Why, what are you thinking of, David? After receiving this telegram?
DAVID: Oh, well, we planned it.
ALICE: Why, as soon as we're married, we're coming directly back here and you're going on with your work.
DAVID: Oh, Alice, gee whiz . . .
ALICE: Now once and for all, David, nothing must interfere with your work.
DAVID: Oh . . .
ALICE: Our marriage must entail no domestic entanglements of any kind.

18. MCU: *Alice and David.*

DAVID: You mean, you mean . . .

ALICE: I mean, of any kind, David.

DAVID: Oh, well, Alice, I was sort of hoping . . . well, you mean, you mean children and all that sort of thing . . .

ALICE: Exactly. *(David mutters to himself.)* This . . .

19. LS: *Alice, La Touche, and David.*

ALICE *(making a large sweeping gesture with her left arm)*: . . . will be our child.

DAVID: Huh? *(He looks above and behind him at the brontosaurus, then turns front, muttering.)*

ALICE: Yes, David, I see our marriage purely as a dedication to your work.

20. MCU: *Alice and David.*

DAVID: Well, gee whiz, Alice, everybody has to have a honeymoon. And . . . and . . .

ALICE: But we haven't time.

DAVID: Oh.

ALICE *(looking at her wristwatch)*: Speaking of time, you have an appointment this afternoon.

DAVID: Oh, have I? Uh, what for? *(He continues to mutter distractedly.)*

ALICE: To play golf with Mr. Peabody.

DAVID: Peabody? What Peabody?

21. MS: *Alice, La Touche, and David.*

ALICE: The Alexander Peabody who represents Mrs. Carleton Random.

DAVID: Now, let me think . . .

ALICE: Who may possibly donate a million dollars to the museum for the completion of all this group. *(She indicates the skeleton.)*

DAVID: Oh, sure, that Mr. Peabody. Yes. A million dollars! Hey! Say, that's pretty white of Mr. Peabody, isn't it?

ALICE: Well, you haven't got it yet. And let me remind you that a lot depends on the impression you make on him.

DAVID: Oh, sure. Aw, don't worry. After I've received this *(indicating telegram).* Say, I feel good for anything. I'll wow him. I'll knock him for a loop!

ALICE: David, no slang! Remember who and what you are!

DAVID *(muttering):* Oh, yeah, that's right.

ALICE: Now do go along. You mustn't keep him waiting.

DAVID *(holding out his hand to shake with La Touche):* Well, well, goodbye, Alice . . . *(Laughs.)* I mean, Professor. *(After shaking hands, David hurries to door.)*

ALICE: And don't forget your golf clubs. Remember . . .

22. LS: *David, at the heavy metal door, observed by a stuffed bird on the far right.*

ALICE *(off):* . . . let Mr. Peabody win.

DAVID: Uh, uh, yes, Alice, yes. Uh . . . *(As he opens the door, he bumps into it.)* Oh, dear, excuse me . . . *(He exits.)*

Dissolve

A Golf Course, day

23. LS: *a golf course, in bright sunlight. Camera dollies ahead of David, Peabody, and their caddies as they walk.*

DAVID: I . . . I can't tell you, Mr. Peabody, how much this endowment would mean to the museum. And to me personally. If you could just give me some assurance that . . . that . . . if you could just give me some assurance that you'd . . . uh . . . consider us first before you donate that million to anyone else, I'd appreciate it.

They have reached Peabody's ball. Peabody exchanges a club with his caddy.

PEABODY: Dr. Huxley, you seem to be under some misapprehension. I haven't got a million dollars.

24. MS: *Peabody leans on his golf club, with David in the foreground.*

PEABODY: I merely represent the possible donor, Mrs. Carleton Random, whose legal advisor I happen to be.

25. MCU: *David.*

DAVID: Oh, yes, yes. I forgot. OK, OK, well, uh, uh, Mr. Peabody, then I wonder . . .

26. MLS: *as in 24. Peabody tries to swing his golf club.*

DAVID: . . . if you could use your influence with Mrs. Random. That would be nice.
PEABODY *(setting his golf club on the ground and leaning on it, addressing David directly)*: Dr. Huxley, when I play golf I only talk golf. And then only between shots. *(He returns to his ball.)*
DAVID: Oh, yes, of course. I'm sorry.
PEABODY: Couldn't we continue this discussion over a whiskey and soda when we've finished our game?

27. MS: *David.*

DAVID: Why, yes, we could.
PEABODY *(off)*: Meantime, I believe you hooked your ball.

28. LS: *as at the end of 23.*

DAVID: Oh, oh, yes. That's right, I did. *(As he starts away.)* Well, I'll be with you in a minute, Mr. Peabody.
PEABODY *(returning to his shot)*: Yes . . . all right . . . all right . . .

29. MS: *David, followed by his caddy. He pauses abruptly, looking off.*

DAVID: Oh, look! Look! You can't . . . *(He points.)*

30. LS: *Susan, with her caddy, preparing to take a shot.*

31. MS: *David, still pointing.*

DAVID *(to his caddy)*: Hey, that's my ball! Just a minute! *(He runs out of the frame, followed by his caddy.)*

32. LS: *Susan is preparing to take a swing as David and his caddy rush toward her from the rearground.*

SUSAN: Well, here's hoping.
DAVID: I say . . . I say . . . just a minute. I beg your pardon . . .

Susan swings at the ball and watches its flight.

DAVID: Oh, dear. *(Clicks his tongue.)*

33. MCU

SUSAN *(turning to face him)*: You shouldn't do that, you know.

34. MCU

DAVID: But that's . . . What shouldn't I do?

35. MCU

SUSAN: Talk while someone's shooting.
DAVID: But that was my ball.
SUSAN *(overlapping)*: Well, anyway, I forgive you . . . *(handing her club to caddy)* . . . because I got a good shot.

36. LS: *camera travels with Susan as she strides across the fairway, followed by David and the two caddies.*

DAVID: But you don't understand.
SUSAN *(still striding)*: See, there it is. Right next to the pin.
DAVID *(striding beside her)*: But that has nothing to do with it.
SUSAN: Oh, are you playing through?
DAVID: No, I've just driven off the first tee *(indicating to his right as they walk)*.

SUSAN: Oh, I see. You're a stranger here. You should be over there *(indicating to the right)*. This is the eighteenth fairway and I'm right on the green.

37. MS: *Peabody watches and waits, as his caddy yawns.*

SUSAN *(off)*: If I sink this putt, I'm gonna beat my record.

38. LS: *as in 36.*

DAVID *(yelling to his right)*: I'll be with you in a minute. *(He is still striding beside Susan.)* What kind of ball are you playing?
SUSAN: PGA. *(She is still on the move.)*
DAVID: Well, I'm playing a Crowflight.
SUSAN: Uh huh, I like a PGA better.

39. MS: *Susan stops and kneels to line up her putt.*

DAVID: No, I'm just trying to prove to you that you're playing my ball. You see, a PGA has two black dots and a Crowflight has a circle. *(He points down toward the ball.)*
SUSAN: Uh huh. *(She prepares to putt.)* I'm not superstitious about things like that.
DAVID: Oh, well, that doesn't have anything to do with it.
SUSAN: Stop talking for a minute, will you please? *(To her caddy.)* Will you take out the pin?

40. MLS: *as the caddy removes the pin, Susan putts the ball. We observe its entire path until it falls into the cup. David runs after the ball toward the cup.*

DAVID: Oh, my. So silly . . . I never saw such a . . .
SUSAN: Hah!

41. MLS: *David and Susan.*

DAVID: There, you see? It's a circle. *(He shows the ball he has taken from the cup.)*
SUSAN: Well, now, of course it is. Do you think it would roll if it was square?
DAVID: No, I have reference to a mark on the ball.
SUSAN *(laughs)*: I know. I was only being silly.
DAVID: *(overlapping)*: That proves it's a Crowflight. That's my ball.
SUSAN: What does it matter? It's only a game, anyway. *(She hands her putter to caddy.)*
DAVID: Well, my dear young lady, you don't seem to realize. You've placed me in a mmmm . . . very embarrassing position.
SUSAN: Oh, really? I'm sorry.
DAVID: The most important corporation lawyer in New York is waiting for me over on the first fairway.
SUSAN: Then it's silly of you to be fooling around on the eighteenth green.
DAVID: You . . . *(holding up the ball in his right hand)* . . . You don't mind if I take this with me?

SUSAN: No, not at all. Tell the caddy master to put it in my bag when you've finished. *(She walks off.)*

42. MCU: *David, holding the ball, his caddy behind him.*

PEABODY *(off)*: Huxley!

David looks to his right.

43. LS: *Peabody on the fairway.*

PEABODY: Huxley! Come on!

44. MCU: *as in 42.*

DAVID: Oh, yes! I'll be with you in a minute, Mr. Peabody. *(David and caddy start off to their right.)*

45. MLS: *a parking lot filled with cars. Susan starts her roadster and drives it forward, bumping the car in front of her.*

46. MLS: *David and caddy walking on the fairway.*

CADDY *(pointing)*: Hey, mister. I think that's your car.

David looks to the right.

47. MCU: *Susan at the wheel. She backs the roadster up, then drives forward quickly. The car comes to a halt with the sound of a banging bumper.*

48. MLS: *as in 46.*

DAVID: Hey! Hey! *(He runs toward his right, then stops.)* Oh. *(He turns and yells to his left.)* I'll be with you in a minute, Mr. Peabody. *(He turns back toward his right, running.)* Hey!

49. LS: *Susan, in the roadster, tries to ease the car out of a tight spot.*

50. CU: *the right rear fender of the car scrapes against a parked car, with a slight scraping sound.*

51. MS: *David, running toward the car as Susan backs it up.*

 DAVID: Hey! Hey! What do you think you're doing?
 SUSAN: I'm trying to unpark my car.

52. MCU: *Susan and David.*

 SUSAN: Oh, hello. It's you. *(She stands up in the car.)*
 DAVID *(overlapping)*: This is my car. *(He indicates the roadster she is driving.)*
 SUSAN: Oh, good. Then, would you mind moving it out of the way?
 DAVID: No. No. *(He points at the car she is in.) This* is my car.
 SUSAN: Yes, I understand that. If you move it back about four feet, why, I'll be able to get out.
 DAVID: Well, I'm afraid you made a mistake. Maybe this is your . . . *(Susan begins to drive again.)* What did you say?

53. MCU: *Susan behind the wheel, David standing next to hood of car.*

 SUSAN: I said *(standing)* if you move it back about four feet, I'll be able to get out. I'm in a terrible hurry and I can't budge.
 DAVID: Oh. You . . . you want me to move your car for . . . *(He touches the other roadster on the right.)*
 SUSAN: Would you mind terribly?
 DAVID: Well, yes I will . . . but . . . but . . . uh . . . *(He points at the car Susan is driving.)*
 SUSAN: That'll be awfully kind of you.
 DAVID: But take it very easy with that car.
 SUSAN: Yes. I'll go slowly.

 David hurries into the roadster on the right.

54. CU: *car moves in reverse; its left fender hits the tree behind with a crash.*

55. MS: *David and Susan simultaneously react to noise off.*

   DAVID: What are you doing?

56. MCU: *Susan at the wheel.*

   SUSAN: Well, I . . . I have to get into position.

57. MS: *David gets into roadster to Susan's right.*

   DAVID: Well, just be careful.
   SUSAN: I will. Now, you say when.

   David starts his roadster.

   DAVID: Yes, all right.

   Susan eases her car forward.

   SUSAN: Am I clear?
   DAVID: Yes, you're clear now.
   SUSAN *(driving forward slowly)*: Clear? *(She drives forward quickly.)*
   DAVID: Oh!

   After another crashing sound, Susan stops her car.

58. CU: *crumpled fenders, a front bumper yanked off by a roadster moving in reverse.*

59. MCU: *David behind the wheel.*

   DAVID: Now look what you've done.

60. MCU: *Susan behind the wheel.*

   SUSAN: Oh, that's all right. I'm insured. *(She backs her car up again.)*

61. MCU: *David behind the wheel.*

DAVID: I don't care whether you're insured or not. *(He rises from the driver's seat, opens the car door.)*

62. MS: *David and Susan.*

DAVID *(stepping on the running board of Susan's roadster)*: Look. Let me drive this car.
SUSAN: Oh, it's all right. It's an old wreck, anyway. It doesn't matter.
DAVID: Well, you don't understand. *This* is my car. *(He points at the front seat where Susan sits)*
SUSAN: You mean this is your car?
DAVID: Of course.
SUSAN: Your golf ball? Your car? Is there anything in the world that doesn't belong to you?
DAVID: Yes, thank Heaven! You!
SUSAN: Now don't lose your temper. *(She prepares to drive off.)*
DAVID: My dear young lady, I'm not losing my temper. I'm merely trying to play some golf!
SUSAN: Well, you choose the funniest places. This is a parking lot.
DAVID: Would you get out of my car?
SUSAN: Will you get off my running board?
DAVID: This is my running board.
SUSAN: All right, honey, stay there. *(She starts to drive car forward.)*
DAVID: Oh . . . Oh . . . Oh, oh, oh . . . *(His arms go flying.)*

63. LS: *David on the running board of the moving car.*

64. MLS: *Peabody and caddy approach the parking lot.*

65. MS: *the upper half of David's body, traveling quickly to the left, is visible above the shrubbery. Sounds of inarticulate cries and an automobile motor.*

SUSAN: If you want to come with me, go ahead!
DAVID: My dear young lady . . .

66. MLS: *Peabody and his caddy.*

PEABODY: Huxley! Huxley!

67. LS: *David, on the running board, as Susan drives the roadster out of the parking lot.*

   DAVID: I'll be with you in a minute, Mr. Peabody.

   Fade out

A Restaurant, night

68. *Fade in.* LS: *the foyer of a fancy restaurant. David, in tails, carrying his top hat, enters through the revolving doors, looks about for someone, then crosses to the headwaiter.*

69. MS: *David and headwaiter.*

> LOUIS: Oh, good evening, sir.
> DAVID: Excuse me. I'm looking for Mr. Peabody. Alexander Peabody. I believe he's dining here.
> LOUIS: Mr. Peabody has not arrived yet.
> DAVID: Oh, is that . . . Well, I'll just wait.
> LOUIS: Yes, sir.
> PATRON: Good evening, Louis.
> LOUIS: Good evening, sir. Right this way. *(He conducts a couple into the restaurant.)*
> PATRON: Thank you.

70. MLS: *camera pans with a hat-check girl who steps up to David.*

> GIRL: May I check your hat, sir?
> DAVID *(deep in thought)*: Excuse me?
> GIRL: Check your hat?
> DAVID: Oh, no, I'd better . . . Well, maybe you . . .

> *He drops his hat. Both of them bend down to retrieve it. They bump heads. He touches the spot on his head where they bumped. As he stoops down to pick up his hat, another hat-check girl joins them.*

> DAVID *(mumbling)*: Well, look at that. *(Aloud.)* I dropped my hat. Well, I'd better hang on to it. *(Another couple crosses in front of him.)*

71. MLS: *Susan, in a shimmering evening dress, sits on a stool at the cocktail bar.*

> JOE: Now watch very carefully.
> SUSAN: I'm watching.
> JOE: I take an olive, see? *(He holds it up.)* And I throw it in that glass. *(He throws it into an empty glass.)*

72. MCU: *Susan and Joe.*

JOE *(holding it up)*: There it is. Now I throw it in that glass. *(He flips the olive into the second empty glass.)*

SUSAN: No. But . . . wait a minute . . . no . . . oh, go on, go on.

JOE: Watch. *(Joe holds out his left hand, palm down, balances the olive on the back of his fingers, sharply slaps his wrist with his right hand, and the olive flies into his mouth.)*

73. MCU: *Susan and Joe.*

SUSAN: Now I know what happens. That's wonderful. *(She reaches into the olive dish.)* You take three, don't you? Only you cheated. Well, you can see me take three now. *(She mutters.)* Now, you throw it in the glass. *(She throws one.)* Take another. Throw it in the glass. *(She does.)* Then you do this. *(She balances a third olive on the back of her palm and slaps her wrist. The olive flies up and falls to the floor.)*

74. LS: *Susan, with Joe behind the bar, and others observing.*

SUSAN: Oh, I . . . *(She stretches to reach the olive.)*

David walks into the frame from the left and takes a flying pratfall.

SUSAN: Ooooh, I'm so sorry. Oh, hello. You're sitting on your hat.

DAVID *(without moving)*: Hm. I know it.

SUSAN: That's silly. *(Holds out her hands.)* Get up.

75. MS: *Susan, standing, helps David off the floor.*

SUSAN: I'm awfully sorry. *(David rises into the frame.)* I couldn't be more apologetic, really.

DAVID: Well, I might have known you were here. I had a feeling, just as I hit the floor.

SUSAN: That was your hat.

DAVID: Yuh, yuh, look at it. Look at it.

SUSAN *(laughing)*: Yes, it's too bad, isn't it? *(Laugh.)* Well, Joe here was showing me a trick and the olive got away.

DAVID: First you drop an olive and then I sit on my hat. It all fits perfectly.

SUSAN: Oh, yes, but you can't do that trick without dropping some of the olives. It takes practice.

DAVID: What? To sit on my hat?

SUSAN: No, to drop an olive. *(David mutters and turns away.)* Now, if you're going to be angry with me, what can I do?

DAVID: Go away.

SUSAN: No. I was here first.

DAVID: Then I'll go away.

76. MLS: *as David walks away from the bar, Susan watches him for a moment, then follows. Camera tracks with her as she walks past tables.*

77. MLS: *David pauses beside a chair, turns toward Susan, and gestures a "shoo" in her direction.*

78. MLS: *Susan, beside the table of Dr. Lehman, picks up an olive from his hors d'oeuvre tray, balances it on the back of her palm, slaps her wrist,*

and opens her mouth to catch it. She picks up another olive from the tray and once again slaps it into her mouth.

LEHMAN: Won't you just take the olive dish?
SUSAN: No, no, it's all right. I'll sit here . . . *(She sits on the arm of the chair.)* You don't mind, do you?
LEHMAN: Not at all.
SUSAN: This is rather difficult. *(She slaps an olive and swallows it.)*
LEHMAN: Thank you.
SUSAN *(laughing)*: Goodness.

79. MCU: *Lehman and Susan.*

SUSAN: You know, your face is familiar. Haven't we met somewhere?
LEHMAN *(removing his monocle)*: Not to my knowledge.
SUSAN: Well, I think you're wrong. My name's Susan Vance. *(She slaps another olive; it misses.)*
LEHMAN *(rising formally)*: I'm Doctor Fritz Lehman. *(He bows.)*
SUSAN: Oh, well, that's all right. You can sit down. I don't mind at all.
LEHMAN *(sitting)*: Thank you. You may have heard me lecture.
SUSAN: What do you lecture about?
LEHMAN: I usually talk about nervous disorders. *(Susan is about to slap-pop another olive.)* I am a psychiatrist.
SUSAN: Oh. *(She puts the olive down.)* Crazy people.

80. CU: *Lehman and Susan.*

LEHMAN: We dislike the use of that word. All people who behave strangely are not insane. *(Lehman suddenly and inexplicably twitches and blinks both eyes grotesquely.)*
SUSAN: Is that so?

81. MCU: *as in 79.*

SUSAN: Oh, umm . . . *(She taps his wrist.)* . . . would you mind if I asked your professional opinion about something?
LEHMAN: Not at all.

SUSAN: Well, now, what would you say about a man who follows a girl around?

LEHMAN: Follows her around.

SUSAN: And when she talks to him, he fights with her?

LEHMAN: Fights with her?

SUSAN: Uh huh.

LEHMAN: Is the young man your fiancé?

SUSAN: Oh, no. I don't know him. I never even saw him before today.

LEHMAN: Oh?

SUSAN: No. He just follows me around and fights with me.

LEHMAN: Well, the love impulse in man very frequently reveals itself in terms of conflict.

SUSAN *(throwing an olive)*: The love impulse?

LEHMAN: Uh huh. Without my knowing anything about it, my rough guess would be that he has a fixation on you, a fixation . . .

SUSAN: No, no, wait a minute. I can't remember any more than that. A fixation—the love impulse in man frequently reveals itself in terms of . . .

LEHMAN: Conflict.

SUSAN: Conflict.

LEHMAN: That's right.

SUSAN *(as both rise)*: Oh, I'm eternally grateful to you. You're absolutely wonderful. Thank you a million times. *(She grabs a purse from the table and rushes off right.)*

82. LS: *Susan approaches David, who is sitting in a corner, his battered top hat on his knees.*

SUSAN: You know why you're following me? *(David rises and backs away in fear.)* You're a fixation.

DAVID: Oh, I'm not following you. *(Camera tracks in.)* I've been sitting here. I haven't moved from this spot. Now, please. You're following me.

SUSAN: Oh, don't be absurd. Who's always behind whom?

DAVID: Now, look, my dear young lady. I haven't been behind anything but what they call the uh . . . uh . . . uh . . . eight ball. I haven't been all day.

SUSAN: You're angry. Aren't you?

DAVID: Yes I am.

SUSAN: Uh huh. The love impulse in man frequently reveals itself in terms of conflict.

DAVID: Excuse me. The what impulse?

SUSAN: Love impulse.

DAVID: Yuh.

SUSAN: Now, you see, the trouble with you is that you have a kind of fix . . .

DAVID: Now, look, look. All I'm trying to do is find the gentleman whom, thanks to you, I abandoned on the golf course today. That's all I'm trying to do here. Now, please, go . . .

SUSAN: But, I . . . *(She notices the purse in her hand.)* Say, this isn't . . . *(She looks to her left.)* Where do you suppose I . . . Here, hold this a minute, will you, please? I'll be right back.

DAVID: Yes. *(He takes the purse and stares at it, as Susan rushes off left.)*

83. LS: *camera tracks left with Susan as she passes Lehman's table. He is trying to slap an olive into his mouth from the back of his hand. As Susan passes his table he slaps his wrist and the olive flies past his mouth.*

SUSAN: Missed.

Lehman laughs. Mrs. Lehman approaches the table as Susan passes.

MRS. LEHMAN: I'm sorry I was so long. *(Lehman rises.)*

LEHMAN: That's quite all right, my dear. *(He holds her chair.)* I had a very entertaining conversation with a young lady who does tricks with olives—when she gets it right.

MRS. LEHMAN: *(laughs—then noticing that her purse is missing)*: Fritz, where is my purse?

LEHMAN: Your purse, dear? I thought you had it with you.

MRS. LEHMAN: No, I left it right here on the table. Oh, my dear, my diamond pin was in it.

LEHMAN: Oh, diamond pin?

84. MS: *David, holding his hat and the purse. He starts to set the purse down, then carries it with him as he walks left, followed by the camera. He passes Mr. and Mrs. Lehman, who are searching for the purse.*

> LEHMAN: You lost a diamond pin; we're going to find it.
> MRS. LEHMAN: I don't understand where it is.
> LEHMAN: All right, don't worry about it.

Mrs. Lehman is blocking David's way.

> DAVID: Excuse me, I . . .
> MRS. LEHMAN: So sorry. *(She looks up.)* Why, there it is. Thank you very much. *(She reaches for the purse.)* Very kind of you.
> LEHMAN *(overlapping)*: Thank you, sir. Very kind of you.
> DAVID: Oh, no.
> MRS. LEHMAN: This is my purse. My diamond pin is in it. *(David won't surrender the purse.)* Will you please give it to me.
> LEHMAN *(overlapping)*: All right, dear. Don't get excited. Just take the purse.
> DAVID: Oh, no, no . . . I'm afraid you . . .
> MRS. LEHMAN: Give me that. *(To Lehman.)* Please do something about it, will you?
> LEHMAN *(to David)*: Will you please hand it over. *(To Mrs. Lehman.)* Will you please keep out of this, darling. Let me handle this. *(To David.)* That was very clumsily done.

85. MS: *at the bar, Joe hands Susan her purse.*

> SUSAN: I did the trick.
> JOE: You did?
> SUSAN: I did it once. *(She turns toward the sounds of the argument. Her smile fades.)* Uh oh. *(She walks off right.)*

86. LS: *Mr. and Mrs. Lehman protest angrily as David grasps the purse. Susan enters from the rearground to observe David protecting the purse.*

> DAVID: I don't mean to be adverse but I'm afraid you've made a slight

blunder. You see, this belongs to . . . *(He sees Susan.)* Oh, there's the
young lady. Now, look, isn't this your purse?
SUSAN *(joining the group)*: No. *This* is my purse.
LEHMAN *(grabbing at the purse in David's hand)*: Now, there you are.
(Lehman and David fight for the purse.)
SUSAN: No. Wait a minute, wait a minute, wait a minute.
DAVID: Now, just a minute. Didn't you give me this purse to hold?

87. MS: *The foursome.*

SUSAN: Yes, that's right, I did. I gave him the purse to hold. You see,
there's been a mistake. I lost my purse and I must have picked up your
wife's purse by mistake.

88. MCU: *The foursome, joined by Louis, who stands behind.*

LEHMAN: Uh . . .
SUSAN: And I wanted him to stay so I gave him your wife's purse to hold
while I went to find my purse. *(David taps Lehman on the shoulder to
get his attention. Lehman shrugs him off to follow Susan's explanation.)*
And I was coming right back. *(David continues to tap Lehman's shoulder.)* Now that's all perfectly clear, isn't it?
LEHMAN: Yeh . . . No, it isn't. *(David still tapping his shoulder.)* You
see, you're going to give me an explanation . . . *(Turns toward David.)*
DAVID: No, no, no. And, my dear sir, it never will be clear as long as
she's explaining it.

89. LS: *as in 87.*

DAVID *(surrendering the purse to Lehman as he backs away)*: Now,
please let me g . . .
LEHMAN: Now just a minute. Oh, no, no, no . . .
SUSAN: He's innocent. He's innocent. *(She steps between Lehman and
David; camera pans with Susan to include more of Louis.)* Now you
have your wife's purse. I have my purse. And Louis here is going to
explain it all to you and everything is going to be all right.[1]

90. MS: *David descends stairs leading to dining room, followed by Susan.*

SUSAN: Now, please, listen to me. You certainly can't think that I did
   that intentionally.
DAVID: Well, if I could think, I'd have run when I saw you. *(He con-*
   tinues down the stairs as Susan follows.)
SUSAN: Now if you'd only wait while I explain. I just gave you my purse
   to ho . . . .

As Susan reaches out her hand to stop David's flight, she grabs hold of
the left tail of his dinner jacket. The coat splits up the center seam with a
loud rip. David stops dead in his tracks, then straightens slowly.

SUSAN: Oh. You've torn your coat.

David explores the ripped seam with his right hand. He turns toward
Susan with menace as she backs up the stairs.

SUSAN: Now, now, I didn't do it on purpose . . . *(Steadily retreating up*
   the stairs as David glares.)

91. MCU: *Susan and David.*

SUSAN: That's not right. That's not right. It's not my fault. I didn't mean
   to do it. I just did it. But I didn't mean to do it. I just caught hold of
   your coattail . . .
DAVID: Look. Will you do something for me? *(They stop but continue to*
   stare at each other.)
SUSAN: A needle?
DAVID: No, it's simpler than that. Let's play a game.
SUSAN: Oh? What?
DAVID: Well, watch, I'll put my hand over my eyes and then you go
   away.
SUSAN: Uh huh.
DAVID: See?
SUSAN: Uh huh.
DAVID *(covering his eyes)*: And I'll count to ten. And when I take my
   hand down, you will be gone. One . . .

92. LS: *Stairs leading to the dining room.*

SUSAN: Well, I like that! I was only trying to be nice.

Susan turns and marches up the stairs, David's hand still over his eyes. As Susan flounces away, there is the sound of another rip. The rear panel of her dress remains under David's right foot, exposing her legs and lingerie to the waist. He uncovers his eyes to note her retreat.

DAVID: Thank you. *(He notices the piece of material at his feet.)* Oh! Oh, just a minute! *(He rushes up the stairs after her.)*

93. MLS

SUSAN: Oh no . . .
DAVID: Just a minute . . .
SUSAN *(turning toward David)*: You can't talk to me that way and then crawl out of it. *(David thrusts his arms around her and backs her against a pillar.)* When I'm mad, I am mad.
DAVID: Something horrible has happened.
SUSAN: Well, don't tell me about it. Just get out of it as best you can.

She starts forward; David cuts off her path with his top hat.

DAVID: Uh, no, uh . . .
SUSAN: And please stop following me around, fixation or no fixation. I've had about enough of it.
DAVID: Please stop talking so that I . . . *(He has maneuvered her back to the pillar.)*
SUSAN: Will you please stop crowding me.
DAVID: No, no, now, look. I'm just trying to tell you that you've torn . . .
SUSAN: Oh, no I didn't! Why, if you hadn't been in such a hurry and had waited for my explanation . . .
DAVID: Not my coat.
SUSAN: Your coat would still be perfectly all right.
DAVID: Oooooh . . .

She stalks away from him into the lounge. David runs after her and slaps

*his top hat over her backside with a loud clap. She stops abruptly. While
David looks around, Susan looks at David.*

SUSAN: What is the matter with you?
DAVID: Well, you see, oh!

*As Susan turns to expose her rear to the lounge, David quickly switches
his top hat to his left hand and clasps it again against her backside.*

SUSAN *(keeping her voice low)*: Do you realize that you're making a
    perfect fool of yourself? *(She walks quickly toward the camera, fol-
    lowed by David.)* Now, look here. You can't tell me that I tore your
    coat. There's such a thing as being fai . . .

DAVID: Oh! *(He clasps his hat to her backside with both hands.)*
SUSAN: Will you please stop doing that with your hat. *(She removes his arms that surround her.)*
DAVID: Well, just stand there, will ya? *(David quickly twirls around her to stand behind her, pressing his body against her back.)*
SUSAN: What in the world is going on here?

Again she turns and again David hops behind her.

DAVID: Oh, no, please don't move.

She twirls away from him, her back once again against the pillar.

SUSAN: Oh, I've had about enough of this!
DAVID: Listen to me. Let's get out of here. Just start walking.
SUSAN *(with a mock laugh)*: Now you want to walk. Well, I'm quite sure that I don't want to walk with you. And I hope you realize that you've made a perfect spectacle of yourself. Have you finished?
DAVID: I . . . Oh, yes, yes, yes. *(He makes a gesture of resignation.)*
SUSAN: Thank you.

As Susan departs briskly, she reaches behind to grasp her train. She stops. She gropes once again for the skirt that is not there. She backs quickly to the pillar.

SUSAN: Oh! Oh! Oh! Help!

94. MCU: *Susan and David.*

SUSAN: Don't just stand there. Do something! Do something! Oh, my goodness.

David moves behind her.

SUSAN: Well, get behind me!
DAVID: I am behind you.
SUSAN: Well, get closer.

DAVID: I can't get any closer. Now, now, are you ready? So, be calm.
Left foot first.
SUSAN: All right.

95. LS: *standing as close together as they can, Susan and David start off on
the same foot and lockstep through the lounge, preceded by the tracking
camera. Patrons at the tables titter and laugh. As they reach the doorway
of the cocktail lounge, David puts on his top hat while Susan smiles
broadly.*

96. CU: *tracking shot continues.*

SUSAN: Keep going straight out the door.
DAVID: But I've got to meet somebody here. Oh, there he is. *(David
points to his left.)*

97. MS: *reverse tracking shot, from Susan's and David's point-of-view, of Mr.
and Mrs. Peabody, standing at the hat-check counter. Peabody opens his
arms in bewilderment.*

SUSAN *(off)*: Don't you dare leave me.
DAVID *(off)*: Oh, I'll be with you in a minute, Mr. . . .

98. LS: *David and Susan in lockstep.*

DAVID: Be with you in a minute, sir. I'll see you in a minute. Uh, I'll
see you in a minute . . .

*David replaces his top hat as he and Susan exit through the revolving
door, sharing the same quadrant, David's split tails hanging down
behind.*

Dissolve

Susan's Apartment, night

99. MCU: *Susan and David sitting in Susan's apartment, Susan sewing
David's coat.*

DAVID: So you see, Miss Vance, it's very important that I meet this man in order to explain to him what happened—although even if I saw him I wouldn't know what to say, I guess.

SUSAN: Well, it's perfectly simple. Just tell him that you met someone that you knew and were detained.

DAVID: Huh. Yeah. I can picture myself explaining our exit from the Ritz-Plaza Hotel to Mr. Peabody.

SUSAN: But it's not Boopie that you're trying to see.

DAVID: Yes, that's right. No. No, his name is Peabody—Alexander Peabody.

SUSAN *(overlapping)*: Alexander Peabody. But that's Boopie and I know him well. I was going to have supper with him tonight. He'll do anything I ask him to. I can wrap him around my little finger. Here.

100. MS: *Susan rises with the repaired coat.*

SUSAN: Now you put on your coat and we'll go over to the Ritz and catch him before he's finished dinner.

DAVID: I'd better go there alone.

SUSAN: And if we miss him there—no, you can't go alone—if we miss him there we'll go out to Riverdale. *(She helps him get his arm in the left sleeve that she seems to have sewn shut.)* There you are.

DAVID: But I couldn't go to Riverdale. I couldn't spend that much time.

SUSAN: Riverdale's only half an hour away. I have my car right outside. I can drive . . .

DAVID: Yes, but I have to go to Carnegie Hall to meet Miss Swallow.

SUSAN: Miss Swallow?

DAVID: Yes, I'm engaged to Miss Swallow.

101. CU: *Susan.*

SUSAN: Engaged? To be married?

DAVID *(off)*: That's right.

SUSAN: That's nice. Then she won't mind waiting, will she?

102. LS: *camera pans as Susan starts toward the door, followed by David.*

DAVID: Oh, I wouldn't like to . . . by Carnegie Hall.
SUSAN *(snatching a fur jacket and slipping it on)*: I mean, if I were
  engaged to you, I wouldn't mind waiting at all. I'd wait forever.
DAVID: Yes, but it wouldn't be right to leave her . . .

Dissolve

Outside Peabody's House, night

103. LS: *camera pans with a station wagon as it comes to a stop in front of a
  darkened mansion. We hear a slight squeak of the brake.*

104. MS: *Susan is behind the wheel, David sitting in the passenger seat.*

SUSAN: Well, I finally got you here, didn't I?

David gets out of the car, Susan follows.

DAVID: Oh, yes. Susan?
SUSAN: Hmm? *(They climb a stairway.)*
DAVID: Susan, do they build all the houses in Riverdale alike?
SUSAN: No, I don't think so. Why?
DAVID: Oh, well, because if they don't, we've passed this one six times
in the last hour.
SUSAN: Oh, but David, it was such a lovely night for a drive.
DAVID: Yeh. Oh, dear.
SUSAN *(running to the front door of the house)*: Come on.
DAVID: Uh, there aren't any lights in the windows. Mr. Peabody must
have gone to bed.
SUSAN: Oh no, they couldn't have gone to bed this soon. It's too early.

105. MLS: *at door—Susan presses the doorbell.*

DAVID: Oh, I don't know. If they expected a visit from you they could—
with the covers over their heads.
SUSAN: Now, David, if you don't stop nagging I won't help you arrange
matters with Boopie.
DAVID: Well, somehow I have a feeling it might be better if you didn't.
SUSAN: Why?
DAVID: Well, I don't think we ought to do this, Susan. Gee, if we wake
him up in the middle of the night he'll be irritable.
SUSAN: Well, I don't think it's going to work anyway, but I know where
Boopie sleeps. *(She moves from the door of the house.)*
DAVID *(following)*: Well, uh, no.

106. LS: *Susan, followed by David, moving along the side of the house.*

DAVID: But Susan, you can't climb in a man's bedroom window.
SUSAN: I know. It's on the second floor. *(Calling up toward darkened
house.)* Boopie! Hey, Boopie!

DAVID: Oh, oh, Susan, please, please. It's too late now, Susan. You can't wake him up.

SUSAN: Oh, can't I? *(She quickly crosses to a nearby tree and bends over.)*

DAVID: Huh, well, what are you doing?

SUSAN: Pebbles.

DAVID: Pebbles? What for?

SUSAN: Well, I've heard that if you throw pebbles up against a window the people think it's hail and then they come and close the window.

DAVID: Uh, uh, uh, uh, uh, uh . . . *(Susan hurls the pebbles.)* Oh!

107. MS: *angling up toward a balcony with darkened French doors—the sound of pebbles clattering against the panes.*

108. MS: *David and Susan, gazing upward.*

DAVID: Oh, oh, I know we ought to go now, but somehow I can't move.

SUSAN: Guess they weren't big enough. *(She stoops to gather more.)*

DAVID: But, uh . . .

109. MS: *as in 107, angling up toward the French doors. They open and a pajama-clad Peabody, yawning, appears.*

PEABODY: What the . . .

110. LS: *as in 108. Susan is still bent over while David notices Peabody.*

DAVID: Oh . . . I . . . I . . .

SUSAN: Oh, here's a pip! *(She straightens up, and, in the same movement, hurls a rock.)*

DAVID: Just a minute, Susan, I . . . Oh!

111. MS: *as in 107, angling up toward the French doors. The rock conks Peabody on the head and knocks him backward through the open door.*

112. MCU: *David and Susan staring upward.*[2]

SUSAN: Jeepers! Let's get out of here.

She grabs David by the arm and they flee toward the rearground, David holding his hat.

Dissolve

Street outside David's Apartment, night

113. LS: *the station wagon pulls up near the curb outside the entrance of an apartment house. Susan is driving.*

114. MCU: *Susan and David in the car.*

SUSAN: Now don't worry, David. Everything's going to be all right.
    (David gets out of the car and stands at open door.) And tomorrow,
    when Boopie's calmed down, we'll go and see him together.
DAVID: Now, just a moment, Susan. Don't think that I don't appreciate
    all you've done. But . . . but . . .
SUSAN: Oh, it was nothing, David, really.
DAVID: Just a moment. But there are limits to what a man can bear. And
    besides that, tomorrow afternoon I'm going to get married.

115. CU: *Susan pauses, takes in a gulp of air, then laughs.*

116. MCU: *David stands beside the car, the passenger door ajar.*

SUSAN *(off)*: What for?
DAVID *(battered top hat in hand)*: Well because, see . . . *(She laughs
    again.)* Well, anyway, I'm going to get married, Susan—and—don't
    interrupt.
SUSAN *(off)*: No.
DAVID: Now my future wife has always regarded me as a man of some
    dignity.

117. CU: *Susan covers her face and laughs into her glove.*

118. MCU: *as in 116.*

   DAVID: Uh . . . Privately, I'm convinced that I have some dignity. Now, it isn't that I don't like you, Susan. Because, after all, in moments of quiet, I'm strangely drawn toward you. But, well, there haven't been any quiet moments. Our relationship has been a series of misadventures from beginning to end. So, if you don't mind, I'll see Mr. Peabody alone—and unarmed.

119. CU: *Susan.*

   SUSAN: Without me?

120. MCU: *as in 116.*

   DAVID: Yes, without you and definitely without you. Now, Susan, I'm gonna say goodnight and I hope that I never set eyes on you again. *(He slams the car door shut.)* Goodnight! *(He tips his battered hat and disappears from the frame—with the sound of a pratfall.)*

121. CU: *Susan leans toward the passenger window to see what has happened.*

122. MS: *David, lying on the sidewalk, glances briefly at the automobile, gets to his feet, brushes himself off a bit, then strides toward the entrance to the apartment house.*

123. CU: *Susan watches, smiles, shifts her eyes from side to side, nods her head affirmatively, then leans back out of the light.*

   Fade out

David's Apartment, day

124. *Fade in.* MS: *David seated beside a table, talking on the phone.*[3]

DAVID: Yes, I did see Mr. Peabody, but I didn't see him. Well, that is, I didn't see him really, I . . . Yes, I, I spoke to him twice, but I didn't talk to him.

125. MS: *Alice on the phone in her apartment.*

ALICE: But, David, I don't understand. Did you see him or didn't you?[4]

126. MS: *David on the phone. The doorbell buzzes.*

DAVID: Whuh, no, I, I don't know . . . Well, . . . *(Another buzz.)* . . . how do I know? Well, because, because . . . *(Camera pans as David rises and crosses to the door, carrying the phone.)* Well, there's someone at the door. That's . . . *(Making sure he doesn't trip over the cord.)* You see, there are some things that are very hard to explain, Alice, and as soon as I, uh . . . *(He opens the door, revealing a delivery man, carrying a box.)* Yes, Ali . . . Oh . . . *(The delivery man leans against the door jamb, watching, chewing gum.)* Now Alice, be . . . before we're married this afternoon, there's one thing we must have clear. I don't want any woman interfering with my affairs. *(He looks at the delivery man, who nods his approval.)* It's fatal.
MAN: That's the stuff, buddy.
DAVID: What do you want?
MAN: Doctor Huxley?
DAVID: Yeah.
MAN *(putting receipt for David's signature on top of the box)*: Sign here.
DAVID: Oh, just a minute, Alice. Have to sign something. *(Signs the receipt.)* Oh! Oh, Alice! Alice, it's arrived! The intercostal clavicle! Yes, isn't that wonderful? Oh, isn't that a marvelous wedding present! *(To delivery man.)* Thank you. You see, I'm going to be married this afternoon.
MAN *(putting the box under David's arm)*: Don't let it throw you, buddy.

The delivery man leaves as David pushes the door closed with his foot and returns to his chair. The camera pans with him.

DAVID: Yes, Alice, yes . . . Yes, isn't that great? Oh, Alice, I'm so excited! Yes, well, I'll tell you what you do. *(He sits.)* You go on down

to the museum and I'll meet you down there right away. Yes, dear,
goodbye. *(He hangs up.)*

127. MS: *David opening the box. The telephone rings. He continues unwrap-
ping the box. The phone rings again. He lifts the receiver.*

DAVID: Hello. *(Pause.)* Oh, it's you. Well, well, I can't hear you very
well. Come closer to the telephone.

128. MS: *Susan, in negligee, sitting at a writing table in her apartment,
talking on the phone.*

SUSAN: I said, "Good morning, David," and I said, "Do you want a
leopard?"

129. MS: *David on phone.*

DAVID: A leopard? No, why should I want a leopard?

130. MS: *Susan on phone.*

SUSAN: Well, for that matter, why should I? But I've got one.

131. MS: *David on phone.*

DAVID: Susan, where would you get a leopard?

132. MS: *Susan on phone.*

SUSAN: Well, I wouldn't get a leopard, David. My brother Mark got
him. He's hunting in Brazil and I guess he caught him.

133. MS: *David on phone, opening the box.*

DAVID: Oh, of course, he's a stuffed leopard.

134. MS: *Susan, on phone, seated. Baby enters from the rearground, strolls
toward the camera.*

SUSAN: Of course not. Why should my brother Mark be hunting stuffed leopards in Brazil when he . . . *(Baby stands beside Susan.) (Addressing Baby.)* You stuffed leopard! . . . when he can find them right here in New York? *(Baby rubs against Susan's knee as she pats its head.)* Well, David, it's lucky I met you yesterday . . . *(Susan rises as she continues to pat Baby.)* . . . because you're the only zoologist I know. *(She holds Baby's tail. Pauses. Laughs.)* Well, of course I know what a zoologist is. *(Susan follows Baby back toward the bathroom door, holding the phone, as the camera tracks with her.)* Get out of here, you . . . No, no, not you, David. Oh, Baby. Get back into that bathroom and stay there. You're making a nuisance of yourself. *(Baby strolls into the bathroom; Susan shuts the door.)*

135. MCU: *Susan.*

SUSAN: No, not you, David. Now, I want you to come right over. Oh, David, don't be irrelevant. The point is I have a leopard; the question is what am I going to do with it.[5]

136. MS: *David on phone, the box open and the bone in his right hand.*

DAVID: Well, Susan, I regret to say the leopard is *your* problem.

137. MCU: *Susan on phone.*

SUSAN: You mean, you refuse to help me?

138. LS: *Susan's living room.*

SUSAN: But David, you can't do that. *(She starts walking from the door.)* You can't leave me alone with a leopard. Now, I'm gonna come and get you in my . . . *(She rushes forward, trips over a lampcord, and falls flat on her face. The lamp and table topple over with a crash.)*

139. MS: *David, phone in left hand, box under right arm, bone in right hand, jumps up.*

DAVID: Susan! *(The sound of moaning comes over the phone.)* What's happened? *(More moaning.)* Is it the leopard?

140. MCU: *low angle, Susan on the floor, clutching the receiver.*

SUSAN: No. No. Nothing happened to me, David. I just fe . . . I mean . . . *(Screams.)* The leopard! David, the leopard! *(She bashes a tray of breakfast dishes off the coffee table and onto the floor.)*

141. MS: *David on phone.*

DAVID: Can you hear me, Susan?

142. MCU: *low angle, as in 140. Susan scrapes the receiver against the fireplace screen.*

SUSAN *(screaming)*: Oh! . . .

143. MS: *David, clutching the box and bone.*

SUSAN *(off)*: Oh!
DAVID: Susan! *(Looks at noisy receiver.)*
SUSAN *(off)*: Oh!

144. MCU: *as in 140.*

SUSAN: Oh! *(She stops to put her ear to the receiver.)*

145. MS: *David on phone.*

DAVID: Susan! Susan, be brave! Be brave. I'll be right there, Susan. *(He rushes off to his right, still holding the receiver.)* Hold on there, Su . . . *(He takes a flying pratfall when he reaches the end of the cord. On the floor, he picks up the receiver.)* Susan! Can you hear me? I'll be there, Susan! *(He throws the receiver on the floor, grabs his hat, and rushes out the door, the box under his arm, the bone in his hand.)*

146. MCU: *low angle, Susan, still holding the phone.*

SUSAN *(purring)*: Oh-h-h. *(She hangs up the phone and stretches on the floor.)*[6]

Dissolve

Hallway and Interior of Susan's Apartment, day

147. LS: *an elevator door opens and David, clutching the box under his left arm, rushes out and hurries to the door of Susan's apartment.*

DAVID *(pounding on the door)*: Susan! Susan! *(Kicking the door.)* Susan!

148. LS: *Susan, in a dark striped dress, carrying her coat, hat, and purse, rushes across her living room as the camera pans. She drops her coat,*

etc., on a chair in passing and continues to the doorway, accompanied by the sound of David's calling, "Susan!" and pounding on the door.

SUSAN: Yes, yes, yes, yes.

As she opens the door, David jumps into the room.

DAVID: Susan!
SUSAN: Yes, David. *(She backs away from him.)*
DAVID: Why, you're all right!
SUSAN: Yes, I'm all right.
DAVID: You lied to me.

Camera pans as David advances, Susan retreats.

SUSAN: No, yes, but I didn't . . .

DAVID: Telling me a ridiculous story about a leopard!
SUSAN *(overlapping)*: Wasn't a ridiculous story. I have a leopard.
DAVID: Well, where is the leopard?
SUSAN: Right in there.
DAVID: I don't believe you, Susan.
SUSAN: But you have to believe me . . .

Camera pans with David as he strides across the room toward bathroom, Susan following.

DAVID: I've been the victim of your unbridled imagination once more.

149. MS: *Baby is seated on the sink. The door jerks open and David takes a step into the room.*

DAVID: Coming all the way for . . . *(He sees Baby. Yelps. Retreats from bathroom, pulling door closed.)*

150. MS: *David at door to bathroom. Silent. Staring.*

151. MS: *Susan turns toward him.*

SUSAN: That will teach you to go around saying things about people. *(She turns away.)*

152. MS: *as in 150.*

DAVID *(shaking his head)*: Susan, you've got to get out of this apartment.

153. MS: *as in 151.*

SUSAN: But, David, I can't. I have a lease.

154. LS: *David outside the bathroom door.*

DAVID: Oh, it isn't that. You've got to get this thing out of here. *(After making sure the bathroom door is closed, he crosses to the phone.)* I'll fix that.

SUSAN *(overlapping)*: Don't worry about him. He's really all right. *(She pursues him to the phone as the camera pans.)* What are you going to do?
DAVID: I'm going to call the zoo.
SUSAN: Oh, no, you can't do that, David! Oh, that's the meanest thing I ever heard. He's a pet. He'd be miserable in a zoo. *(She picks up a piece of paper from the desk.)* Listen. From my brother, Mark, from Brazil. *(Reads.)* Dear Susan, I'm sending you Baby—*(Indicating bathroom.)* that's Baby—*(Pointing at the letter.)*—leopard I picked up. Guard him with your life. He's three years old, gentle as a kitten, and he likes dogs. I wonder whether Mark means that he eats dogs or is fond of them? Mark's so vague at times.
DAVID: Vague!
SUSAN *(returning to letter)*: He also likes music, particularly that song, "I Can't Give You Anything but Love, Baby."
DAVID: Oh, that's absurd.
SUSAN: No it isn't, David. Really. Listen.

Camera pans with her as she crosses to start a portable Victrola. "I Can't Give You Anything but Love, Baby" blares out.

155. MCU: *Susan and David.*

DAVID *(sitting in a chair, holding his box)*: This is probably the silliest thing that ever happened to me.
SUSAN: I know it's silly, but it's true. He absolutely adores the tune.
DAVID: What's the difference whether it adores it or not?

156. LS: *Susan at Victrola, David seated.*

SUSAN: It's funny he should like such an old tune, isn't it? But I imagine that down in Brazil they got . . . *(She turns quickly to look at the bathroom door.)* Look!
DAVID: Oh, stop it, Susan!
SUSAN *(running to the bathroom door)*: Oh, David, let me show him to you.
DAVID *(jumping up, following her to the bathroom)*: Oh, don't do that, Susan! Don't go near the do . . . !

Susan opens the door; Baby strolls out. David hops up on a coffee table.

DAVID: Oh, dear, dear, dear. *(He lifts the box above his head.)*
SUSAN: Awwwww . . .

157. CU: *at Victrola. Baby walks up to it, raises himself, and sniffs the record.*

SUSAN *(off)*: Now watch, David, you'll see. He'll go right toward the music. Look at that!

158. MS: *Susan.*

SUSAN: Isn't this remarkable! It loves it.

159. MCU: *David aloft, holding his box over his head.*

DAVID: Susan, if we put the Victrola in the bathroom, will it go back in?

160. MS: *Baby turns away from the Victorola and starts toward David on the coffee table.*

SUSAN *(off)*: Oh, yes. But the music sounds better out here. And besides, he likes it.

161. MCU: *as in 159.*

DAVID: Oh, here it comes.

162. CU: *Baby at David's feet.*

DAVID *(off)*: Oh, now, go away. Oh, oh, please, go away.

Baby nuzzles David's right calf.

163. MCU: *as in 159.*

DAVID: Oh my, go 'way. I'm going to get out of here. *(He starts down off the coffee table.)*

164. CU: *as in 162.*

> DAVID *(off)*: Oh, oh. Susan, I don't like leopards.

> *Baby is nuzzling and nipping at David's left pant leg.*

> SUSAN *(off)*: Just think of him as being a housecat, David.

> *Baby tugs at David's left cuff playfully.*

> DAVID *(off)*: Well, I don't like cats either.

165. MS: *Susan and David.*

> SUSAN: Stand still, David. Don't be nervous.
> DAVID *(holding box aloft, trying to free himself from Baby)*: Oh, oh, make him stand still.

166. MCU: *low angle, Baby playing with David's cuff, as Susan crouches, watching.*

> SUSAN: Don't be silly, David. You can't make a leopard stand still.

167. MCU: *David.*

> DAVID: *(still holding his box above his head)*: Susan, do something. Turn off that Victrola.

168. MS: *Susan.*

> SUSAN *(standing and moving to Victrola)*: I don't think it's the music, David. I think it's you. *(She snaps off the machine, then straightens.)* David, I think you've found a real friend.

169. CU: *Baby on his back, playing with David's left shoe.*

> SUSAN *(off)*: Look, isn't it affectionate! Just like a little baby kitten.

170. LS: *David backs away, box aloft.*

> SUSAN: I never saw anything take such a liking to anyone in my life. It
> would follow you anywhere.
> DAVID *(overlapping)*: I wish it wouldn't . . .
> SUSAN: We shan't have any trouble taking it to Connecticut.
> DAVID: Connecticut!
> SUSAN: My farm in Westlake, Connecticut.
> DAVID: Westlake! Well, I'm not going to Westlake, Connecticut!
> SUSAN *(putting on her coat)*: But, David, you've got . . .

171. MCU: *Susan and David.*

> DAVID: Susan, I will not be involved in any more of your harebrained
> schemes.

SUSAN: It's not a harebrained scheme. Imagine Aunt Elizabeth coming to this apartment and running smack into a leopard! That would be an end of my million dollars.

DAVID *(overlapping)*: Aunt Elizabeth? . . .

SUSAN *(speeding onward)*: If you had an aunt who was going to give you a million dollars if she liked you and you knew she wouldn't like you if she found a leopard in your apartment what would you do?

DAVID: I don't know. *(He goes for his hat.)*

SUSAN: Oh, David, you have to help me!

DAVID: Oh . . . oh . . . There are only two things in the world I have to do—finish my brontosaurus and get married! At three o'clock.[7]

172. CU: *David's legs start out the door, followed by Baby, then by Susan's legs.*

SUSAN *(off)*: Go on, quitter!

173. MLS: *David comes through the door of Susan's apartment into the hallway.*

DAVID: Well, it's no good calling me names, Susan, because I won't argue with you anymore. *(Baby comes through the door, following David to the elevator.)* I don't want anything to do with a leopard.

The elevator doors open and David steps in. Just as the elevator doors close, Baby reaches them.

174. MS: *The hallway.*

SUSAN: Go on, Baby. Down the stairs.

175. LS: *camera pans as Baby heads for the stairs and trots down them.*

176. LS: *Susan closes the door of her apartment and hurries toward the stairs.*

177. LS: *the elevator door opens and David emerges, clutching his box. Camera pans as he crosses to the street door. As he passes the stairway,*

Baby arrives to follow the unsuspecting David out the door. Susan comes down the stairs and hurries toward the door.

178. MS: *camera pans as Susan leaves the building, rushing toward her station wagon, parked at the curb. A doorman stands at the entrance, looking to his right. Susan looks in the same direction.*

    SUSAN: Morning. *(Susan slides into the station wagon and begins to drive it forward.)*

179. MLS: *camera tracks with David, walking along the street, his box under his left arm, oblivious of the fact that Baby is walking directly behind him, to his right. Susan's station wagon pulls into the frame.*

180. MS: *Susan behind the wheel.*

SUSAN: Good morning, Professor.

181. MCU: *David walking as the camera pans.*

   DAVID: Good morning. *(Starts to tip his hat, then shakes his head.)*
   Oh . . .[8]

182. MCU: *Susan behind the wheel.*

   SUSAN: You'd better change your mind about coming to Connecticut.

183. MS: *David and Baby walking, camera tracking.*

   DAVID: Susan, we've settled that question once and for all.

184. MCU: *as in 182.*

   SUSAN: But, what . . . what about my leopard?

185. MS: *tracking, as in 183.*

   DAVID: Hmm, that's your problem.

186. MCU: *as in 182.*

   SUSAN: It's not *all* my problem.

187. MS: *tracking, as in 183.*

   DAVID: Susan, will you please go away?

188. MCU: *as in 182.*

   SUSAN: All right, David. Since he likes you so much, I've decided to
   give him to you.

189. MCU: *David walking.*

DAVID *(smiling smugly)*: I won't take him.
SUSAN *(off)*: Ha, ha! You've got him.

David hears the sound of a snarl nearby.

190. MLS: *David looks down to see Baby by his side. He gasps.*

DAVID: Oh, Su . . . Su . . . *(The sound of a snarl.)* Susan! Don't go away! I've got the leopard! *(Baby lies down on the sidewalk beside David's right foot.)* Susan, bu . . . Oh, dear, dear . . .

Dissolve

Susan's Station Wagon, day

191. MCU: *David and Susan in the front seat of the station wagon, Susan behind the wheel, Baby in the back seat.*[9]

SUSAN: No, David, all I was doing was driving along. That's all I was doing. You were standing on the sidewalk yelling and looking very silly and I came to your rescue . . .
DAVID *(overlapping)*: Now, you know very well you tricked me into this trip.

Baby leans toward them from the back seat, poking his head between them, nuzzling the seat cushion.

DAVID: Uh huh, huh . . . look, look . . . eating your car.

Susan turns to look at Baby. David grabs the wheel.

DAVID: Oh, oh, look at the road!

192. CU: *David.*

DAVID: Oh! *(He shakes his head.)* Oh, dear. I have a feeling something horrible is gonna happen.

193. CU: *Susan.*

   SUSAN: Oh, no, David. Everything's going to be all right.

194. CU: *as in 192.*

   DAVID: I don't care anymore.

195. MS: *Baby pops up behind David and Susan, resting his paws over the back of their seat.*

   DAVID: Oh!
   SUSAN *(to Baby)*: Hello. Aww, what's the matter? Did you get lonely?
   DAVID: Susan, if you know any shortcuts, please take them.

Baby stares in David's face.

SUSAN: We're gonna be there in no time now, David, really.
DAVID: Because all I want to do is deliver this leopard, take the first train back to town and forget the last twenty-four hours ever happened.

Baby still leans between them, attending to the discussion.

SUSAN: Oh, well, now, what's wrong with the last twenty-four hours? I've had a wonderful time.
DAVID: Su . . . Susan, I don't know. You . . . you look at everything upside down. I've never known anyone quite like you.
SUSAN: You've just had a bad day, that's all.
DAVID: Oh, well, that's a masterpiece of understatement. Now, look. *(He looks at Baby.)* Uh . . . Well, I can't, I can't discuss anything with you with Baby breathing down the back of my neck!
SUSAN *(turning to Baby)*: Hey! Hey! Get down! Go on! Go on! Go on! Now, lie down!

196. MLS: *moving shot, rear view of an open-backed truck laden with crates of fowl.*

197. MS: *David and Susan in the station wagon. Susan is still looking at Baby. David grabs for the wheel.*

DAVID: Susan! Duck!

198. LS: *the station wagon swerves just in time to avoid hitting the poultry truck, but manages to sideswipe it. As the station wagon skids forward, crates of fowl topple over the side of the truck as it comes to a halt.*

199. MS: *Susan brings the station wagon to a stop with a jerk. Susan and David look behind.*

200. LS: *flying and cackling fowl—on the ground and in the air.*

201. MS: *Baby strains forward out the rear window of the station wagon.*

202. MCU:

    SUSAN *(grabbing Baby's tail)*: Oh—oh, no . . .
    DAVID: Oh, never hang on to a leopard's tail, Susan.
    SUSAN *(holding on)*: Sing, David. *(She begins to sing.)* "I can't . . .

203. CU: *Baby straining forward.*

    SUSAN *(off)*: . . . give you anything . . . *(David joins.)* . . . but love,
    Baby.

204. MS: *Susan and David.*

    SUSAN AND DAVID *(singing and holding on)*: That's the only thing I've
    plenty of, . . .

205. CU: *Baby leaps from car.*

    SUSAN AND DAVID *(off)*: . . . Baby . . .

Dissolve

Susan's Station Wagon, day

206. MCU: *David stares silently ahead. Feathers on his hat and jacket fly in
the breeze of the moving car.*

    SUSAN *(off)*: Well, anyway, David, I still insist that he was right in the
    middle of the road. I've never hit anything that was in the right place.

207. MS: *Susan and David.*

    DAVID: That wagon was on the *side* of the road, Susan.
    SUSAN: It certainly was not. It was straight ahead of me and that's why I
    bumped into it.
    DAVID *(feathers still floating in the breeze)*: What time is it?

208. MCU: *Susan.*

SUSAN: Well, David, we'll be there in no time. We just have to stop at Westlake to get some meat for Baby.

209. MCU: *as in 206.*

DAVID: Yeh . . . *(Looks at Baby in the back seat.)* Oh!

210. CU: *Baby lying in the back seat, shaking off some feathers.*

DAVID *(off)*: Why, he's already had an assortment of ducks and chickens.

211. MS: *as in 207.*

DAVID: Not to mention a couple of swans.
SUSAN: All feathers.
DAVID: Yeh, well, very expensive feathers. Look, I don't see how any pair of swans could cost a hundred and fifty dollars. That was a gyp.
SUSAN: Well, if you'd run as I told you to, we shouldn't have had to pay for them.

212. MCU: *as in 206.*

DAVID: Susan, when a man is wrestling a leopard in the middle of a pond he's in no position to run![10]

Dissolve

Westlake, day

213. LS: *the station wagon drives along the main street of a small town, moving toward the camera. The faint sound of a calliope can be heard in the distance. Susan pulls the station wagon into an available parking space.*

214. MS

SUSAN *(bringing her car to a stop)*: There it is, David. Please, hurry up.

David opens the car door, steps out, and notices the music.

DAVID: Oh . . . Susan. Why, of all places, when you have a leopard in
  the car, did you have to stop in a town where there's a circus.
SUSAN: But David, I didn't stop because there's a circus. But Baby's
  going to be hungry and we'll have to feed him. Now, please hurry,
  David. If Baby wakes up, we'll be in real trouble.
DAVID: Well, I don't suppose it makes any difference to you, but you're
  parked in front of a fireplug.
SUSAN: Uh huh. *(She nods.)* I know it. But don't worry about that, David.
  I'm going to take care of everything. You go ahead.

*Camera pans with David, still carrying his box under his right arm, as he
crosses the sidewalk and enters the market.*

215. MLS: *camera pans with David, who walks in the door and crosses to the
  meat counter. To his right, at the far end of the meat counter, Doctor
  Lehman waits for his purchase.*

  CLERK *(returning change to a woman customer)*: Fifty . . . one dollar.
    Thank you. *(To David.)* Yes, sir. What can I do for you?"
  DAVID: I want thirty pounds of sirloin steak, please.

216. MS: *the clerk behind the meat counter, David on the other side.*

  CLERK: Did you say thirty pounds?

217. MS: *reverse of 216.*

  DAVID: Yes, that's right. Thirty pounds.

218. MCU: *Clerk, as in 216.*

  CLERK: How will you have it cut?

219. MS: *as in 217.*

  DAVID: Oh, just in one piece.

220. MCU: *as in 218.*

    CLERK: Are you gonna roast it or broil it?

221. MLS: *as at the end of 215.*

    DAVID: Neither. It's going to be eaten raw. *(David nods.)*
    CLERK *(pausing a beat)*: Yeah.

    The clerk walks back to the refrigerator. David looks toward the street, then turns back to address the clerk, only to discover he has departed.

222. MLS: *Slocum, walking in front of Jergen's Market, hands in pockets, whistling. He kicks a piece of something into the gutter, then notices a car parked at the fireplug.*

223. LS: *Susan perched on the running board of her car, looking off right. Circus music off.*

    SLOCUM *(snapping his fingers)*: Hey, uh, lady!
    SUSAN: Huh?
    SLOCUM *(indicating hydrant)*: That's a fireplug.
    SUSAN *(laughs)*: I know it—*(She continues to look off.)*
    SLOCUM: It's against the law to park alongside a fireplug.
    SUSAN: I know it.
    SLOCUM: Come here. *(Beckons with his left hand.)*
    SUSAN: Who, me? Why?
    SLOCUM *(pulling back his coat lapel to reveal his badge.)*: I'm Constable Slocum.

224. MCU: *Susan.*

    SUSAN: Oh. Is that so? *(She steps down from the running board.)*

225. MS: *Susan and Slocum on sidewalk.*

    SUSAN *(crossing to Slocum)*: How do you do? I'm Susan Vance.

SLOCUM: How do you d . . . , Now, listen, I don't care who you are. I just
want to let you know that you can't park alongside of a fireplug.

SUSAN: Yes, well, you see, I was just watching the parade.

SLOCUM: Oh, you were.

SUSAN: I suppose you get free seats to the circus.

SLOCUM: Well, Elmer and I usually get a coup . . . Now, listen, young
lady, that has nothin' to do with it. *(A clerk leaves the meat market,
carrying packages.)* [12]

226. CU: *Baby lifts his head in the back seat of the station wagon.*

SLOCUM *(off)*: I'm just gonna give you a ticket.

SUSAN *(off)*: Oh, . . .

227. MS: *as in 225.*

SUSAN: . . . Well, thank you very much, Constable. I'd love to go to the
circus. But you'd better keep your tickets because I'm busy tonight.

SLOCUM *(writing)*: Yeah, well, it ain't that kind of a ticket.

Susan glances toward the station wagon.

228. MS: *Baby leaps from the window of the station wagon into the window of
a limousine, parked alongside to the left.*

229. MS: *as in 225. Slocum still writing, his attention on the pad.*

SUSAN: Oh, jeepers!

SLOCUM: Young lady, it might interest you to know that you're under
arrest!

SUSAN: Oh, well . . . *(She turns from Baby to Slocum.)* I mean, why?

SLOCUM: For parking alongside of a fireplug!

SUSAN: Oh. *(shakes her head.)* But I'm not parked next to a fireplug.

230. MLS: *Susan and Slocum.*

SLOCUM: You ain't? Well, what do you call that? *(Indicates fireplug.)*

SUSAN *(looking at the fireplug)*: Oh, well, you mean that you think that this is my car. *(She touches the spare tire on front fender of the station wagon.)*
SLOCUM: Well, ain't it?
SUSAN: No. *(Indicates limousine.) That's* my car.
SLOCUM: Well, why didn't you say so in the first place.
SUSAN: Well, you didn't ask me.
SLOCUM: Oh . . . Uh . . .

He turns and walks away. Susan darts toward the limousine.

231. MS: *David and the clerk at the meat counter, Lehman observing. David's large package of meat lies on the counter.*

CLERK: Say, do you grind this up before you eat it?
DAVID: Oh, oh, this isn't for me. It's for Baby. *(He puts the large package under his left arm, the box still under his right.)*
CLERK: Oh, I see. Huh? . . .

David walks out the door as Lehman watches.

232. LS: *David at the curb, carrying the large bundle of meat, Susan seated behind the wheel of the limousine.*

SUSAN: Hurry up, David. Get in!
DAVID: But, but, but . . .

The car begins to back away from the curb.

SUSAN: Jump on.
DAVID *(running after the car)*: But that isn't your car.
SUSAN: No, but it's my leopard.

David hops onto the running board, carrying the package of meat, tossing his box into the car. As the car pulls away, Lehman rushes into the vacated parking space, pointing.

LEHMAN: Hey! Hey, wait a minute! Hey! Wait a minute! That's my car! Come back here! Come back . . .

Slocum, with his sidekick, Elmer, joins Lehman in the vacated parking space.

SLOCUM *(overlapping)*: Hear that? What're you yelling about?
LEHMAN: They stole my car.
SLOCUM: Stole your car?
LEHMAN: Last night they tried to steal my wife's purse.
SLOCUM: What!
LEHMAN: Now, don't stand there. Do something! Go out and catch them!
SLOCUM: Well, Elmer, bless me. *(Claps his hands.)* Hey! Bring back that car!

The three of them run in the direction in which the car sped off.

Dissolve

Stables at Aunt Elizabeth's House, day

233. LS: *the limousine in a stable. Susan gets out to join David. Both are singing, "I Can't Give You Anything but Love, Baby." They sing the following words to its tune.*

DAVID *(singing)*: I'm glad we finally got here.
SUSAN *(singing)*: I know. But isn't it wonderful? *(Closes the car door.)* We could put him in that box. No, wait a minute. *(Still sings while David hums.)* Don't open the door until you close those. *(Indicates the stable doors.)*
DAVID *(singing)*: I think that is a good idea too.

He runs to close the stable doors while Susan opens the door of a stall. A light change indicates the stable doors are closed. Both continue to sing. David moves to the stall door as Susan crosses to the car door.

SUSAN *(singing)*: Get by that door and I'll open this one. *(She opens limousine door and Baby saunters out.)* Come on, Baby. Go on. *(Baby makes a wrong turn.)*

DAVID *(singing, box under his arm)*: Just go in the right stall, Baby.

SUSAN *(singing)*: Right in there, right in there, ri-ight in there.

After she guides Baby into the stall, she and David quickly close the door and latch it.

SUSAN *(still singing)*: Now everything is quite all right.

DAVID *(singing)*: No everything is not all . . . *(He shakes his head.)*

234. MS: *David and Susan.*

DAVID *(no longer singing)*: Everything is not all right, Susan. It may be all right for you, but now I've got to get back to New York.

SUSAN: Oh, David. *(Stamps her foot.)* What a one you are! No sooner do you get one thing settled than you start worrying about something else. Now, come into the house . . .

DAVID *(overlapping)*: My heavens, Susan, one of us should worry. *(He retreats from her advance.)* Because on top of all that's happened, we've stolen a car. *(Points at it with his left arm, the box still under his right.)* Look.

SUSAN *(crossing to car for her purse)*: Oh, well, that's all right. I'll send it back. I don't like it anyway.

DAVID: Uh huh. I suppose you'd like me to leave it with the constable on my way back to New York.

SUSAN *(brushing some feathers from the left shoulder of his jacket)*: No. That wouldn't be safe. You might be arrested. Besides, it's a hot car. *(Still brushing feathers from his coat.)*

DAVID: Uh, huh, yes, I know. You're going to file the numbers off the engine.

SUSAN: No. That would be dishonest. I'll have the gardener take it back after it's dark. *(David stops her fussing with the feathers on his coat.)* But wait! You're, you're . . .

DAVID *(overlapping)*: Stop it, Susan! Stop it! *(He backs away and slaps her hand away.)*

SUSAN: . . . shedding.

DAVID: Now, where's a telephone?

SUSAN: Out that door. *(Points to her right.)*

DAVID: Well, that's all I want to know. Thank you. *(He moves toward the door.)*

SUSAN *(running after him, as the camera tracks with them)*: No, but David, what I want to suggest is . . .

DAVID *(still moving)*: Now, Susan, I don't want any more suggestions from you. My fiancée is waiting for me in New York, and in order to get married, I have to get to New York. *(He opens the door, through which Susan glides first.)*

235. MLS: *Susan and David outside the stable door.*

SUSAN: Oh, well, David, I want you to be married. *(They walk together down a path.)* I think you should be married. I think every man should be married. *(The camera pans with them as they walk.)* But I don't think that any self-respecting girl will marry you looking the way you do.

DAVID *(overlapping)*: Where is the telephone?

SUSAN: In there. *(They continue to walk toward the house.)* But David, look at yourself. You're filthy . . .

DAVID *(overlapping)*: Well, what's the matter with me? My . . . *(Looks down at himself.)* Oh, my . . . I am dirty, aren't I?

SUSAN: There, you see. Now, what I want to suggest is that you come into . . .

236. MS: *Susan and David.*

DAVID: Ah! The only way you'll ever get me to follow another of your suggestions is to hold a bright object in front of my eyes and twirl it. *(He starts toward the house.)*

SUSAN: Yes, I understand that. *(She is running after him.)* I simply wanted to suggest . . .

DAVID: I don't want any suggestions. All I want to do just now is to clean up. *(He holds out his arms imploringly, the box still under his right arm.)* Where is there a shower, please?

SUSAN: That's what I was going to suggest. A shower.

DAVID: Huh? Oh . . .

She walks toward the house as David follows.

Dissolve

Aunt Elizabeth's House, day

237. CU: *David under the shower.*

238. MS: *a door opens. Susan, wearing a bathrobe, peeps into the guest room. The camera pans with her as she runs to the foot of the bed and scoops up David's clothes, including his shoes and his hat, which she puts atop her own head. Camera pans with her as she races out of the room.*

239. LS: *camera pans with Susan, carrying David's clothes, as she races from the guest room through the living room and dining room.*

240. MLS: *the door to the kitchen opens as Susan races in, carrying David's clothes.*

SUSAN: Hannah!

Camera pans with Susan as she races to the kitchen table in the center of the room. Hannah is busy at the stove nearby.

SUSAN: Hannah, I want you to send these things to town and have them cleaned and pressed.
HANNAH: But, why send them into town? I can do them here. *(Susan has put them on the table.)*
SUSAN: Now, don't argue with me, Hannah. Into town. And have them cleaned and pressed.
HANNAH: It'll take a lot longer . . .
SUSAN *(moving again as the camera pans with her)*: Oh, well, there's no hurry, Hannah. No hurry at all. *(She leaves the kitchen and closes the door.)*

241. LS: *as in 239, camera pans as Susan runs through living room and dining room.*

242. MS: *Susan appears at the door of the guest room, pauses, then crosses into the room as the camera pans with her.*

SUSAN: Hurry up, David.
DAVID *(off)*: I am hurrying.

Susan sits on the bed and idly picks up David's box, lying beside her. She sets it in her lap.

SUSAN: David?
DAVID *(off)*: What?
SUSAN: 'S in the box?
DAVID *(off)*: What did you say?
SUSAN: What's in the box?
DAVID *(off)*: Oh, that's the intercostal clavicle of a brontosaurus.
SUSAN: Oh, really? *(Opens box.)* Oh, it's just an old bone.

243. MS: *the door leading to the bathroom opens slightly, and David looks out through the crack.*

DAVID: Yes, Susan, it's just an old bone. Put it down gently and go
    away.

244. MS: *Susan seated on the bed.*

SUSAN: All right, David. *(She sets the box on the bed, rises, and leans on the bedpost.)* Is there anything else I can do for you?
DAVID *(off)*: Oh, yes. Hand me my clothes, will you?
SUSAN: Well, David, they aren't, they aren't here. They're being pressed.
DAVID *(off)*: What?
SUSAN: I mean, well, I mean, the gardener's taken them into town.

245. MS: *as in 243.*

DAVID *(peering through the crack of the bathroom door)*: Oh, uh, well,
    stop him! I can't wait! I must leave here immediately!

246. MS: *Susan at the bedpost.*

SUSAN: David, you can't leave without your clothes. *(She starts to leave.)*

247. MS: *as in 243.*

DAVID: Well, I know that. Bu . . . Where are you going?

248. MLS: *Susan at guest room door.*

SUSAN: I'm going to take a shower. *(She leaves.)*

249. MS: *as in 243.*

DAVID: Oh, Susan! Susan! Don't leave me here like this!

250. MLS: *Susan pinning up her hair as she crosses toward her own bathroom.*

SUSAN: Don't be impatient, David. We'll talk it over after I've finished. Everything's gonna be all right . . .

251. MS: *David at the crack in the bathroom door.*

DAVID: Yeh. Everything's gonna be all right.

Through the partially open bathroom door we see his shadow on the wall as he slips into something to wear.

DAVID *(off)*: Oh, certainly. Everything's gonna be all right. Everything's gonna be . . . Oh, I'm losing my mind, that's all. Huh, huh. Roaming around Connecticut without any clothes on. I'll go crazy. How can all these things happen to just one person?

He comes through the bathroom door wearing a very frilly, feminine, white negligee, but not wearing his glasses. Camera pans with him as he gallops toward the adjoining room.

DAVID: Susan! Susan!

252. MLS: *David in front of Susan's bathroom door.*

DAVID: Susan! Susan, where are you?
SUSAN *(off)*: Huh?
DAVID *(speaking to the closed bathroom door)*: Susan, will you come out of there and help me find some clothes or must I come in and get you?
SUSAN *(off)*: Oh, David, you wouldn't.

253. MCU: *David outside bathroom door.*

DAVID: Oh, yes I would. *(Strides to the bathroom door. Then stops.)* Oh, maybe I wouldn't. *(Retreats from the door, then turns back to address it.)* Susan, where's the gardener's room?
SUSAN *(off)*: Why?
DAVID: Because he must have some clothes. Where's his room?
SUSAN *(off)*: What? I can't hear you.
DAVID: You can hear what you want to hear.
SUSAN *(off)*: No, really, I can't. What'd you say?
DAVID: I just said, uh . . . never mind. I'll find the place myself. *(He leaves the frame.)*

254. MLS: *panning with David as he leaves the adjoining room.*

DAVID: The gardener must have clothes. Clothes are clothes.
SUSAN *(off)*: The gardener's in town.
DAVID: Well, he couldn't have taken all his clothes with him!
SUSAN *(off)*: Oh, yes he could!
DAVID: Of all the conceited, spoiled, little scatterbrains . . . *(He rushes toward the living room.)* My goodness, the man who gets . . . *(The doorbell rings just as David reaches the entry hall.)* The man who gets you is gonna have a lifetime of misery! *(Camera pans with David as he crosses to the front door.)* *(Mocking her.)* Everything's gonna be all right. Yes, everything's gonna be . . . *(He throws open the door. Aunt Elizabeth steps over the threshold.)* What do you want?
AUNT: Well, who are you?
DAVID: Who are you?
AUNT: But, who are *you?*

255. MS: *David and Aunt Elizabeth at the front door.*

> DAVID: What do you want?
> AUNT: Well, who *are* you?
> DAVID *(sighing deeply)*: I don't know. I'm not quite myself today.

256. MCU: *Aunt Elizabeth, seen over David's shoulder.*

> AUNT: Well, you look perfectly idiotic in those clothes.

257. MCU: *reverse shot of 256.*

> DAVID: These aren't my clothes.
> AUNT: Well, where are your clothes?
> DAVID: I've lost my clothes.

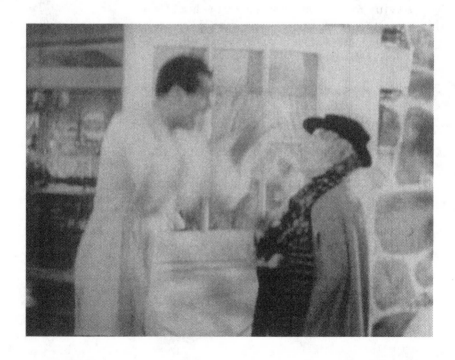

258. MS: *as in 255.*

> AUNT: But, why are you wearing these clothes?
> DAVID: Because I just went gay . . . *(He leaps into the air as Aunt Elizabeth recoils.)* . . . all of a sudden.

259. MLS: *David and Aunt.*

> DAVID: Oh, excuse me. I'm sorry.

He turns away and crosses toward the staircase as Aunt follows and camera pans.

> AUNT: Now, see here young man, stop this nonsense!

David sits on a lower step of the staircase.

> AUNT: What are you doing?

260. MCU: *David on staircase.*

> DAVID: I'm sitting in the middle of Forty-second Street, waiting for a bus.

261. MS: *George trots into the open front door, wags his tail, and barks three times.*

262. MCU: *David stares gloomily ahead; George's barking continues off.*

263. MLS: *as at the end of 259. George runs in, barking continuously at David.*

> DAVID: Shoo!

Hannah enters from the living room as George's barking continues.

> AUNT: Come here. Who is this man?

HANNAH: I don't know.
AUNT: Stop it, George! Well, what's he doing here?
HANNAH: I don't know.

264. MLS: *Susan, still in a bathrobe, runs through a door toward the barking noise.*

SUSAN: Uh oh. *(She turns to go back into the bedroom.)*
AUNT *(off)*: Susan! Susan! Come back here!

265. MLS: *as in 263.*

AUNT: Stop it, George. Susan, come here and tell me about . . .

266. LS: *camera pans as Susan runs toward her aunt, arms outstretched, and embraces her. George is still barking, David is still sitting on the lower stair, his head in his hands, staring at George.*

SUSAN: Why, Aunt Elizabeth. Why, it's you! Well, I've never been so thrilled in my life. This is amazing to see you here. *(Bends down.)* And George. Dear little George. *(George's renewed yelping drowns out Susan's bubbling chatter.)*
AUNT: Quiet, George.

267. MS: *Susan and Aunt Elizabeth.*

AUNT: Now, stop gushing and tell me: who is this man? *(Susan's continuous chatter overlaps the din.)*

268. MCU: *David raises his head to speak but gives up trying to pierce the chatter and barking with a word.*

AUNT *(off)*: Who is this man? *(More chatter from Susan and barking from George.)* Where'd you get him?
SUSAN *(off)*: He's a friend of Mark's.
AUNT *(off)*: What's he doing here?
DAVID *(finally getting a word in)*: Susan brought me! *(He nods victoriously.)*

AUNT *(off)*: I don't doubt it, but why?

269. MLS: *Susan and Aunt standing, David seated on the stair, his head in his hands.*

   SUSAN: You see, I had a letter from Mark from Brazil. He said that David was an old, old friend of his. *(David returns his head to his hands.)* He'd been working very very hard in town. And that he was on the point of having a nervous breakdown. *(She makes a screwy twisting of her right index finger.)*
   DAVID: Well, that's it. Oh, now I'm a nut from Brazil!

270. MCU: *Susan and Aunt Elizabeth.*

   SUSAN: Well, he's very excitable. He must be allowed to do whatever he wants to do.
   AUNT: Where are his clothes?

271. MCU: *David's head resting on his hands.*

   DAVID: Susan took them.
   SUSAN *(off)*: His clothes?
   HANNAH *(off)*: Gogarty's taken them into town.
   AUNT: *(off)*: What's he doing in that thing?
   SUSAN *(off)*: Oh, well, Mark says he should be allowed to wear a negligee if he . . .

272. MCU: *as in 270.*

   SUSAN: . . . wants to wear a negligee. Because there's no telling, Mark says, what will happen if he doesn't have his own way.

273. MS: *reverse of 272.*

   AUNT: Does he want to wear those clothes?

274. MCU: *as in 271.*

DAVID: No, I don't want to wear this thing! I just want to get married!
(He bounces up and down on the stair; George barks.)

275. MS: *Susan smiling down at David, Aunt Elizabeth exasperated.*

AUNT: Susan, I forbid it!

276. MCU: *as in 271. David alternates between trying to explain and putting his chin on his left fist.*

AUNT *(off)*: I absolutely put my foot down! The idea!
SUSAN *(off)*: Oh, Auntie, you don't understand! You've made a terrible
mistake.
AUNT *(off)*: I won't permit it! The very idea! Marrying a man . . .

The off-frame dialogue becomes unintelligible, punctuated by George's barking. David has finally had it.

277. MLS: *David rises and moves to group.*

DAVID: Quiet! Quiet! *(Aunt and Susan continue to bicker.)* QUIET!!!
SUSAN *(overlapping)*: David, don't talk so much.

David raises his left foot and stomps it on Susan's toes. Susan yelps and and grabs her right foot. She sits on the stair in pain as David advances on Aunt and Hannah. Even George is silent.

278. MS: *David, Aunt Elizabeth, and Hannah.*

DAVID: Perhaps you can help me. *(Coolly and deliberately.)* Perhaps you
can help me find some clothes.
AUNT *(fidgeting with her gloves)*: Why, yes, yes. *(Laughs nervously.)*
Must be some of Mark's things around . . . somewhere . . . under
some . . . *(Prods Hannah with her left hand.)*
DAVID *(to Hannah)*: Are there?
HANNAH: Well, uh, well, uh, oh, yes! There are some in Mr. Mark's
room, sir. *(Indicates.)* Yes, sir.

DAVID: Which is Mr. Mark's room?

HANNAH *(indicating again)*: Well, it's at the end, sir. Yes, sir.

DAVID *(to Hannah)*: Thank you. *(To Aunt.)* Thank you. *(Aunt Elizabeth recoils from the sharp tone.)*

279. LS: *David turns and stalks away from the group, camera panning with him. George follows at his heels, barking loudly.*

DAVID: Go 'way. Go 'way. Go 'way. *(David runs to escape the beast, dashing into Mark's room, George right behind him. David runs out of Mark's room and George follows.)* Oh, go away!

As George readies to run back into Mark's room, David, inside the room, swings the door shut, leaving George alone, barking noisily.

280. MCU: *Susan sitting on the stairs, counting on her toes. Her aunt's shoes, hands, and skirt are visible behind her.*

SUSAN: He loves me—he loves me not—he loves me—he loves me not—he loves me—David! Where'd he go?

AUNT *(off)*: Went to get some clothes.

281. LS

SUSAN: If he gets some clothes he'll go away. *(Rises.)* And he's the only man I've ever loved. *(Camera pans with her as she runs toward Mark's room.)* David! Oh . . .

As Susan turns and rushes through the door of the guest room, George follows her, barking.

282. MS: *panning with Susan on the run.*

SUSAN: Oh, stop it! Get away from me.[13]

Susan hurries to a closet to grab some clothes. George jumps up on a bench at the foot of the bed, watching Susan, barking.

SUSAN: Oh, George, please keep quiet. *(Camera pans with Susan as she rushes out of the bedroom.)*

283. MCU: *George, barking, sees David's box and leaps on the bed. After sniffing the box, he takes out the bone, leaps off the bed, and scurries out the door with the bone in his mouth.*

284. MS: *camera panning as George runs through the living room, carrying David's bone, out the front door.*

Dissolve

Aunt Elizabeth's House, day

285. MLS: *camera pans with Susan, in slacks and a loose blouse, carrying a straw sunhat. She comes out of the bedroom, runs to the door of Mark's room, and raps on the door.*

SUSAN: David?
DAVID *(off)*: What?
SUSAN: Can I come in?

286. LS: *a form is barely visible behind the door of the closet in Mark's room.*

DAVID: I don't care what you do.
SUSAN *(off)*: Thanks.

The door opens and Susan enters the room.

SUSAN: Where are you?
DAVID: Here I am. What do you want? *(David appears from the closet, wearing a hunting coat and breeches, carrying a pair of riding boots in his left hand and a pair of sandals in the right. He is without glasses.)*
SUSAN: Oh, jeep . . . *(She can't stop herself from laughing.)*
DAVID: Oh, go on and laugh. I know it looks ridiculous but I'm past caring.
SUSAN: Oh, no, I don't mean . . . What are you gonna do?

DAVID: What I've been trying to do. Get back to New York. *(He sits on a chair beside the bed to measure the sole of the boot against his foot.)*

SUSAN: But David, you can't go to New York dressed that way. You might be . . .

DAVID: They're all I could find. And clothes are clothes. And I'm going. I'm going back to New York . . . *(He throws the boot down.)* . . . if only to repair the damage that's been done since I've known you. *(Bends over to tie on the sandals.)* My goodness, the damage I've done to Miss Swallow, to the museum, to Mr. Peabody, and everybody else I've known in all my life . . .

SUSAN: Mr. Peabody? But, David . . . *(She squats down beside him.)*

287. MCU: *David, bending over to put on his sandals, while Susan kneels in front of him.*

SUSAN: . . . the one way for you to get to Mr. Peabody is through Aunt Elizabeth.

DAVID: I don't want to hear.

SUSAN: Please listen to me for one second. Now, he'll do anything that she tells him to. He'll even like you. He's Aunt Elizabeth's lawyer. *(David looks up from his lacing.)* He's her lawyer. Mr. Peabody.

DAVID *(stopping and gulping)*: What's your aunt's name?

SUSAN: Elizabeth.

DAVID: No, she has another name.

SUSAN: Yes, of course she has. It's . . .

DAVID: No, no, never mind, never mind. Don't tell me. *(He puts his left hand to his forehead.)*

SUSAN: Well, why not? It's Random. Mrs. Carleton Random.

DAVID: Yes, I know, I know. I knew that was coming.

SUSAN: Well, what's the matter?

DAVID *(muttering, as he rises and walks out of the frame)*: Out of seven million people, why did I have to run into you yesterday?

SUSAN: Well, what have I done?

288. MS: *David near windows.*

DAVID: Susan. Mrs. Random is gonna give away a million dollars.

SUSAN *(off)*: I know.
DAVID: I wanted it for the museum.

289. MS: *Susan squatting on the floor.*

SUSAN: Oh! David! Well, I'm afraid that you've made a rather unfavorable impression on Aunt Elizabeth.

290. MS: *as in 288.*

DAVID: Yeh, I quite realize that. *(He kneels down.)*

291. MS: *David and Susan.*

DAVID: Susan. Susan, listen to me.
SUSAN: What?
DAVID: Now, a lot of things have happened but we'll forget all about
them because this is serious.
SUSAN: What, David? *(She moves closer.)*
DAVID: Well, can you concentrate for just a moment? *(He holds her
shoulders.)*
SUSAN: Uh huh.
DAVID: There's only one thing to be done.

292. MCU: *Susan over David's shoulder.*

DAVID: And this is important to me and to my work.
SUSAN: O-o-o-h-h.
DAVID: What?
SUSAN: You're so good-looking without your glasses.

293. MCU: *reverse shot of 292.*

DAVID *(shaking his head)*: Susan, listen to me. And try and remember.

294. MCU: *as in 292.*

SUSAN: What?

DAVID: Well, you see, I've made a horrible mess of things.

SUSAN: Uh huh.

DAVID: And your aunt must never find out who I am. You do understand all that, don't you, Susan?

SUSAN: Yes, David.

295. MS: *David holds Susan's shoulders, she looks into his eyes.*

DAVID: You can tell her that I'm a friend of Mark's. That I have bats in the belfry. But don't ever tell her my name is David Huxley. Now, can you remember all that, Susan?

SUSAN: Yes, David.

296. MCU: *as in 292.*

DAVID: You sure?

SUSAN: Yes, David. But you *are* good-looking without your glasses.

297. MCU: *as in 293.*

DAVID: Oh, never mind, Susan. Susan, never mind.

298. MLS: *David rises and moves toward the bedroom as Susan follows.*

SUSAN: What'd I say? What'd I say? What'd I do?

299. MLS: *David, Susan following close on his heels, enters the bedroom. Camera pans as he crosses to the mantel to retrieve his glasses.*

SUSAN: What'd I say? What'd I say? What'd I do, David?

David puts on his glasses, crosses to bed, and picks up his box.

DAVID: Susan, I just asked you to remember one thing . . .

He sees that the box is empty. Susan follows him to the bed.

SUSAN: I know, David. And I swear I'm going to remember it.
DAVID: Where is it?
SUSAN: I know exactly what you told me to say. It's lucky my mind . . .
DAVID: Where is it?
SUSAN: Where's what?
DAVID: My intercostal clavicle!
SUSAN: Your what?
DAVID: My bone! It's rare. It's precious. What did you do with it?
SUSAN: The bone! *(She removes the packing paper from the empty box.)*
DAVID: Susan, you had it. Give it to me.
SUSAN: No, I haven't got it. I really haven't got it.
DAVID *(grabbing her left wrist)*: Well, did you carry it somewhere?
SUSAN: No, David. What would I be doing carrying a bone around?
DAVID *(dropping her wrist)*: But I, I wouldn't dare give a reason for
   anything you do. *(He backs off and kneels down, looking under
   the bed.)*
SUSAN: Well, I guess you have to find another one.
DAVID: Wuh, it took three expeditions and five years to find that one.

300. MCU: *Susan.*

SUSAN: Well, David, now that they know where to find them, couldn't
   you send them back to get another one?

301. MCS: *David and Susan holding the bedpost between them.*

DAVID *(getting to his feet and crossing to her)*: Susan, look. You had it.
   You took it out of the box. Now, where did you put it?
SUSAN: I put it back in the box.
DAVID: Well, was there somebody else in the room?
SUSAN: No, David, there was nobody else in the room, but . . . *(She
   stops.)* David, George!
DAVID: Who's George?
SUSAN: The dog. You know? Don't you see? Dog—bone. Dog—bone.
DAVID: O-o-o-o-h-h-h.

He rushes off, followed by Susan.

302. LS: *David running out of the guest room with Susan on his heels. Camera pans with them as they race around living room.*

DAVID: George!
SUSAN: George!
DAVID: George!
SUSAN: George!
DAVID: Geor . . .
SUSAN: George!
DAVID *(stopping)*: Oh, stop it, Susan. You sound like an echo. *(On the run again, Susan behind him.)* George!
SUSAN: Nice George!

303. MLS: *David and Susan running through the dining room.*

DAVID: George!
SUSAN: Nice George!
DAVID: Nice George!
SUSAN: George!

David rushes back into the living room, Susan following, where they encounter Aunt Elizabeth.

DAVID: Did you see him?
AUNT: See who?

304. MS: *David, Susan, and Aunt Elizabeth.*

DAVID: George.
AUNT *(pointing at David's outfit)*: Are those the only clothes you could find?

David quickly shakes her outstretched finger and runs out the front door. Susan shakes it too and runs out.

AUNT: Susan! Susan! *(Claps her hands.)* Come back here! Come back here this minute! *(Susan returns.)* What are you doing?

SUSAN: Hunting for George.
AUNT: Why?
SUSAN: David wants him, David loves him, David thinks he's such a
   nice dog. *(Ties on her sunhat.)*
AUNT: George is a perfect little fiend and you know it!
SUSAN: But David doesn't. *(She runs out the front door.)*
AUNT: Come here, Susan! Oh! *(She raises her fists.)* Oh! Oh!

305. MLS: *camera pans with David, walking on the garden path, wearing his
   hunting outfit with sandals and white socks. Susan rushes toward him.*

SUSAN: David!
DAVID *(whistling)*: George!
SUSAN: He's definitely not in the house. That's settled. *(David whistles.)*
   Don't do that, David. If he knows you want him, he'll hide.
DAVID: Well, Susan, where's he apt to go?
SUSAN: George is apt to go anywhere.
DAVID: Oh, I don't mean that. Where does he hide things?
SUSAN *(giggling)*: Oh, now David, how can I tell that?
DAVID: Well, you ought to know. *(A piercing bark off.)* Oh! There he is!
   George! George! *(David points and rushes to his left.)*

306. LS: *a running David and Susan encounter the trotting George, who
   enters the frame from the opposite direction.*

DAVID: Oh, my goodness, look at his nose. He's been digging. He's
   buried it.

George looks up at David and wags his tail.

SUSAN: David, there are twenty-six acres in this garden!
DAVID: Well, that's awful! Now, George. *(He kneels and points. George
   yaps. David withdraws his finger.)* Where did you hide that bone?
SUSAN: No, no, David—not that way, now.

307. MS: *Susan kneels down beside David and George.*

SUSAN: Now, George, we're not angry. No. David and Susan need that
  bone. It's a nasty old bone. It's hundreds of years old. That's David's
  bone. *(George lies down.)* Now, Susan'll get you a nice fresh bone if
  you'll just show us where it is.
DAVID: Oh, look at the nasty little cur.
SUSAN: No, no, no, you'll ruin everything. Spell it. Now, George, don't
  be stubborn. Susan loves you. Now, where'd you put it? *(Mimes digging.)* Don't you remember? Where'd you dig?
DAVID: He's not paying a bit of attention . . .
SUSAN: Where'd you dig? Yes, he is.

George springs up and trots off. Susan and David leap to their feet and follow.

DAVID: Oh, George! George!

308. LS: *George, with David and Susan rushing behind, runs toward a tree trunk in the foreground.*

SUSAN: See? It's all very easy if you know how to handle him.

309. CU: *George in a flowerbed.*

SUSAN *(off)*: Everything's going to be all right, David. This must be the spot.

310. MS: *Susan and David watching George.*

SUSAN: He's gonna start digging in a minute. I can tell. There he goes. That's right, George. That's right. *(They bend down to watch closely.)*

311. CU: *George digging.*

SUSAN *(off)*: Nice George. You see, it's all very simple if you keep your head.

312. MS: *as in 310.*

DAVID: I do hope he doesn't hurt that bone.
SUSAN *(overlapping)*: Isn't he a nice little dog? Isn't he a strong little man, David? Oh, he's got something!

313. MLS: *Susan and David crouching over George.*

SUSAN: He's got something!

Susan and David drop to their knees and dig alongside George.

SUSAN: Come on, little digger. Dig!

DAVID: I'm digging. *(George yelps.)*

SUSAN: Oh, I feel something! I feel something!

DAVID: Oh, I hope it isn't hurt.

Susan pulls up an old shoe.

SUSAN: Oh, look, David, a boot.

DAVID *(taking it from her)*: A boot. *(He makes a motion as if to hit her with it.)*

SUSAN: Don't hit George, David.

DAVID: I wasn't gonna hit George.

SUSAN: Now, George, that was fine. But, now you've got to concentrate again. David has to find his bone. *(George sniffs the hole.)* No, not in there.

George runs off to the right. David and Susan leap up to follow.

314. LS: *David and Susan run around a tree as the camera pans.*

SUSAN: Isn't this fun, David? Just like a game.

DAVID: Oh, yes.

SUSAN: Now, George, if you get tired of digging, you just tell David and Susan where you hid it and they'll dig.

Dissolve

The Garden, day

315. CU: *George, lying in a shallow hole, panting.*

DAVID *(off)*: Susan?

SUSAN *(off)*: What?

316. MLS: *David standing with a shovel, Susan digging with a spade, while George lies nearby.*

DAVID: Do you think George is really trying?

SUSAN: Well, David, almost every place he's taken us we've found something.

DAVID: But nothing here. *(He throws aside a small bush.)*

SUSAN *(laughing)*: Oh, look, David, another boot. *(She holds it up, then tosses it aside.)*

DAVID: Oh, another boot! That makes three pair. Now, come on George. Quit stalling! Where is it? *(Leans on the shovel.)*

SUSAN *(rising and moving to David)*: Oh, don't be discouraged, David. Now, George, concentrate. *(Kneels down.)* Bone—not boots.

George leaps up and trots off.

DAVID: Oh, there he goes.

SUSAN: Ah! You see? He's got the idea.

DAVID *(following George)*: I'm getting tired of all this digging.

SUSAN: Yes, what we need is a plow.[14]

317. MLS: *another part of the garden.*

AUNT: Susan!

318. MLS: *at a stream. Susan and David have just followed George across some stepping stones.*

AUNT *(off)*: Susan!

SUSAN: Oh, jeepers! Aunt Elizabeth!

George makes a sudden dash to the left.

DAVID *(overlapping)*: There he goes! *(David rushes after him.)*

SUSAN: Follow him, David! Don't let him get away.

319. MLS: *as in 317.*

AUNT: Susan!

320. MLS: *as in 318.*

SUSAN: Yes, Auntie! I'm coming.

Camera pans as Susan rushes to her left, while Aunt Elizabeth meets her from the opposite direction.

AUNT: Susan!
SUSAN: What?
AUNT: What on earth are you doing? What, what, what, what are all these?
SUSAN: Those? Oh, they're holes.
AUNT: Well, holes. Of course. I can see they're holes. How'd they get here?

321. MS: *Susan and Aunt Elizabeth.*

SUSAN: Well, uh, David and George and I were digging.
AUNT: Who is this David?
SUSAN: He's a . . . friend of Mark's.
AUNT: Is that all you know about him?
SUSAN: No. I know that I'm gonna marry him. He doesn't know it, but I am.
AUNT: Now, see here. If you're planning to marry him on my money you're very much mistaken. I don't want another lunatic in the family. I've got lunatics enough already. When are you going to marry him? What's his name?

322. MCU: *Susan and Aunt Elizabeth.*

SUSAN: It's . . . uh . . . Bone.
AUNT: Bones?
SUSAN: One bone.
AUNT *(overlapping)*: What a ridiculous name. Well, one bone or two bones. It's a ridiculous name. What does he do?
SUSAN: . . . He hunts.

AUNT: Hunts? Hunts what?
SUSAN: Well, animals. *(With a laugh.)* I should think.
AUNT: Big-game hunting, huh?
SUSAN: Yes. Very big.
AUNT *(indicating to the left)*: You call that big-game hunting?

323. LS: *David, on his hands and knees, follows George around a tree and into a shrub.*

AUNT *(off)*: Look at that!
SUSAN *(off)*: Well, Auntie, he's just playing with George.
AUNT *(off)*: Well, he's not going to play with George another minute.[15]

324. MS: *as in 321.*

AUNT: Tell him dinner's at half-past eight sharp, and not to keep us
   waiting.

325. MLS: *David and George crawling through shrubbery.*

AUNT *(off)*: George! Come here, this minute. George!

George scampers off as David lunges for him, misses, and sprawls.

326. MLS: *Susan and Aunt Elizabeth, joined by George.*

AUNT: Come along, George. *(She turns and leaves with George at
   her heels.)*
SUSAN: Oh! Oh, David! *(Susan turns and runs off to her right.)*[16]

Fade out

Aunt Elizabeth's House, night

327. *Fade in.* MS: *David is seated, talking on the phone, wearing his own
   clothes and his glasses.*

DAVID: Yes, Alice, that's where I am. In Connecticut. But I can't get in because I've been unavoidably detained.

328. MLS: *camera pans as Susan runs through the living room to the guest room door.*

    SUSAN: David, listen.

329. MS: *as in 327.*

    DAVID *(putting his hand on mouthpiece, he glances toward muffled sounds coming through the door)*: Susan, I can't hear you. I'm talking. Go away. I'll be with you as soon as I'm finished.[17]

330. MS: *Susan outside the bedroom door.*

331. LS: *she dashes across the living room, camera panning with her, to an extension phone on a table beside the front door. She picks up the receiver.*

    SUSAN: Now, David, you have to listen to me.

332. MS: *as in 327.*

    DAVID: Yes, I know that . . . *(Looks at the receiver.)* Susan, will you please get off the phone.

333. MS: *Susan on phone.*

    SUSAN: No, but David, you don't realize how important this is. It's about the leopard. He's making the most terrific ruckus out there. He's hungry and we've got to feed him.

334. MS: *as in 327.*

    DAVID: Well, I can't help that . . . uh, uh . . .[18] What, Alice dear?[19] No, it's somebody on the line. Keep quiet, Susan.[20]

335. MS: *as in 333.*

> SUSAN: David, you've got to help it. This can't wait. There are eight
> million people in this house and if they hear him, why, they'll think
> that something terrible has happened.

336. MS: *as in 327.*

> DAVID: Oh, now, Susan, get off the line, plea . . . Hello, Alice. Hello.
> Uh, what? Oh, well, I don't know what time it is.

337. MS: *as in 333. Susan picks up a pencil from the table.*

> SUSAN: *(into phone, imitating an operator)*: When you hear the tone, the
> time will be 7:37 and one-quarter . . . *(She lowers the pencil toward a*
> *brass ashtray on the table.)*

338. MS: *as in 327. After the bong of a metallic stroke, David holds the*
receiver away from his ear.

> DAVID: Oh, Susan. Please. Please. Alice, you see, I can't hear you.[21]

339. MS: *as in 333.*

> SUSAN: When you hear the tone, the time will be 7:40. *(Another bong*
> *with the pencil.)*

Camera pans away to reveal Major Applegate, his face visible through
the glass panes of a Dutch door.

> SUSAN *(off)*: When you hear the tone, the time will be 7:40 and one-half.
> *(Another bong.)*

Applegate takes out his watch, looks at it, and shakes his head.

> SUSAN *(off)*: When you hear the tone, the time will be 7:41.

Applegate pushes back the top portion of the Dutch door.

APPLEGATE: Eh, pardon me. *(Bong.)* The time is 8:10. Heh, heh. *(Nods.)*

SUSAN *(off)*: When you hear the tone, the time will be 7:41 and three-quarters.

APPLEGATE *(overlapping)*: No . . . the time . . . my watch shows 8:10 and a quarter . . . I, uh . . .

SUSAN *(the back of her head leaning into the frame)*: Who're you?

APPLEGATE: Who'm I? I'm 8:10. Uh, uh . . .

SUSAN *(off, overlapping)*: When you hear the tone, the time will be 7:42.

APPLEGATE: I'm Major Applegate. I, uh, I, uh . . . *(Climbs over lower half of door and sits on it.)*

340. MLS: *Susan, with Applegate on the Dutch door.*

SUSAN *(with another bong)*: What do you want?

APPLEGATE: Uh, uh, Mrs. Random invited me to dinner. Would you please find out if she still wants me?

SUSAN: She's hung up. *(Susan replaces receiver.)*

APPLEGATE: Whush, sheh. Oh, well, heh, heh, so am I.

AUNT *(off)*: Why, Horace.

341. LS: *camera pans as Aunt Elizabeth crosses to Applegate and Susan at the doorway.*

AUNT: What are you doing? Are you coming in or going out?

APPLEGATE *(returning to the floor)*: Heh, well, uh, I . . . I . . .

SUSAN: He's coming in to dinner. This is Major Applegate. How do you do. I'm Susan Vance. *(He doesn't know whose hand to shake.)*

APPLEGATE: How do you do, Miss Susan? Hello, Elizabeth.

AUNT: You know you're much too big to swing on gates.

APPLEGATE: Yes, I found that out . . . I . . . heh, heh . . .

Susan walks off toward the bedroom.

342. MLS: *David, putting on his coat, comes out the bedroom door toward which Susan is walking.*

AUNT: *(off)*: Susan. Come back here! Where are you going?

SUSAN: Oh, I'm just going . . .

DAVID *(overlapping)*: Susan, I've had enough of this. You should be watching George. Not playing around with telephones . . . Oh, excuse me.

AUNT *(off)*: George is fast asleep in my room.

Susan tries to whisper something to David.

AUNT *(off)*: Now, come here, young man. And don't be afraid. Come here.

David walks away from Susan.

343. MLS: *David and Susan join Applegate and Aunt Elizabeth in the entry hall.*

AUNT: Oh, you look much better in those clothes, young man.

DAVID: Thank you.

AUNT: I want you to meet Mr. Bone.

DAVID AND APPLEGATE *(simultaneously)*: How do you do, Mr. Bone. *(They shake hands.)*

AUNT: No. *(To David.)* You're Mr. Bone.

Susan, at David's back, tugs on his coat to attract his attention.

AUNT: This is Major Applegate.

APPLEGATE: Yes. I'm Major Applegate. Heh, at least, I'm pretty sure I am. Heh, heh. That is, I was this morning. Heh, heh, heh.

DAVID: Uh, uh, there must be some mistake.

AUNT: There isn't any mistake. I've known Major Applegate for twenty years. Haven't I, Horace?

While Aunt Elizabeth turns to Applegate, Susan kicks David's leg. He turns toward her.

APPLEGATE: Well, uh, twenty-two to be exact, I think, Elizabeth. It was long about, uh . . .

Susan mimes to David that he is Mr. Bone.

DAVID: Oh! *(Turns back to Applegate.)* Oh, excuse me. How do you do, Mr. Applegate? *(He offers his hand.)*

APPLEGATE: Well, how do you do again. Thank you. *(They shake hands.)*

SUSAN: Yes. Now, Mr. Bone, we'll go for a nice, long walk. *(She takes his arm.)*

DAVID: Well, I'd like to have a chance to explain to you . . .

SUSAN: You don't need to explain anything to them. They understand perfectly.

Susan takes David into the dining room as Aunt and Applegate watch.

APPLEGATE: It's perfectly all right. I understand. I understand all right. Yes. Yes. Goodbye, er, Major Applegate . . . er . . . Mr. Bo . . . er . . . er . . .

David and Susan leave.

344. MS: *Aunt and Applegate.*

APPLEGATE: A strange young man, isn't he? Eh, eh, is he suffering from something?

AUNT: He's had a nervous breakdown.

APPLEGATE: Had or has?

AUNT: Had.

APPLEGATE: Oh.

AUNT: And it's left him sort of . . . *(She makes screwing gesture with her right index finger.)* . . . you know.

They move forward to the bar, camera dollying ahead of them.

APPLEGATE: Oh, my, my, my. What a pity. And so young, too.

AUNT: The trouble is my niece, Susan, seems to be showing the same tendencies.

APPLEGATE: Is that so? You're all right, though?

AUNT: Well, I hope so.

APPLEGATE: Yeh, well, eh . . .

AUNT: Here, have a drink. Help yourself.

APPLEGATE: Thank you. Thank you.

AUNT: Now, conversation at the dinner table may be a trifle difficult on account of this young man. So I want you to sort of draw him out.

APPLEGATE: Eh, draw him out? I don't know what you mean. *(Mixes a drink.)*

AUNT: Yes. Talk to him about something he understands. Big-game hunting, for instance. You know, he's a big-game hunter like yourself.

APPLEGATE: You don't say. Well, then, Elizabeth, you've come to the right man.[22]

Dissolve

Stables at Aunt Elizabeth's House, night

345. MLS: *David is seated on a bale of hay in the stable as Susan comes out of Baby's stall. She closes and latches the door.*

SUSAN: There, he's fed. Now, I'm sure he's going to be quiet, David. Well, come on, let's go in to dinner. *(David starts to speak, then doesn't.)* Well, what's the matter? Why are you just sitting there?

DAVID: Well, well, I'm just trying to figure out how I ever got mixed up in all this. *(Clicks his tongue.)* Mr. Bone! Isn't that amazing?

SUSAN: Well, David, you told me not to tell Aunt Elizabeth what your real name was.

DAVID: Look, look, I didn't tell you to think up a name like Bone. You know, that's hard to do to . . . to . . . *(He points to his left.)* Oh . . . oh . . . oh . . .

Camera pans as David rises and crosses to George, who is standing to their left.

DAVID: Well, now, George. George. Stay there, George. *(Picks George up.)* Hold on, George. Quickly. Let's get out of here. Oh . . . *(He rushes toward the door with George under his arm.)*

346. MS: *as Susan closes the stable door, David holds George under his right arm, his left hand at George's mouth.*

DAVID: Quick! Shut the door! Shut the door!

SUSAN: What's the matter? What's the matter?

DAVID: What's the matter? Did you ever stop to think what would happen if Baby and George got together?

SUSAN: Oh, they'd probably like each other.

DAVID: And, if they didn't?

SUSAN: If they didn't, why Baby would eat George.

DAVID: Yeah, well, that's what I mean.[23]

Dissolve

Dining Room, night

347. MLS: *Aunt, Applegate, Susan, and David are seated at the dinner table, eating their soup. George lies in a chair by the wall, midway between Susan and David.*

APPLEGATE: And there it was, straight before me, crouching as tigers do before the kill, you know. But I was ready for him. I drew a bead, levelled away and caught him right between the eyes. *(David is staring intently at George.)* Oh, my, my, it certainly was a thrilling experience, heh, heh, heh. As I'm sure you'll all agree. Hmmm? Or do you, Mr. Bone? Hm?

348. MCU: *Applegate, with Aunt Elizabeth, and David at the table.*

APPLEGATE *(glancing at Aunt Elizabeth, then continuing in a high-pitched voice)*: Have you ever been . . . Oh, pardon me, I'm . . . *(Clears his throat.)* . . . so sorry. Uh, have you ever been in Arabia, Mr. Bone?

349. MS: *David returns to his soup without a reply.*

APPLEGATE: I, uh, said, have you ever been in Arabia, Mr. . . . ?

DAVID: No.

APPLEGATE: Oh, I suppose you've spent most of your time in Africa. Hm?

DAVID: No.
APPLEGATE: Eh, eh, Tibet, perhaps?
DAVID: No.

350. MLS: *as in 347.*

APPLEGATE: Uh, Malay Peninsula, perchance? Hm?

David sees George leave his chair and trot out the entry door.

DAVID: Excuse me. *(David rises, holding his spoon and napkin, to follow George out the door.)*
APPLEGATE: Uh, heh, heh, heh. *(They observe David's departure.)*

351. MCU: *Applegate.*

APPLEGATE: Heh, well, at least that got a rise out of him. Hm, hm . . .

352. MS: *Applegate, Susan, and Aunt Elizabeth.*

SUSAN: Well, you see, you shouldn't have mentioned the Malay Peninsula. He was horribly clawed there by a tiger. He doesn't like talking about it.

353. MLS: *Dinner table.*

APPLEGATE: I had a gun-bearer once who was clawed by a tiger. He . . . the foo . . .

Aunt Elizabeth, Applegate, and Susan look toward the living room as George trots in followed by David, still carrying his napkin and spoon. George hops back on his chair.

354. MS: *David returns toward the group at table.*

SUSAN: I was just telling Major Applegate that you were horribly clawed by a tiger in the Malay Peninsula.

355. MCU: *David returns to his place at the table, still holding his napkin and spoon.*

DAVID: I've never been there.

356. MS: *as in 348.*

APPLEGATE: You . . . You've never, uh . . . oh, well, no matter, no matter. Heh, heh . . .

357. MLS: *Dinner table.*

APPLEGATE: Uh, what type of gun do you use in hunting tigers, Mr. Bone?

David is staring at George on his chair.

358. CU: *George on his chair.*

APPLEGATE *(off)*: I, uh, I personally use a bold-action Mauser . . .

George leaves his chair.

359. MLS: *Dinner table.*

APPLEGATE: . . . with a very large bore. I find . . .
DAVID *(rising to follow George)*: Excuse me.

David, holding soupspoon and napkin, follows George out the door as Aunt Elizabeth, Applegate, and Susan watch.

AUNT: Huh! Susan! Imagine giving a dinner party with your husband stalking like Hamlet's ghost all through the meal.[24]

360. LS: *George trots in the garden with David following close behind, carrying his napkin and spoon. Camera pans with them as they pass Gogarty, sitting in a chair, smoking his pipe, observing.*

361. MCU: *Gogarty.*

> GOGARTY: Well, give me patience. No, this is too much. *(He rises.)* I
> can't stand it.[25]

362. MLS: *George, followed by David, returns to his place. Aunt Elizabeth,
Susan, and Applegate are still seated at the table while Hannah serves
vegetables.*

> APPLEGATE: Oh, uh, we were uh, we were talking about the jungle
> while you were away, Mr. Bone.
> DAVID *(returning to his place with spoon aloft)*: My soup is gone.
> AUNT: It was cold.

363. MLS: *Gogarty in the stable approaches the door to the stall where Baby
is imprisoned.*

> GOGARTY: Digging trenches . . .

364. MS: *Gogarty enters the pen and looks in the haybox.*

> GOGARTY *(grumbling)*: Spying on an innocent dog. Did anyone ever
> hear such nonsense. *(He bends, strains, and pulls a bottle from the
> haybox.)* Enough to drive a man crazy. And then they say, "Keep away
> from the bottle. Don't drink." No, not even a wee drop to steady a
> man's nerves. *(He drinks.)*

365. LS: *interior of stables.*

> GOGARTY: If one more thing happens, I'll quit. I'll quit. *(He walks
> away from the stall toward door leading outdoors; Baby follows.)* And
> where Aloysius Gogarty goes, Mrs. Aloysius Gogarty goes too.

366. MS: *Gogarty emerges from the stable door, muttering. He goes off to the
left. Baby emerges through the open door and trots right.*

367. MLS: *the dinner table, where Hannah is serving David.*

APPLEGATE: Just picture it: a vast, mysterious silence, vibrant with life . . .

368. MS: *as in 362.*

APPLEGATE: . . . strange cries . . . *(A strange cry erupts on the sound track.)* . . . in the night.

All react to the strange cry, including George. Susan and David exchange glances.

AUNT: Good gracious! What was that?

APPLEGATE: Uh, that was a loon, Elizabeth. Loon. *L*, double *o*, *n*. Yes. I'm sure that once you got the jungle in your blood, I wouldn't be able to keep you out of it, you know. Heh, heh, heh.

369. MS: *reverse shot of 368. There is another strange cry in the night as David continues eating.*

AUNT: Susan, did you hear that?
SUSAN: I didn't hear a thing.
APPLEGATE: You did . . . ? Oh, my . . .
AUNT: Horace, are you quite sure that was a loon?
APPLEGATE: Oh, yes, indeed, Elizabeth. I've heard many a loon, and if there ever was a loon, that is a loon. Heh, heh . . .

370. MLS: *Dinner table.*

APPLEGATE: Uh, isn't it, Mr. Bone?
DAVID: No.
APPLEGATE: Uh, hm, uh, well what do you say it was?
DAVID: A leopard.

371. MS: *as in 369.*

AUNT: Oh, don't be ridiculous. Major Applegate would know a leopard's cry if he heard it.
APPLEGATE: Well, thank you, Elizabeth. I'm an authority on animal cries.

372. MCU: *Applegate, Susan, and David with George seated between.*

APPLEGATE: Now you take . . . *(Susan gives David a quick nudge as George observes from his chair.)* . . . the rogue elephant, for instance.
DAVID: Oh, excuse me, Major. You're right. It is a loon.
APPLEGATE: Oh, thank you. Thank you. Hmm. The leopard's cry is something once heard, you can never forget.
DAVID: Oh, yes. I know.

373. MCU: *Applegate.*

APPLEGATE: Eh, eh. Oh. You . . . *(Clears throat.)* You know? Thank you. It, uh, of course, it varies at, uh, different seasons. Uh, let me see. Now, what month is this?

AUNT *(off)*: June.

SUSAN *(off)*: June.

APPLEGATE: Eh, eh, June? Well, it would go, it would go something like this. *(Clears his throat.)*

374. CU: *David looking at George.*

APPLEGATE *(off)*: I must prepare for it, you know. Heh.

375. MCU: *as in 373.*

APPLEGATE: Eh, now let me see. *(Applegate rubs his fingers.)* Uh, there

we have it. *(He clears his throat, raises his hands to his mouth, and expels a piercing cry.)*

376. MS: *Susan, George, and David all react to the shriek with amazement. Applegate's howl becomes a cough.*

APPLEGATE: Oh, pardon me, I . . .

DAVID: It's still a loon.

APPLEGATE *(coughing)*: Well, of course, I haven't practiced the leopard cry in a long time. I'm . . . *(Cough.)* . . . slightly out of voice. *(He takes a sip of water.)*

AUNT *(off)*: Try again. Try again.

APPLEGATE: Yes, I shall. I shall. *(He clears his throat several times.)*

377. MS: *as in 369. Applegate raises his fingers to his mouth, but before they reach his lips another cry sounds in the night. He lowers his hands.*

APPLEGATE: Eh, heh. Well, now, I didn't do that.
SUSAN: It was probably an echo.
APPLEGATE: Eh, yes, well it was a long time coming back, wasn't it? I'm . . . hm, hm . . .
AUNT: Well, try again. Try again.
APPLEGATE: Yes. Yes. I . . . I shall. *(Raises his fingers and makes a blood-curdling howl.)*

378. MS: *as in 368.*

APPLEGATE: There. That's better. *(David shakes his head.)*

An answering cry silences the group.

APPLEGATE: Now, that's peculiar. There aren't any leopards in Connecticut, are there?
DAVID: Yes.
SUSAN: No.

379. MLS: *Dinner table.*

AUNT: Of course not.
APPLEGATE: Why do you say yes, Mr., uh, Bone?
DAVID: Well, you see . . . *(David sees George jump off the chair and head for the door.)* Excuse me. *(He rises to follow George.)*
SUSAN *(jumping up to follow)*: Excuse me.
AUNT: Susan! Susan! Sit right down and finish your dinner. And stop this nonsense!
SUSAN: All right. I'll sit down. You'll be sorry. *(She sits.)* But I'll sit down.[26]

380. MLS: *Gogarty closes the kitchen door and walks on the porch. Camera pans with him as he grumbles.*

GOGARTY: I can't . . . I can't stand it. I . . . I've got to get away from it! I've got to get away from it!! *(Sits on a bench.)*

381. MCU: *Gogarty.*

GOGARTY: Instead of sitting decently at the table eating their dinners, they're howling and roaring at one another like a lot of banshees.

382. MLS: *as in 380.*

GOGARTY *(standing)*: And then they say . . . *(Looks toward the kitchen door.)* . . . "Gogarty, you mustn't drink. Gogarty, you must keep away from the bottle." *(He looks off in the opposite direction.)* The bottle!

Camera pans with him as he walks along the porch to a table and chair.

383. MS: *porch.*

GOGARTY *(pulling a bottle from behind the chair)*: As if a man didn't need something to listen to them. I'm within me rights. I'm perfectly within me . . . *(Takes a long drink.)* . . . rights. *(He sits.)* If one more thing happens . . . *(Baby jumps over the porch railing and lies on the table beside Gogarty.)* . . . to upset me, I'll . . . I'll be seeing things. I'll be seeing . . . *(He turns his head and sees Baby staring at him. He stops and stares back. He slowly uncrosses his legs and sneaks out of his chair, withdrawing toward the wall of the house.)*

384. CU: *Gogarty makes an inarticulate cry and a frightened grimace.*

385. CU: *Baby stares back quietly.*

386. MS: *Gogarty drops the bottle with a crash. Camera pans as he makes a dash for the kitchen door.*

GOGARTY: Hannah! Hannah! Hannah Gogarty! Hannah Gogarty!

387. MLS: *Gogarty rushes through the kitchen door and slams it. Camera pans as he races across the room.*

GOGARTY: Me gun! Me gun! *(He grabs Hannah, knocking the tray out of her hands with a terrific crash.)*

388. MLS: *Aunt Elizabeth, Applegate, and Susan, seated at the table, respond to the crash. David, napkin in hand, stands beside George.*

AUNT: Good gracious! Now what's happened?

Camera pans as they hurry toward the kitchen, where angry voices continue off-frame.

GOGARTY *(off)*: This is no time for personalities. Where's me gun! Where's me gun!

389. MLS: *Aunt Elizabeth opens the door to the kitchen.*

HANNAH *(off)*: What would you be wanting with a gun now?

Aunt Elizabeth, Applegate, Susan, and David move toward the argument as the camera pans.

GOGARTY: Me gun! Hand me me gun!
AUNT *(clapping her hands)*: Be quiet, both of you!

390. MS: *Aunt Elizabeth, Gogarty, and Hannah.*

AUNT: Now, Gogarty, What is all this?
GOGARTY: I saw it. I saw it outside.
AUNT: Saw what?
GOGARTY: A cat! As big as a cow. With eyes like balls of fire.

391. MS: *Susan and David in the kitchen doorway. Susan presses her hand to David's shoulder. He looks at her hand. She pushes him backward into the dining room.*[27]

AUNT *(off)*: Hannah, clean up this mess. And serve the next course.[28]

392. MS: *Susan, pushing David away from the kitchen door, backs him into*

*the dining-room table. The argument in the kitchen continues under their
dialogue.*

SUSAN: Jeepers, David! Do you realize what's happened? *(David brushes
her hand off his chest.)* Baby's escaped!
DAVID: Well, I don't care.
SUSAN: Come on. We've got to catch him. *(She pulls him toward the
entry door.)*
DAVID: I've got to watch George.
SUSAN: You're not gonna stay here?
DAVID *(overlapping)*: Yes, I . . .
SUSAN: If you stay here I'm gonna tell Aunt Elizabeth that your name is
Doctor David Huxley!
DAVID: Oh, you wouldn't do that, Susan.
SUSAN: Right now. *(She makes a move toward the kitchen.)*
DAVID *(pulling her back)*: Oh, oh, Susan, don't do that. All right. I'll do
anything you say. I'll go with you. I'll . . .
SUSAN *(overlapping)*: Oh, you changed your mind. All right. *(Pulls
David toward the entry door.)*
DAVID: George, stay there. *(Calling.)* Oh, Major Applegate. Uh, uh,
keep an eye on George. Thank you.

Susan pulls him through door and they run into the night.[29]

393. MLS: *David and Susan dash through the open door of the stable as the
camera pans.*

SUSAN: Baby! Baby! Oh, the door's open. *(They arrive at the empty
stall.)* Yup, he's gone, all right. Oh, dear, now Aunt Elizabeth is . . .
absolutely . . .
DAVID: But don't lose your head, Susan. Don't lose your . . .
SUSAN: Don't lose my what?
DAVID: Don't lose your head.
SUSAN: I've got my head. I've lost my leopard! Oh, dear! Oh, dear!
DAVID: Now, now, wait a minute. Nothing's gonna be gained . . .
SUSAN: What're we gonna . . .
DAVID: Nothing's gonna be gained by uncontrolled hysteria. *(He is still
clutching his dinner napkin.)* Now, compose yourself.

SUSAN: But what shall we do?[30]

394. MS: *Susan and David in the stable.*

> DAVID: Now, look. I'll call the zoo, tell them we saw a leopard and they'll come and catch him. Now, come on.
> SUSAN: All right.

Camera pans as they rush out the open stable door.[31]

395. MLS: *Aunt Elizabeth and Applegate are seated at the table, George on his chair. Susan comes through the door toward the table, while David, outside, walks quickly past the door.*

> APPLEGATE: It, eh, it . . .
> AUNT: Well, Susan, I do hope this time you've come to stay.

In her haste, Susan collides with the table.

> SUSAN: Yes. *(She sits.)* I've come to stay, Auntie. *(Applegate makes a polite half-rise, then sits.)* We've just been walking. Walking up and walking down and . . . *(She looks off toward her left as Aunt Elizabeth follows her look.)*

> AUNT: Where's that young man going now?
> SUSAN: He's just going in to take a rest. He . . . he has to take frequent rests. The doctor says, uh, have you ever had jungle fever, Major?

396. *Applegate, Susan, and Aunt Elizabeth.*

> APPLEGATE: Eh, eh, well, I, uh . . .
> SUSAN: Oh, you have? Then, of course, you realize how important rest is.
> APPLEGATE: Eh, I, uh, well, of course.

Hannah approaches the table with an envelope, which she hands to Aunt Elizabeth.

HANNAH *(overlapping)*: This just came, Ma'am. *(She leaves.)*
SUSAN *(while Aunt Elizabeth opens the envelope and reads)*: Now, with
Mr. Bone, in his case, it's rather difficult 'cause he has two doctors.
One says rest, one says exercise. Which do you prefer?
APPLEGATE: Well, I think that perhaps . . .
SUSAN: Well, neither can he make up his mind . . .
AUNT: Wait, Susan, listen to this.
SUSAN: What?
AUNT: This is a cable from Mark.

397. MS: *reverse shot of 396.*

SUSAN: Mark?
AUNT: Not a particle of sense in it, you know.
SUSAN: What does it say? What does it say?
AUNT *(reading)*: Are you pleased with Baby?

398. MCU: *Susan.*

SUSAN: Baby?
AUNT *(off)*: Love, Mark.
SUSAN: Mark?
AUNT *(off)*: Yes. And not a word about my leopard.
SUSAN: Le . . . *Your* leopard?

399. MLS: *Dinner table.*

AUNT: I've always wanted a leopard.
SUSAN: Oh. *(She rises.)* Excuse me.
AUNT: You know, he promised it . . .

Susan dashes off toward the living room as Applegate rises politely.[32]

400. MS: *David is seated in an armchair, talking on the phone.*

DAVID: Thank you very much. Thank you. *(He hangs up.)*

Susan opens the door, still holding her dinner napkin, and enters the bedroom.

SUSAN: Don't call the zoo.
DAVID: Well, I just . . .
SUSAN *(closing the door and hurrying to him)*: Don't call the zoo!
DAVID: Well, look, I've just called them. It's all fixed.
SUSAN *(holding the phone)*: Call them back and unfix it!
DAVID: Well, why?
SUSAN: Don't ask questions! Call them back!
DAVID: But I've just told them they could have the leopard if they found him.
SUSAN: You've given away Baby?
DAVID: Yeah.
SUSAN: You had no right to do that! He doesn't belong to you. Oh, it's all your fault. You've ruined everything.
DAVID: It's all my . . . Oh, I've had enough! I quit. *(He starts out of chair; Susan pushes him back down.)*
SUSAN: You can't quit. Call them back.
DAVID: But you told me to call them in the first place.
SUSAN: Everything's changed. I just found out that that leopard belongs to Aunt Elizabeth.
DAVID: Aunt Elizabeth? You said it was yours.
SUSAN *(overlapping)*: Never mind. I'll explain later. Just call them back and tell them that you were mistaken! *(Still holds the phone out to him.)*
DAVID: But, Susan, I've only just managed to convince them that I did see a leopard. They'll never believe me now.
SUSAN *(overlapping)*: Oh, I can fix that, David. I'll tell them that you're a drug addict. That you're always seeing things. What's the number? *(She holds the base of the phone to her ear.)*
DAVID: Oh, is that what . . . Oh, never mind. Give me that phone. *(He takes the phone from her.)*
SUSAN: Hurry up.
DAVID: You'll do nothing of the sort.

401. MCU: *David and Susan.*

DAVID: Hello? Hello, operator?

SUSAN: Calm down.

DAVID: Get me Westlake 2-8-4. I don't know what I'm going to tell the man, but I'm . . .

SUSAN: Oh, never mind, David, what you're going to . . .

DAVID: Hello? Hello? Is that zoo? . . . Well, nobody's talking baby talk. Well, I'm the man that called up about the leopard. You don't have to do anything about it. It's all been a mistake. Yes. Uh . . . Oh, well, stop them.

SUSAN: What's the matter?

DAVID: Oh, my. *(He hangs up.)*

DAVID: Oh, it's too late. It was the night watchman. He says everybody's gone. They're all out leopard hunting.

SUSAN: Oh, jeepers!

402. MS: *as in 400.*

SUSAN *(throwing down her dinner napkin)*: You've gotten us into a wonderful mess.

DAVID: I've gotten us? . . . Well!

SUSAN: Well . . . *(She paces.)* . . . let's think before we act.

DAVID: You, you think. You can think faster than I can.

SUSAN: Thank you, David. Now, what do you take with you when you go to catch a leopard?

DAVID: A bigger leopard.

SUSAN: Well, one thing's certain—we've got to catch him before they do.

She pulls him out of the chair and toward the door. The dinner napkin on his lap flies to the floor.

DAVID: Oh, I've got to watch George. I can't be . . .

SUSAN: We'll take George with us.

DAVID: All right.

They run through the door.

403. MLS: *camera pans with David and Susan as they hurry into the dining*

room as fast as they dare without arousing suspicion. Aunt Elizabeth and Applegate are still at the table. Applegate rises as Susan approaches.

SUSAN: Auntie, Mr. Bone and I are going to take George for a walk. Where's a leash?
AUNT: Leash? . . .
DAVID *(backing away from George's empty chair)*: Oh, my goodness.
SUSAN: What's the matter?
DAVID: Well, where's George?
SUSAN: Where's George?
AUNT: Now, why this morbid interest in George?

Susan bends to look under the table; so does David. Applegate sits.

DAVID: Well, I've got to find him.
AUNT: What for?
DAVID: Oh, because he knows where my intercostal clavicle is.
AUNT: Your what?

Applegate stirs the coffee in his demitasse.

DAVID: Uh . . .
SUSAN *(overlapping)*: David, don't talk to . . .
DAVID: Major Appletree, you promised to watch George.
APPLEGATE: Uh, well, I did do that.
SUSAN: But you didn't.
APPLEGATE: Oh, yes, I did. *(About to drink from his demitasse.)*
DAVID: Well, where is he?
APPLEGATE: Uh, he's gone.
SUSAN: Gone where?
APPLEGATE: Yuh, out that door. *(He sips.)*

David and Susan babble as they race toward the entry door from the dining room to the garden.

APPLEGATE: No, no. Uh, not that door. *(Points toward the living room.)* That door.

Susan and David dash into the living room.

DAVID: Thank you.
APPLEGATE: Yes, that's right. Heh, heh, heh. That's . . . hm.

They rush out the living room door.

AUNT *(rising)*: Oh, I can't stand this another moment. Horace, come
along. Let's get some fresh air.
APPLEGATE *(rising)*: Yes. Shall we run?
AUNT: Yes.
APPLEGATE: Yes.

They trot out the entry door toward the garden.

Dissolve

The Garden, night

404. MLS: *Aunt Elizabeth and Applegate are walking from the house toward
the camera, which pans with their stroll.*

APPLEGATE: I can't understand, Elizabeth, why a loon would answer a
leopard's cry. Uh, there's something wrong, you know.
AUNT: They both sound exactly alike to me.
APPLEGATE: Oh, no, uh, no, pardon me, Elizabeth, please. I'd, huh . . .
the leopard's cry is entirely different, you know. As I explained to you
in there, the leopard's cry goes like this. *(He sucks in a deep breath,
raises his fingers to his mouth, and emits a blood-curdling cry.)*

405. MCU: *Applegate clears his throat after the howl.*

AUNT: What a terrible noise. I don't see how you do it.

406. MS: *Baby prowls near some bushes.*

APPLEGATE *(off)*: It's done largely with the palate, . . .

407. MCU: *as in 405.*

APPLEGATE: . . . you see. Of course, the hands play an important part in the resonance and carrying power.

AUNT *(placing her thumbs together)*: But why do you put your thumbs together like that?

APPLEGATE *(demonstrating as he explains)*: Well, well, you see, the thumbs, it is very necessary that the base of the thumbs are close together like that. You see, that brings out a sort of a pear-shaped tone. You see? Now, having done this, you take a deep breath, keep the throat well open, and out comes . . . *(He sucks in a breath, raises his fingers to his lips, and sends forth a leopard cry—that collapses into a cough.)*

From off-frame comes the answer of a gargling cry. Aunt Elizabeth stands still with her hands near her chest.

APPLEGATE: Oh, my, why that's fine Elizabeth . . .

408. MCU: *reverse shot of 405.*

APPLEGATE: . . . for one who hasn't had any practice. *(Aunt Elizabeth stands still and stares, her fingers still pressed together.)* Really it is. I think you've got something there.

AUNT: Got what?

APPLEGATE: The mating cry.

AUNT: Now don't be rude, Horace.

APPLEGATE: Well, Elizabeth, I'm not rude. I was merely alluding to the scream that you did just now.

AUNT: I didn't scream.

409. MCU: *as in 405.*

APPLEGATE: Uh, you didn't scream?

AUNT: I certainly did not.

APPLEGATE: You didn't scream?

AUNT: No. I ought to know if I screamed.

APPLEGATE: Well, then, there must be something wrong here. I . . .
I . . .
AUNT: Wrong? Well, I should say so . . .

Applegate's eyes open in terror as he spies something off-frame.

410. MCU: *Baby beside some bushes.*

AUNT *(off)*: Why, I never in my life have known anything like it . . .

411. MCU: *as in 405. Applegate's eyes are still popping.*

AUNT: Ever since I came into the house there's been something wrong.
It's been bedlam.
APPLEGATE *(clearing his throat)*: Elizabeth, Elizabeth, don't you think
it's time we went in the house?
AUNT: No. We've only just left the house.
APPLEGATE: But don't you think it's, eh, eh, a good idea to go back?
AUNT: No. I think it's a good idea to continue our walk.
APPLEGATE *(maneuvering her toward the house as the camera pans)*:
But, don't you find it a bit chilly . . .
AUNT: No, I . . .
APPLEGATE: . . . without a gun, Elizabeth.

He propels the protesting Aunt Elizabeth in a race toward the house.[33]

412. LS: *David, armed with a rope and a croquet mallet, and Susan carrying
a butterfly net, rush down a hill in a forest. The camera pans with them
as they walk.*

SUSAN *(singing)*: That's the only thing I've plenty of, Baby.
DAVID *(whistles)*: George!
SUSAN *(singing)*: Dream awhile. *(Stops singing.)* Why don't you sing,
David?
DAVID: Well, I can't sing.
SUSAN *(singing)*: Scheme awhile. *(Speaks.)* Yes, you can. You have a
fine strong voice.

DAVID: Yes, but not for singing.

SUSAN *(stopping and turning to David)*: It's not fair. You're just being stubborn.[34]

Two yaps from George punctuate the conversation from off-frame. Susan and David quickly turn to the left, from which the barks seem to have come.

DAVID: That's a dog!

Two more barks from off-frame.

SUSAN: George!

Susan runs off-frame to the left.

DAVID *(running after her)*: Oh . . .

413. MLS: *Susan and David rush down a hill through shrubbery.*

DAVID: George! George!

Susan stops abruptly.

DAVID: What's the matter?
SUSAN: Something moved in that bush.
DAVID: Oh—oh. Let me go first.

David steps in front of her and creeps cautiously toward the camera, his stalking motion followed and echoed by Susan.

414. MLS: *David and Susan stalk silently through the bushes.*

415. MCU: *they walk silently through shoulder-high bushes, David in the lead. A branch, recoiling from David's shoulder, smacks Susan in the face.*

416. CU: *David walking.*

SUSAN *(off, in a whisper)*: David.
DAVID: Sh-h-h.

417. CU: *Susan walking; another branch smacks her in the face.*

SUSAN: David, don't you think it'd be better if I went first?

418. CU: *as in 416.*

DAVID: Oh, Susan, no. You might get hurt.

419. CU: *as in 417. Another branch whacks Susan in the face.*

SUSAN: Thank you, David. *(She drops to her knees below the branches and crawls onward.)*

420. CU: *low angle on David's legs moving through the bushes, Susan creeping behind them.*

DAVID *(off)*: I can't see a thing.
SUSAN: Neither can I.

421. MCU: *David's head, shoulders, and uplifted croquet mallet in a sea of tall bushes.*

DAVID: Susan, are you sure you saw something moving in here, because I can't . . . ? *(He turns, looks around, and sees nothing but bushes.)* Well, Su . . . Susan, where are you?

422. CU: *as in 417.*

SUSAN *(looking up from below)*: Here I am.

423. MCU: *as in 421.*

DAVID: Susan, this is no time to be playing squat-tag!

424. CU: *as in 417.*

SUSAN: I'm not playing.[35] *(She closes her mouth and shakes her head. She starts to rise.)*

425. MLS: *Susan and David among the reeds.*

SUSAN: Oh, I'm caught on something. David, help me, will you? Uh . . .
DAVID: No.
SUSAN *(struggling to get free)*: Help me, will you?
DAVID: No. Huh, huh. That's poison ivy.
SUSAN: I'll bet you wouldn't treat Miss Swallow this way.
DAVID: I'll bet Miss Swallow knows poison ivy when she sees it.

426. MCU: *Susan.*

SUSAN: Yes. I'll bet poison ivy runs when it sees her.

427. MS: *Susan and David, with croquet mallet aloft.*

DAVID: I didn't come out here to discuss Miss Swallow. I came out to look for George and I'm going to find him if I can ever get to . . . *(David turns, takes a step away from Susan, and suddenly slips down a steep embankment, sliding speedily on his backside, the camera tilting down with him.)* Oh! *(He hits bottom with a thud.)*

428. MLS: *Susan runs to the edge of the embankment, looking down.*

SUSAN: Oh, David. Are you all right? *(She bursts into a laugh.)*

429. MS: *David, on his backside, looks up toward Susan, whose laughter continues off.*

DAVID *(pausing, with his mouth open, then shaking his head)*: Oh, don't laugh.

430. MCU: *Susan, laughing.*

SUSAN: Can't help it. *(Still laughing.)* You look so silly. *(Susan jerks as she feels herself slipping.)* Ah!

431. MLS: *embankment from above. Susan slides down on her backside.*

SUSAN: Ah! Oh!

432. MS: *Susan comes to an abrupt stop beside David at the bottom of the embankment. As she does, she bags David's head in the butterfly net.*

SUSAN: Ah! *(She bursts into peels of laughter.)* Uh!

David sits frozen with the net over his head, staring at Susan, who continues to laugh hysterically.

433. MCU: *David continues to stare at the giggling Susan. And stare. And stare. He silently taps her on the left arm with his right hand, then points at the net over his head. Susan, still laughing, lifts it off his head, catching his nose on the meshes. She throws the net to the ground. Her laughter stops abruptly as David lunges toward her with his hands spread, as if to throttle her. He clasps his hands around his head instead. Baby's off-frame cry makes Susan sit up.*

SUSAN: Wait a minute. Did you hear that? That's Baby!

Two yaps from George from off-frame.

DAVID: It's George, too.

434. LS: *Susan and David.*

SUSAN: Oh, you don't suppose that . . .

They rise and dash off to the left, as the camera pans with them.

SUSAN *(singing)*: I can't give you anything but love . . .
DAVID: Shut up.

As they run, George barks once from off-frame.

435. LS: *another off-frame bark. David and Susan come to a stop at the bank of a river.*

     DAVID: Oh, oh, look! *(He points.)*

436. LS: *George and Baby wrestling. George barks while Baby growls.*

437. MS: *David and Susan watching.*

     SUSAN: Look, David. *(She taps his arm.)* They like each other.
     DAVID: Yes, but goodness knows how long that's gonna last.

438. CU: *Baby and George wrestle playfully with barks and growls.*

439. MS: *as in 437.*

     DAVID: Oh, in another minute my intercostal clavicle will be gone
       forever.

440. CU: *George and Baby wrestling more ferociously. George seems to be getting the best of a submissive Baby.*

441. MS: *as in 437.*

     SUSAN: Here, George! Here, George! Come here.
     DAVID: No. Ho . . . Sh-h-h. Sh-h-h, Susan.

442. CU: *as George and Baby wrestle, Baby tumbles to the ground and lies on his back submissively, extending a paw toward George.*

443. MS: *as in 437.*

     DAVID: Susan, is there any way to cross this stream?
     SUSAN: Oh, surely. It's shallow. We can wade across.
     DAVID: Oh.

444. MLS: *Susan and David beside the river.*

DAVID: So glad.

Camera pans with them as they step into the water and immediately disappear beneath the surface. A second later their two heads bob up.

DAVID: Oh, yuh . . .

445. MS: *Susan and David in the river.*

DAVID: Susan!

They begin swimming back to the riverbank.

SUSAN *(coughing)*: The riverbed's changed.
DAVID *(sarcastically, as he swims)*: Oh! The riverbed's changed!
SUSAN *(still coughing, she reaches the bank and slides up it on her backside)*: Did we get across?
DAVID *(pulling himself up on the bank, on his knees)*: No, Susan. We're right back where we started. Only we're wet.
SUSAN: Oh.
DAVID *(looking across the river)*: Oh. Now George and Baby have disappeared.
SUSAN *(another cough)*: Well, while you were about it, you might as well have gotten to the other side.
DAVID: While I'm wet, I'm gonna go to the other side. *(He lunges out of the frame with a splash.)*
SUSAN: Oh, well, don't leave me! *(She dives in after him. Camera pans as they swim to the opposite bank.)*
SUSAN: Oh!
DAVID: Come on!

They climb up on the bank.

SUSAN: Oh!

DAVID *(calling)*: George—George—

Dissolve

The Woods, night

446. MLS: *David is standing with his back to a campfire, drying his shirt-tail. Susan is seated on a stump, bending toward the fire, drying her hair. Some of their clothing hangs on twigs.*

SUSAN: You know, David, if we'd had a bathhouse by this wouldn't have been so complicated.
DAVID: Hm. Next time I'll try and arrange one. Or perhaps there are portable bathhouses for people like you. There must be. Must be.

SUSAN: Oh, David, don't be so grouchy. *(She picks up a twig bearing one of David's socks, and holds it over the fire.)* We could have such fun. This moonlight and everything is so lovely. And I do so like being with you. *(The sock dangles from the stick into the fire.)*

DAVID *(toasting his hands)*: You do? Well, I like peace and quiet.

SUSAN: But it's peaceful and quiet here.

DAVID: Oh. Well, let's just stay here and let George and Baby . . .

447. MS: *Susan and David by the campfire.*

DAVID *(sitting on a fallen log)*: . . . look for us.

SUSAN *(laughs, then notices his flaming sock)*: Oh, David, your sock's on fire.

DAVID: Oh, that's all right. I don't care any more.

SUSAN *(dropping the burning sock into the fire)*: Well . . . *(She grabs its mate and tosses it into the fire too.)*

DAVID: Uh huh. That's fine. Throw the other one in.

SUSAN: Oh, that's true. You could have . . . Oh, well, don't be upset, David.

DAVID: Oh, well, who wouldn't be?

448. MCU: *David.*

DAVID: My goodness, Susan, here I am, trying to help you find a leopard so that your Aunt Elizabeth won't be angry at you. And then she'll probably give you the million dollars that I need for my museum. Well, if you'd planned it, you couldn't have ruined my chances more completely.

449. MCU: *Susan, her cheek resting on her right hand.*

DAVID *(off)*: You told your aunt I was crazy, didn't you?

SUSAN *(nodding)*: Uh-huh.

450. MCU: *as in 448.*

DAVID: You told her my name was Bone and you didn't tell me.

451. CU: *Susan nodding in agreement.*

DAVID *(off)*: You told her I was a big-game hunter and you didn't tell me. You'd tell anybody anything that comes into your head and you don't tell me.

452. MS: *as in 447.*

SUSAN: Uh-huh. *(She rises.)* Well, here's something else I didn't tell you either. *(She walks over to David's drying jacket.)*
DAVID: What . . . what now?
SUSAN: Boopie—Mr. Peabody—is coming to see Aunt Elizabeth tonight.

453. MS: *David.*

DAVID: Oh, dear. *(He puts his hand over his forehead.)* Oh, well, that's the end. That's the end, that's all. Peabody's sure to tell your aunt who I am. Yeah. He'll never remember those four years' hard work I put in on that brontosaurus. No. No, all he'll remember is that I conked him on the head with a rock last night—he thinks.

454. MS: *from the distance comes strains of calliope music.*

SUSAN *(handing David his tie)*: Here. *(She looks up.)*
DAVID *(taking the tie)*: Oh.
SUSAN: Where's that music coming from, David?
DAVID: Westlake. There's a circus there. A circus.[36]

Dissolve

Circus Midway, night

455. LS: *animal cages in the foreground, a sideshow in the rearground, where the silhouette of a hoochy-coochy dancer is clearly visible. Her music and the pitch of a barker accompany her on the soundtrack. Two men enter the frame in the foreground.*

456. MLS: *the two men in workclothes converse with a man in a white hat, suit, and tie, surrounded by onlookers. The cooch dancer's silhouette continues in the left rearground, a leopard observes from a cage in the right rearground.*

> MANAGER: Joe, we got a job for you. Boss wants you to take this leopard over to Bridgeport.
> JOE: What happened?
> MANAGER: Just gave that new trainer a going-over.
> JOE: Hurt him bad?
> MANAGER: Bad? You don't think three minutes alone with that cat did him any *good*, do you?
> MAN TO HIS RIGHT: Aaah, they should have shot him last summer when he ripped up Caldoni.
> JOE: Well, what do we do with him?
> MANAGER *(taking slip of paper from his pocket)*: Here. Deliver him to this address. They got a gas chamber. I phoned over. You go along too, Mac. *(He starts to leave.)*
> MAC: Who, me?
> MANAGER *(stopping)*: You heard what I said.
> JOE: Where is Bridgeport?
> MANAGER: How should I know? Somewhere out on the State Highway. Ask somebody. And get going. *(He resumes his walk.)*[37]

Dissolve

The Woods, night

457. MLS: *David, holding the rope and croquet mallet, is just finishing stamping out the fire. Susan is putting on her shoes.*

> DAVID: Well, that's that. Come on, Susan, let's get going.
> SUSAN: All right. *(She gets up, holding the butterfly net.)*
> DAVID: You sure you don't want my coat?
> SUSAN: No, David. I'm completely dry, really.

They start forward.

DAVID: Well, let's go.

They stop as some headlights from the highway strike them in the face.

SUSAN: Hey. Wonder what that is.

458. MLS: *the cage-truck drives past a tree and comes to a stop near a signpost.*

JOE: Hey, Mac. See what that sign says. *(The passenger door of the truck opens.)*[38]

459. MS: *Susan and David looking toward the highway.*

SUSAN: David, it's the zoo truck.
DAVID: Is it?
SUSAN: They've got Baby.
DAVID: Oh! Oh! Is George with them?
SUSAN: No. I can't see George. But we've got to get Baby away from them.
DAVID: Oh, no. All I promised to do was help you find Baby. Well, you've found him.
SUSAN: Now, listen.
DAVID: There. *(Nods and points.)*
SUSAN: All you have to do is to go and talk to those men in the front of the truck while I let Baby out the back. Give me that rope, you take this. *(Takes the rope from him and hands him the butterfly net.)*
DAVID: Well, I know, but what'll I say to them?
SUSAN: Well, well, they're from the zoo. Tell them you're a zoologist. Talk about zoos. *(Urges him forward.)*
DAVID: Well . . .
SUSAN: Go ahead. Go 'head. Go on.
DAVID: Oh . . .

David walks off as Susan watches.

460. MLS: *Joe and Mac, in front of the truck, are studying the map in the*

truck's headlights. David, holding the butterfly net, approaches the truck from the background.

JOE: But I can't find Bridgeport.
MAC: Well, you got the map upside down.

David approaches carrying the butterfly net.

DAVID: Good evening, gentlemen.
JOE: Hello.
DAVID: Uh . . . *(Climbs over a wooden fence.)* May I help you?
JOE: Yeah. Do you know the way to Bridgeport?
DAVID: Oh, uh . . .

461. MS: *David, Mac, and Joe.*

DAVID: I'm not going to Bridgeport.
MAC: No, not you. We're going to Bridgeport. Do you know which way
    it is?
DAVID: Yes.
JOE *(indicating to his left)*: It's that way, ain't it?
DAVID: Yes.
JOE: You see?
MAC: But I thought it was that way. *(Indicates with his thumb to the right.)*
DAVID: Uh . . . weh . . . yes, it is.
MAC: There, I told ya.

462. MS: *Susan, at the rear of the truck with her rope, removes the bolt from
    the cage and opens the door. David's interview with the drivers continues
    mutedly off-frame.*

SUSAN *(whispering)*: Now, come on. Come on. *(The leopard comes
    forward to the open door.)* Get this around your neck. That's a good
    boy. Come on. Put your head through. Come on. *(The leopard snarls
    at her.)* Hey! *(Another snarl.)* Hey, what's the big idea? Go 'way from
    me. Put your head through again and I'll take you back home. Come
    on, sweetie. Come on. Oh!

The leopard avoids the noose and jumps to the ground.

463. MLS: *Susan follows the leopard with the noose. As the leopard slides through the fence and into the woods, Susan takes a pratfall over the wooden fence.*

   DAVID *(off):* . . . when New York is straight ahead.
   JOE *(off):* This guy ain't got all his buttons.
   DAVID *(off):* Well, I . . . you see . . .[39]
   SUSAN: David! *(She runs off to her left.)*

464. MS: *at the front of the truck, David, sitting on the bumper, holds Joe's and Mac's attention.*[40]

DAVID: Now, we have found distinct evidence . . .

Susan rushes in to join the men.

SUSAN: David.
DAVID: Yes, dar . . .
SUSAN: He's escaped.
DAVID: Oh, I was just explaining to these gentlemen . . .
SUSAN: No, you see, he's escaped!
JOE AND MAC: Oh! He's escaped!
SUSAN: Yeah. *(David stands up.)*
MAC: Shall we help you tie him up, lady?
DAVID: Oh, oh, no. Not me. No. No. You're mistaken, gentlemen. Not
. . . Well, goodnight, gentlemen.
SUSAN *(overlapping)*: Come on. No. Thank you. *(She pulls David to-
ward the woods.)*[41]

465. MS: *a leopard climbs onto a stone fence and utters a cry.*

466. MLS: *David and Susan rush into a clearing with rope, croquet mallet,
and butterfly net. They stop, looking for the source of the sound.*

SUSAN: Over there. Oh, we're on the right track now, David, I'm sure.

They run off.[42]

467. LS: *at the stone fence, a leopard prowls the foreground side of the fence,
as David and Susan appear in the background, running toward the fence.*

SUSAN: Do you see him, David?
DAVID: No, I think he's farther down this way.

The leopard stands close to the fence, as Susan leaps upon it.

SUSAN: Well, I'll try over there anyway.

Just as Susan is about to bring her legs over the fence, David stops her.

DAVID: Well, Susan, I'm absolutely certain the sounds came from down this way.

A gunshot explodes from off-frame, followed by two more bursts.

DAVID: Well, what's that?
SUSAN: Somebody's shooting at him.

She jumps off the wall; she and David run off to the left, while the leopard stands calmly in the foreground.

468. MLS: *in the woods.*[43]

GOGARTY: You'll miss it again.
APPLEGATE: Quiet!

Applegate raises the gun, takes aim, and fires. Susan and David rush in.

SUSAN: Major Applegate, don't shoot! Don't shoot!
APPLEGATE: Please stand back. Please. Please. Please. I . . . I won't miss him this time.
SUSAN: No, but you don't understand! We're trying to catch that leopard.
APPLEGATE: Ha, ha, ha. Well, so am I.
DAVID: It's a tame leopard.
APPLEGATE: Yes, but, I don't like to say so, sir, at this moment, sir, but everybody knows you're crazy. *(Raises gun and takes aim.)*
SUSAN *(grabbing the gun)*: Oh, please, don't do that!
DAVID: Susan! Susan!

469. MS: *David, Susan, Applegate, and Gogarty.*

DAVID: Well, Susan, why don't you explain to Major Applegate and then perhaps you'll catch your leopard.
SUSAN: Yes, Major Applegate. You know that Aunt Elizabeth was expecting a leopard from Brazil, don't you?
APPLEGATE: I had heard that, yes.
SUSAN: Well, that's her leopard, and it's tame.

APPLEGATE: Impossible. There can be no such thing as a tame . . . *(He stops and shakes his head.)* A tame leopard?
SUSAN: A tame leopard. We had it locked up and it escaped.
APPLEGATE: Are you sure it's quite harmless?
SUSAN: Absolutely.
APPLEGATE: Well, my goodness, why didn't you say so in the first place?
SUSAN *(overlapping)*: Well, I've been trying . . .
DAVID *(overlapping)*: We've been trying to tell you . . .
APPLEGATE: Well, I . . . I . . . I apologize to you, Mr. . . . eh . . . Mr. Boney. I really do.
DAVID *(overlapping)*: Well, thank you very much.
APPLEGATE: Even though it is tame, I think we should try to catch it, don't you?
DAVID: Yes, but which way did it go?
SUSAN *(overlapping)*: Now, which way did it go?
APPLEGATE AND GOGARTY: Uh . . . uh . . . uh . . . That way. *(They point in opposite directions.)*
DAVID: Oh.
SUSAN: Well, we'll go in that direction—you go in that one. Come on, David. *(As she and David start off.)* Remember, don't shoot!
APPLEGATE: Oh, no, no, no. Of course not.[44]

470. LS: *Susan and David running through the forest with rope, butterfly net, and croquet mallet. The camera pans with them.*

DAVID: George!
SUSAN: George!
DAVID: George! George! George!

471. MLS: *Applegate, carrying the gun, and Gogarty, walk beside the stone fence.*[45]

GOGARTY: I knew all the time he was tame.
APPLEGATE: Oh, is that so?

Gogarty sits on the fence.

GOGARTY: Yes. I patted him on the back.

APPLEGATE: Um-hm.

GOGARTY: Stretched me hand right out . . .

472. MCU: *a leopard prowling near the fence.*

GOGARTY *(off)*: . . . and patted him on the back.

APPLEGATE *(off)*: Well, well, well, well.

GOGARTY *(off)*: He's gentle as a kitten. *(The leopard snarls.)*

APPLEGATE *(off)*: Gentle as a kitten?

473. MCU: *Gogarty and Applegate on the stone fence.*

APPLEGATE: Well, of course, I don't see why you didn't mention all this
be . . . *(Applegate looks off to his left at the sound of another snarl.)*

GOGARTY: There he is.

APPLEGATE: Hm. Oh, well, this will all be quite simple. Hm, hm. Let me
have that rope, will you? Hm, hm. *(He takes the rope from Gogarty.)*
There. Now you hold the gun. We shan't need that any further. *(As he
ties a noose with the rope.)* Now, Gogarty, you stand perfectly still and
leave everything to me. I've . . . had vast experience in these matters.
*(Applegate advances with the noose, as a low snarl accompanies
their walk.)*

474. LS: *camera pans as Applegate, holding the rope in front of him, Gogarty
behind him, sneaks toward the leopard.*

APPLEGATE: Here, kitty, kitty, kitty, kitty, kitty. Come, kitty, kitty, kitty,
kitty, kitty. *(As Applegate extends the noose, the leopard snarls. Applegate retreats.)* Hm. Hm. Heh, heh, heh. Don't you fool me. Heh, heh.
You're not afraid of me, now, are you? Come, puss, puss, puss.

Again the leopard snarls.

475. MCU: *the men draw back with a gasp.*

APPLEGATE: Er . . . er . . . er . . . You say you patted this beast?

GOGARTY: Well, in a manner of speaking, I did.

476. CU: *the leopard snarls.*

477. LS: *the two men retreat further.*

> APPLEGATE: Er . . . eh . . . eh . . . Personally, Gogarty, I think you're a liar.

> *As the leopard advances slowly, the men turn and run off to the left. The leopard follows.*

478. LS: *Applegate and Gogarty dash madly through the forest screaming inarticulately, followed by the leopard.*

479. LS: *Applegate and Gogarty running.*

> APPLEGATE: The gun, man. Use the gun! The gun!

> *They run off, the leopard in pursuit.*[46]

480. MLS: *Susan, rushing through the forest, followed by David.*

> SUSAN: You see him, David?
> DAVID: No.
> SUSAN: Oh, dear, I seem to have lost my sense of direction. I wonder where we are. *(She scrambles up a slight incline.)*
> DAVID: Well, my rough guess is somewhere near the Canadian border by now. *(He removes his glasses to clean them.)*
> SUSAN: Oh, no, David . . . *(She slides down the incline and plunges into David's back, sending him sprawling into a ravine.)*
> DAVID: Oh!
> SUSAN *(tumbling to the ground beside him)*: So sor . . . Uh.

481. MS: *Susan and David lying side by side on the ground.*

> DAVID: Oh! Oh! My glasses! Don't move, Susan. My glasses!
> SUSAN: Oh, here they are, David. Here they are . . . Oh, David, they're broken. I'm sorry.

DAVID *(on his knees, tossing his right hand in the air)*: Oh, it doesn't make any difference. Hm. The things I've been doing today I could do just as well with my eyes shut.
SUSAN *(handing the glasses to him)*: Well . . .

482. LS: *David grabs the glasses and flings them away.*

SUSAN: Well, anyway, David, you look much handsomer without them.

They both get to their feet. David strides toward the camera with Susan following.

DAVID: Oh, stop it!
SUSAN: Oh, look, David, I've lost my heel! I lost my heel! Look at me walk.

She walks with a hippity-hoppity bounce, bobbing up and down. She giggles and continues to march, humming "The Spirit of '76."

DAVID: Susan! *(Watches her.)* Susan!
SUSAN: Born on the side of a hill.

483. MS: *Susan and David.*

SUSAN: I was born on the side of a hill. *(Bouncing up and down beside him.)*
DAVID: Susan, stop! Now . . . Oh . . . Oh, now look, Susan, we're not getting anywhere like this. Now . . . now . . . you must be very tired and I suggest that you go home.
SUSAN: Oh, but David, we can't quit now. Why, we've let a wild animal loose on an innocent countryside. *(David tries to interject.)* We . . . we can't just go home and sleep. It wouldn't be right.
DAVID: Su . . . Susan, you misunderstand me. I want *you* to go home.
SUSAN: But, Da . . . *(A pause.)* You mean you want *me* to go home?
DAVID: Yes.

484. MCU: *Susan over David's shoulder.*

SUSAN *(near tears)*: You mean you don't want me to help you any more?
DAVID: No.
SUSAN: After all the fun we've had?
DAVID: Yes.
SUSAN: And after all the things I've done for you?
DAVID: Well, that's what I mean.
SUSAN: Well, all right. I know enough to go when I'm not wanted. And . . .

485. MS: *Susan and David.*

SUSAN: And don't you worry about me. I'll take care of myself.

She backs away from him with a hippity-hop and suddenly falls over a tree branch. The camera tilts down with her. David scrambles over the branch to her side.

SUSAN AND DAVID: Oh!
DAVID: Oh, my goodness. Susan, Susan, are you all right?

486. MCU: *Susan and David.*

SUSAN *(weeping)*: Yes, I'm all right.
DAVID *(overlapping)*: Did you hurt yourself?
SUSAN *(overlapping)*: No, I didn't hurt myself. *(Still weeping.)* It's not
    that. It's just that I'm miserable. Because you don't like me anymore.
    (Weeps, her head on his shoulder.)
DAVID: Oh, yes, I do, Susan.
SUSAN: You tried to get rid of me. And you just don't think of me. And
    you don't like me anymore.
DAVID *(overlapping)*: Nah, nah. *(Dabs her eyes with his handkerchief.)*
    Oh, your face is dirty, Susan.
SUSAN: Oh. Oh. Now you're being nice to me. And after all the horrible
    things I've done to you. I just can't bear it. *(Collapses on his shoulder,
    weeping.)*
DAVID *(overlapping)*: Oh, now, Susan. Oh, stop crying. Susan, please.
SUSAN: It's just that everything I do with the best intentions seems to
    turn out badly.

DAVID: Yes, it does, doesn't it?

SUSAN: Oh, David, please let me come with you. *(She raises her head; their lips almost touch.)* Oh, David.

David moves to kiss her, then draws back. Susan sighs.

DAVID: Uh-uh. Well, all right, Susan. You can come with me.

SUSAN: Are you sure you want me?

DAVID: Yes. Yes.

SUSAN: Positive?

DAVID: Yes. You can come. Come on.

487. MS: *they rise, camera tilting up with them.*

SUSAN: Well, don't you worry, David. Because if there's anything that I can do to help you, just let me know and I'll do it. *(She starts to walk toward the camera.)*

DAVID: Uh, . . . *(He puts his hand on her arm.)* . . . don't do it until I let you know.

SUSAN *(shaking her head)*: Uh-uh.

DAVID: Oh, yeh. Fi . . . *(They move toward the camera.)*

Dissolve [47]

Dr. Lehman's House, night

488. LS: *George seated on the lawn in front of a house, barking. David and Susan approach him. David drops the croquet mallet and butterfly net. George runs over to David, wagging his tail.*

DAVID: Come on. Come on, George. Ah. *(Picks George up.)*

SUSAN: Oh, look, David. Baby's on the roof!

David looks up, accompanied by snarls on the soundtrack.

489. MS: *Baby prowls on the gable of a roof.*

SUSAN *(off)*: Come on, Baby. Come on down. Come on.

490. MS: *David, holding George, and Susan.*

> SUSAN: Oh, David, make him get down.
> DAVID *(holding George in his arms)*: I suppose you'd like me to climb
> up and push him down. Oh. *(Shakes his head.)*
> SUSAN: Well . . . uh . . . well . . . maybe we'd better sing. *(Sings.)* I
> can't give you any . . . *(Stops singing.)* Well, sing, David.
> DAVID: Uh.
> DAVID AND SUSAN *(singing close harmony in thirds)*: I can't give you
> anything but love, . . .

491. MCU: *Susan and David singing, as David holds George in his arms.*

> DAVID AND SUSAN: . . . Baby. *(David beckons toward the roof with his
> finger.)* That's . . . *(George joins to make it a trio.)* . . . the only thing
> I've plenty of, Baby. Dream awhile, scheme awhile, . . .

492. MS: *Baby on the roof joins the song with a yowl.*

> ALL *(off)*: You're sure to find . . .

493. MCU: *as in 491.*

> ALL: . . . Happiness and I guess
> All those things you've always pined for.

494. MCU: *Baby on the roof.*

> ALL *(off)*: Gee, it's great to see you looking swell, Baby.

495. MCU: *as in 491.*

> ALL: Diamond bracelets Woolworth's never sell, . . .

496. MCU: *an upstairs window of the house.*

> ALL *(off)*: . . . Baby.

A light comes on in the window, which opens. Dr. Lehman peers out monocle in hand.

497. MS: *as in 490.*

    ALL: Till that lucky day . . .

Susan recognizes Lehman and pokes David.

    DAVID *(still singing)*: You know darn well, . . .
    SUSAN: Hey. *(She points.)*
    DAVID *(seeing and recognizing Lehman)*: Oh, Baby! *(He rushes off to his right accompanied by barking from George.)*
    SUSAN *(singing)*: Baby. *(She chases after David.)* Oh, David, where're you going?
    DAVID *(off)*: I'll be back.

SUSAN: Oh, dear. *(Returns to finish the refrain.)* I can't give you anything but love, . . .

498. MS: *Lehman in the window.*

SUSAN *(off)*: Not you, it. *(Lehman looks around; Susan sings again off.)*
I can't give you . . .
LEHMAN: What are you doing, may I ask?
SUSAN *(off)*: Singing. *(Her singing overlaps his interrogation.)* . . .
anything but love, Baby.
LEHMAN: If you are paying a bet . . .

499. MS: *Susan, singing, cups a hand over her ear.*

LEHMAN *(off)*: . . . there must be somewhere else you can pay it.
SUSAN *(singing)*: That's the only . . . *(Stops singing.)* I'm not paying a
bet. There's a leopard on your roof.

500. MS: *Lehman in the window.*

SUSAN *(singing, off)*: . . . of, Baby.

Mrs. Lehman appears in the window beside Lehman.

LEHMAN *(overlapping)*: I'm not going to bandy words with you at this
time . . .

501. MS: *as in 499.*

LEHMAN *(off)*: . . . at night.
SUSAN: Dream awhile, scheme awhile . . . *(Stops singing.)* There is a
leopard on your roof and it's my leopard and I have to get it. And to get
it I have to sing. *(Sings.)* You're sure to find, . . .
LEHMAN *(off, overlapping)*: There's nothing on my roof.
SUSAN *(speaking)*: Come on, you fool. There's nothing on your roof.
LEHMAN *(off)*: No!
SUSAN *(laughs)*: All right, there's nothing on your roof. *(Sings.)* Hap-
piness and I guess . . .

502. MS: *Dr. and Mrs. Lehman in the window, looking down.*

> SUSAN: *(off, singing):* . . . All those things you've always pined for.
> MRS. LEHMAN *(shaking her head, overlapping):* Poor girl. You'd better
> go down, Fritz.

Lehman disappears from window.

> SUSAN *(singing, off):* Gee, it's great to see you . . .
> MRS. LEHMAN *(overlapping):* Sing if you like, dear.

503. MS: *as in 499.*

> SUSAN *(singing):* . . . looking . . . *(Speaking.)* Thank you.
> *(Singing.)* . . . swell, Baby. *(Speaking.)* You can sing, too.
> *(Singing.)* Diamond bracelets Woolworth's . . .

504. MLS: *lights come on inside the house and on the front porch. The door
opens and Lehman rushes out, slamming the door.*

> SUSAN *(off, singing):* . . . never sell, Baby.

505. MLS: *Susan looking up toward the roof. Lehman hurries to her.*

> SUSAN: Oh, Baby, don't . . . Oh, why did you have to do that? You've
> frightened him away.
> LEHMAN: Sh-h-h. Quiet. It's all right.
> SUSAN: It's not all right.
> LEHMAN *(taking her hand):* Don't worry.
> SUSAN: Well, I have to worry. I've lost my leopard. Oh, please help me
> find him.
> LEHMAN: I certainly will. You just come with me. *(Leads her toward
> the house, as the camera pans.)*
> SUSAN: But you don't understand. He went that way. *(Points behind her.)*
> LEHMAN *(leading her forward toward the house):* Oh, no he didn't.
> SUSAN: Oh, yes he did. I saw him.
> LEHMAN: Oh, you're wrong. He's up there. *(Points toward the roof, his
> monocle glittering.)* See him?

SUSAN *(looking up)*: Wh . . . ?
LEHMAN: There.
SUSAN: Where?

506. MCU: *Susan and Lehman.*

LEHMAN *(pointing upward)*: There. Peeking around the corner. See it?
SUSAN *(staring hard)*: No, I don't . . . *(Looks at Lehman to examine him.)* Hey! Hey! There's nothing there! There's nothing there!

507. MS: *As at the end of 505.*

LEHMAN: *(holding her arm tightly as she tries to pull away from him)*: Oh, yes there is.
SUSAN *(overlapping)*: Now, you let me go. You let me go.
LEHMAN *(pulling her toward the house as the camera pans)*: You just come into the house and we'll find him.
SUSAN *(resisting)*: I don't want to go in your . . .
LEHMAN: Will you come along?
SUSAN: You don't seem to understand that there's a million dollars at stake.
LEHMAN: A million dollars!
SUSAN: Yes.
LEHMAN: Well, you'll get it. We have it right in there. All in one-dollar bills. Now you just come along. *(He drags her toward the door, which has been opened by Mrs. Lehman.)*
SUSAN *(overlapping)*: Oh, no. Don't do this to me. Oh, let me go. Oh, this is awful.

Lehman pulls her into the house and closes the door.

508. MLS: *David peers around a corner of the garden, carrying George. He moves toward the house.*[48]

509. LS: *a vintage touring car pulls up in front of a gate. Slocum and Elmer get out of the car and move toward the gate.*

SLOCUM: Pssst. *(Whispers.)* Elmer, look.

510. MLS: *David, holding George, stands at a lighted window, peering into house.*

511. MS: *Slocum and Elmer looking off to their right.*

> SLOCUM *(whispering)*: You know him?
> ELMER: No. Looks like a Peepin' Tom.
> SLOCUM: Peepin' Tom, eh? *(Taps Elmer's shoulder.)* Get your gun out and we'll nab him.

> *They draw their guns and move toward the house.*

512. LS: *Slocum and Elmer, with guns drawn, move across the lawn toward the house, camera panning with them. As they reach the porch, camera picks up David standing at the window.*

> SLOCUM: Stick 'em up! I got you covered!

> *David quickly turns and raises his hands, dropping George. George barks and runs off.*

> SLOCUM: Come on, grab him, Elmer. Grab him. *(David moves to catch George.)*
> DAVID: But my dog . . .

> *Elmer grabs David and carries him into the house.*

> DAVID: I have to get my dog. George! Don't go away, George.
> SLOCUM: Don't argue. Don't argue. Inside!

> *Dissolve*[49]

Westlake Jail, night

513. MCU: *David, behind bars, seated on a cot, chin in his hands, staring. A sound attracts his attention.*

514. MCU: *Susan, picking at the lock of her cell door.*

515. MCU: *as in 513.*

> DAVID: What are you doing?

516. MCU: *as in 514.*

> SUSAN *(working on the lock)*: I have a hairpin.
> DAVID *(off)*: Aaaah!
> SUSAN: Well, I did it once with a trunk. Anyway, David, when they find
> out who we are, why, they'll let us out.

517. MCU: *as in 513.*

> DAVID: When they find out who you are, they'll pad the cell. *(He returns
> his chin to his hands.)*

518. MCU: *as in 514.*

> SUSAN *(curling her lips sarcastically)*: Humph.

519. MLS: *Slocum, seated at his desk, talking on the phone. Lehman, Elmer,
and a policeman are grouped around.*

> SLOCUM *(into phone)*: We picked up a girl who says she's your niece.
> Now the question is, have you or have you not got a niece?

520. MS: *Aunt Elizabeth on the phone.*

> AUNT: Of course I have a niece. But she's not singing around under
> windows.

521. MCU: *a dirtied Applegate at the bar, downing a drink.*

> AUNT *(off)*: She's decently in bed.[50]
> APPLEGATE: I . . . I wouldn't be too sure, Elizabeth.

AUNT *(overlapping, off)*: Of course, I . . . Oh, Horace, do be quiet. I'll talk to you presently. *(Applegate takes another gulp of his drink.)*[51]

522. MS: *as in 519.*

SLOCUM *(into phone)*: Now lady, do you definitely refuse to come down and identify this girl?

523. MS: *Aunt on phone, Applegate beside her.*

AUNT: If you continue to annoy me about this girl who is no responsibility of mine . . . *(Applegate tries to stop her with his hands, she pokes him back with her elbow.)* . . . I'll have you arrested. *(Returns the receiver to the hook.)* The idea!

524. MS: *as in 519.*

SLOCUM: Hello. *(Hangs up.)* She says her niece is in bed.
LEHMAN: Uh huh. Just what I expected. That girl is lying.
SLOCUM: Doc, I think you're right. *(He raps his desk with his right knuckle.)* I think they're both lying.[52]
LEHMAN: Now, what are you going to do about it?
SLOCUM: Well . . . uh . . . What would you do?
LEHMAN: Find out the truth.
SLOCUM: You're right. *(Rises, as he raps again on the desk.)* I'll go back and have a little talk with them. Come on, Elmer. Open 'er up.

525. MLS: *the men stand behind the barred gate, as Elmer opens the door. The camera pans with them as they cross to Susan's and David's cells.*

SLOCUM: Now, uh, look here you two. Get your ears up like a rabbit 'cause I've got something to tell you. *(David stands up in his cell.)* And if you ever want to get out of this jail, you better listen.
SUSAN *(standing, her hands on the bars of her cell)*: I'm listening.
SLOCUM: Quiet, young lady. I'm gonna get to you later.

526. MS: *David and Susan, holding the bars of their cells, Slocum addressing David.*

SLOCUM: Now I want you to tell me the truth, the whole truth, and nothing but the truth.

DAVID: We . . .

SUSAN *(overlapping)*: Well, what did my aunt say?

SLOCUM: Uh, quiet please.

SUSAN: What did my aunt say?

SLOCUM: Your aunt? Why she said . . . . Now, young lady, you haven't got an aunt!

SUSAN: But I certainly have got an aun . . .

SLOCUM: Quiet! Quiet please! *(Steps toward David.)* Now, look here, young fella, I want you to tell me just exactly what were you doing tonight?

DAVID: Well, I . . . I . . .

SUSAN *(overlapping)*: Well, we were hunting for a leopard.

SLOCUM: You were hunting for a leopard! A leop . . . Now, now, now, look here, look here, young lady. Now you know that's silly. There never was a leopard in the whole State of Connecticut.

SUSAN: Well, there is now.

SLOCUM: Yeh . . . Now, young lady, listen here. *(Slaps his hands.)* I'm going to stay here if it takes all year. I am waiting for you . . . *(Slaps his hands.)* . . . to tell the truth.

SUSAN: Well . . .

DAVID *(overlapping, finally seizing the chance to speak)*: Oh, if you're gonna wait for her to tell the truth, you'll have a long gray beard. Down to here *(indicates his waist)*.

SLOCUM: You know, it's a funny thing. My grandfather had a . . . Quiet. *(Slaps his hands.)* Young man, listen. I don't want any more slick remarks out of you. This is a jail, and I want you to have a little respect for the Law.

DAVID: I'm just trying to explain, Mister Constable. You see, it . . . it all started over at my aunt's . . . at her aunt's house.

SLOCUM: Her aunt's house. Yes, yes.

DAVID: You see, her aunt promised to give me . . .

SLOCUM: Uh, hold on, hold on there, Bub. Just a minute. She hasn't got an aunt.

SUSAN: I certainly have. She's my father's sister. Now, look here, Constable. Come over here. *(Pulls Slocum to her cell.)*

SLOCUM: Young lady . . .
SUSAN: Stop wasting your time. Now quiet.
SLOCUM: Yeh, yeh, yeh . . . *(David mutters incomprehensibly.)*
SUSAN: Now, look here. You want us to get out of here, don't you?
SLOCUM: Oh, lady, yes, I certainly do.
SUSAN: Now, I gave you my aunt's telephone number, didn't I?

David points and raises a finger, hoping to utter a word.

SLOCUM: Yup.
SUSAN: And you called her up, didn't you?
SLOCUM: I sure did.
SUSAN: And what did she say?
SLOCUM: Well, uh, she said that you were home in bed.

527. MCU: *Susan and Slocum.*

SUSAN: Then what am I doing here?
SLOCUM: Well, you're here because you're . . . you're . . . you're . . . .
   your aunt, she said . . . Now, confound it, lady . . . *(Slaps his hands.)*
   . . . you know that you haven't got an aunt!

528. MCU: *David in his cell, trying to get a word in edgewise as Susan and
   Slocum argue.*

SUSAN *(off)*: But if I did have an aunt?
SLOCUM *(off)*: She'd muzzle you!
SUSAN *(off)*: Now, look here. You can't talk to me that way. Now, how
   do you know we were going to get to wander around . . .

*David gives up trying to make a point. He shakes his head and leans
against the bars.*

DAVID: I don't know.
SLOCUM *(off, overlapping, trying to interrupt)*: I don't like to see young
   people in trouble. I have children of my own.
SUSAN *(off)*: Listen, I don't care anything about your family. All I want

to do is get out of here. I haven't got time to waste sitting around in a
jail in Connecticut.

SLOCUM *(off, overlapping)*: Only if we arrive at some definite conclusion here.

*David discovers the cell door isn't locked. He pushes it open and crosses to
Slocum, as the camera pans with him. David taps Slocum on the shoulder.*

SUSAN *(overlapping)*: We'll arrive at a definite conclusion when you
have the brains . . .

SLOCUM: One second. Now, go 'way. Go 'way, please.

SUSAN: Oh, shut up, David.

SLOCUM: Now, David, please be quiet.

SUSAN *(overlapping)*: When you have the brains to listen to me . . .

DAVID *(overlapping)*: I can explain the whole thing to you if you just
listen to me. Susan, please.

SUSAN *(overlapping)*: Now, let me tell you what happened. We left New
York at eleven o'clock this morning in a Ford station wagon . . .

SLOCUM: Huh? What?

DAVID: Now, now. You see, you're not going to get anywhere with her.
I'll give you . . . You just come with me.

SLOCUM: Well, that's better. If one of us talk at a time, now we're really
getting somewhere.

*David leads Slocum by the arm back to his cell, as the camera pans with
them.*

DAVID: Just be calm.

SLOCUM: Now, then, speak up, speak fast.

DAVID: I'll explain . . .

SLOCUM *(suddenly realizing he is inside David's unlocked cell)*: OH!!!
(Slocum dashes out of the cell and closes the door.) Elmer! Elmer! Get
the key here! Quick! Lock him up! Lock him up!

*Elmer rushes in to lock the door. Slocum pulls the keys away from the
fumbling Elmer. He takes the key and leaves it dangling in the lock.*

DAVID: Well, now, please . . .

SLOCUM: Fine officer you are! Locking up a dangerous criminal without locking him up.

DAVID: It's not locked.

SLOCUM: Huh?

DAVID: Not locked.

SLOCUM: Oh. Thank you. *(He turns the key.)*

529. LS: *a motorcycle cop opens the door to the outer office of the jail. Another cop enters, shoving a protesting Gogarty ahead of him. Camera pans with them as they cross to cell corridor, Gogarty yelling inarticulately.*

GOGARTY: You have absolutely no right to do that . . .

SLOCUM *(off)*: Here, here. What's the commotion out there?

530. MLS: *the cop propels Gogarty to Slocum, Lehman, and Elmer, picking him up and dropping him to the floor.*

COP: Here's something for you, Constable.

SLOCUM: Well, what's the charge?

COP: We caught him just as he was driving up in front of a meat market in Dr. Lehman's stolen car.

GOGARTY: I . . . I . . .

SLOCUM: Oh ho, so you're a car thief, huh?

GOGARTY: Car . . . *(He stops, jerks off his hat, and throws it to the floor.)* No man is going to call Aloysius Gogarty a car thief. *(He puts up his dukes and begins waltzing around to battle anyone in the group.)* Come on. Come on. Come on.

SLOCUM *(overlapping.)*: Here, here. Stop this. Now you've had it.

The cop picks Gogarty up by the seat of his pants.

SLOCUM: Lock him up. Lock him up.

Camera pans as the cop carries Gogarty into a cell.

GOGARTY: Let go. Let go.
SLOCUM *(overlapping)*: There you are, young fella . . . *(Slocum closes the cell door and locks it.)* This will hold you for a while.

531. CU: *Susan in her cell, waving.*

SUSAN: Hello, Gogarty.

532. MS: *Gogarty at the door of his cell.*

GOGARTY: Ah, Miss Susan. How did you get in?

533. MS: *David and Susan in their cells, their arms wrapped around the bars.*

DAVID *(smiling)*: Influence.
SUSAN *(smiling)*: Don't worry, Gogarty. I'll get you out.
DAVID *(still smiling)*: Oh, sure, sure. Look. She got me out.

534. MS: *Slocum at Gogarty's cell, Lehman behind.*

SLOCUM: Say, hold on there. Do you know this young lady?
GOGARTY: Of course I do. Don't I work for her aunt?
SLOCUM: Yuh . . . You what?
GOGARTY: Don't I work for her aunt?
SLOCUM: Now look here. *(Clears throat.)* If one more person mentions that she's got an aunt I'll put you all on bread and water for thirty days. *(Clears throat.)*[53]

535. LS: *as in 529. The door to the jail opens from the outside and Aunt Elizabeth enters, followed by Applegate, carrying the gun. Camera pans with them as they cross the room.*

AUNT: Well, where is everyone? Who's in charge here?
COP *(indicating behind him)*: Right in there. Hey, Constable.

The cops move toward the door. Lehman enters.

AUNT *(to Lehman)*: What do you mean by locking up my niece? I won't stand for it! Give me the keys! Come along, come along, come along!

Slocum, Elmer, and a cop join Lehman.

LEHMAN *(overlapping)*: Madam, madam, madam, you are hysterical!
SLOCUM: Say, what is it you want?
APPLEGATE *(holding the gun)*: Uh . . . Uh . . . she wants her niece.

536. MS: *Aunt, Slocum, Lehman, Applegate, and others.*

AUNT: I certainly do. I want my niece right here.
SLOCUM: Well, who is your niece?
LEHMAN: You give us a description of her and they find her.
APPLEGATE: Uh . . . she's about so tall . . . *(Indicates.)*
SUSAN *(off, overlapping)*: Aunt Elizabeth! Aunt Elizabeth! Is that you?
AUNT: There she is now! *(She starts forward.)*
SLOCUM *(stopping her)*: Eh-eh-eh-eh-eh. Hold on here. Hold on now. Just a minute, lady. Tell me, who are you?
AUNT: I am Mrs. Carleton Random and I want my niece.
SLOCUM: Oh, so you're Mrs. Carleton Random.
AUNT: I certainly am.
SLOCUM: And you say your niece is here?
AUNT: She certainly is!
SLOCUM *(slapping his hands)*: Hah! That's where I got you. The young lady we got here ain't got no aunt, . . .

537. MCU: *Slocum, with Applegate and others.*

SLOCUM: And you're not Mrs. Carleton Random because I talked to Mrs. Carleton Random on the telephone not ten minutes ago!

538. MS: *reverse shot of 537.*

AUNT: Well, I ought to know who I am!
APPLEGATE: Uh . . . yes, you should, Elizabeth, I think. You did talk to her ten minutes ago on the telephone. That's right.

SLOCUM: How do you know?

APPLEGATE: Be . . . uh . . . I was there.

SLOCUM: And who are you?

APPLEGATE: I'm the niece. Uh . . . uh . . . um . . . I'm the aunt. Uh
. . . I'm Major Horace Applegate of the Explorer's Club . . .

SLOCUM: Say, uh, what're you doing with that gun?

APPLEGATE: The guh . . . uh . . . I have been hunting a leopard.

539. MCU: *as in 537.*

SLOCUM *(pausing, raising his eyebrows)*: Oh, uh. You've been hunting
leopards.

APPLEGATE: I said so. I have been hunting leopards. Yes.

SLOCUM: Any luck?

APPLEGATE: Uh, well, not what I'm accustomed to. No.

540. MS: *as in 538.*

APPLEGATE: I have been a bit confused regarding leopards . . .

SLOCUM: Boys.

APPLEGATE: The leopards here.

SLOCUM: Boys. *(They move toward Applegate.)*

APPLEGATE: Uh . . . You have something on your mind, haven't you?

*Elmer and the Cop grab Applegate. They struggle for possession of the
gun. Aunt joins in the fight, batting Slocum with her purse. A cacophony
of voices rises from the fray.*

Dissolve

Westlake Jail, night

541. MS: *Slocum sitting on the edge of his desk, talking over the phone.
Lehman and Elmer standing by.*

SLOCUM: Not so fast. Not so fast, lady. We just want to find out. This
old battleaxe we got here keeps yelling that she's Mrs. Random.

542. MS: *Hannah Gogarty in the kitchen, her hair in curlers, on the phone.*

> HANNAH: Well that's ridiculous! Mrs. Random is in bed. And don't you
> be calling up here again! Goodnight! *(She slams down the receiver.)*

543. MS: *as in 541.*

> SLOCUM: Goodnight. *(Hangs up.)* Well, just as you said, Doc. They're
> all lyin'.
> LEHMAN: Obviously. I have no doubt you will find you've made a very
> important haul.
> SLOCUM: Yeah. Thanks to you, Doc.
> LEHMAN: If you get their confessions, Constable, there'll be a lot of
> things you'll turn up.
> SLOCUM: Yeah. Well, I'll try it again. Come on, boys.

They move toward the cell corridor.

544. LS: *Slocum, Elmer, Lehman, and a cop stride through the gate in the
background and walk down the corridor to a point between the four cells.*

> SLOCUM: Now, you folks . . .

A cacophonous din of voices rises from the cells.[54]

> SLOCUM *(slapping his hands)*: Quiet! Quiet!!! QUIET!!! Now, look here.
> I warn ya—the first one that lets a squeak out of 'em, I'm gonna put in
> solitary confinement. I'm gonna ask this young man a few questions,
> and I want absolute quiet. Now, young man . . . *(He moves to his right.)*

545. MS: *at David's cell. David seated on his cot, Susan standing at the door
of her cell. Lehman stands behind Slocum with a pad of paper. Susan
moves to observe the examination from her cell.*

> SLOCUM: Said your name was Bone. Do you stick to it?
> DAVID: Well, I . . .
> SLOCUM: Won't do any good. We don't believe you. We know that's an
> alias. Now, we know that ain't your right name.

LEHMAN: They're all impersonating somebody.
SLOCUM: What were you doing, trying to break into Dr. Lehman's house?
DAVID: I was after a leopard.
SLOCUM: Leopard! There you are, Doc. They still stick to it.
LEHMAN: They've all agreed on one story.
SLOCUM: Uh . . . Uh . . . How about that bank robbery in Oldtown?

546. CU: *David.*

DAVID: Oh, what about it? How much did they get?

547. MCU: *reverse shot of 546. Slocum and Lehman.*

SLOCUM: Oh, they got a pretty penny. Must have got five thousand, six hun . . . Say, who's asking these questions? You or me?

548. CU: *as in 546.*

SLOCUM *(off)*: Who was with you last month in Rockdale on that mail-truck job?[55]
DAVID: Mickey-the-Mouse and Donald-the-Duck.

549. MS: *Slocum and Lehman.*

SLOCUM: Mickey-the-Mouse and Donald-the-Duck. Doc, make a note of them names.

550. MS: *Slocum and David, Susan observing from behind.*

SLOCUM: Now, you're beginning to talk. We're getting someplace. Now, young fella, speak up.
SUSAN *(squatting in a chair and assuming a tough pose)*: Say!
SLOCUM *(overlapping)*: Quiet, lady. I'm waiting for ya.
SUSAN: HEY!
SLOCUM: Quiet lady! Speak up now.
SUSAN: HEY—FLATFOOT!!!!!
SLOCUM: Yeh . . .

David and Slocum turn to look at her with utter amazement.

SUSAN *(in the voice of a moll)*: You ain't gettin' no place. Come here!
SLOCUM: Me?
SUSAN: Yes, you. Come on. Haul it over. Haul it over.

Camera pans as Slocum steps to Susan's cell and she rises from her chair.

SUSAN: You want someone to talk, don't ya?

551. MCU: *Susan and Slocum.*

SLOCUM: Well, it's about time. I certainly do.
SUSAN: Yeah. Well, get me out of this cooler and I'll unbutton my puss and shoot the works![56]

552. CU: *David, astonished.*

SLOCUM *(off)*: You'll, uh . . . Say, hold on, lady, I thought that you were . . . but . . .

553. MS: *as in 551.*

SLOCUM: Hey, you ain't no lady.
SUSAN: Yeah. I kinda had you fooled for a minute, didn't I?
SLOCUM: You sure did.
SUSAN: I always could make a sucker out of a copper.

554. CU: *David, amazed.*

SUSAN *(off)*: What did I tell you my name was?
SLOCUM *(off)*: Why, your name is . . . uh . . . uh . . . uh . . .

555. CU: *Aunt and Applegate, who turn to one another amazed.*

SLOCUM *(off)*: Doc, what's her name?
LEHMAN *(off)*: Susan Vance.

556. CU: *Susan and Slocum.*

> SUSAN: Vaunce, kiddie, Vaunce. That's my society moniker. But the mob all calls me "Swingin'-Door Susie."
> SLOCUM: Swingin'-Door Susie.
> SUSAN: Now do you peg me? Come on, toots. *(She chucks Slocum under the chin.)* Open up. Open up.
> SLOCUM: Ey, ey, ey, ey, ey. Stop . . . Stop . . . Stop that. Stop that. *(Brushes her hand away.)* I'm not opening any doors 'round here till you promise to talk.
> SUSAN: Listen, I'll talk. I'll talk so much it'll make your hair curl.
> SLOCUM: You'll talk? You hear that, Doc? She's promised to talk.

557. CU: *David, seated on his cot.*

> SLOCUM *(off)*: All right, I'll open 'er up.
> DAVID: Susan. *(Shakes his head.)* It won't work. Whatever it is, it won't work.

558. MS: *Susan, her feet planted on the bottom rungs of her cell door, swings out in a wide arc, as the camera pans with her motion.*

> SUSAN: Swingin'-Door Susie hasn't flopped yet. *(The moving door squeaks as she ends up in front of David's cell and steps off the door.)* I'm out this far, ain't I?

559. MLS: *the corridor between the cells.*

> SUSAN: Well, so long, gang. I'm not takin' the rap for this job. It's every man for himself.

As Susan and Slocum turn to walk away, those in the cells send forth loud protests. David leaps up from his cot to the door of his cell.[57]

> SLOCUM *(returning to the center of the corridor)*: Now, here. Quiet! Quiet! You know what I told you and I meant it. *(To David.)* And you too.

SUSAN *(stepping beside David)*: Aw, quit beefin'!

560. MCU: *Susan and David.*

SUSAN: Get wise to yourself. The heat's on, Jerry.

561. CU: *Slocum.*

SLOCUM *(a take of astonishment)*: Jerry? Jerry? Ain't his name Bone!

562. MCU: *as in 560.*

SUSAN: Bone!? Aaaaah.
DAVID *(overlapping)*: Of course it isn't Bone . . .
SUSAN: You mean to say you don't remember "Jerry the Nipper"?

SLOCUM *(off)*: Jerry the Nipper? Make a note of that, Doc.
DAVID: Constable, she's making all this up out of motion pictures she's seen.
SUSAN: Oh, I suppose I saw you with that redheaded skirt in a motion picture!
DAVID: Redhead . . .
SLOCUM *(off)*: There you are, Doc. Another woman.
SUSAN: Sure. I wouldn't be squealing if he hadn't given me the runaround for that other twist.

563. MS: *Slocum, Lehman, and the Cop.*

SLOCUM: Oh. So he's a lady-killer.

564. MS: *Susan and David.*

DAVID: Uh . . .
SUSAN *(overlapping)*: A lady-killer? Why, he's a regular Don Swan.
DAVID: Oh . . .
SUSAN: Loves the ladies. Don't you honey? He bops 'em over, . . . *(Snaps her fingers.)* . . . one—two—three—boom. *(David follows Susan's hands with his eyes.)* Just like that. *(She mimes the twisting of a neck and tossing the carcass away.)* He's a wolf!
DAVID: Oh! Now I'm a wolf! *(He flings himself down on his cot, his hands over his head, as the camera tilts down.)*[58]
SUSAN: Come on, son, we're wasting time.[59]

565. LS: *Susan at the entrance to the corridor of cells.*

SUSAN: I'll send you a box of birdseed.

Camera pans as Slocum and Susan leave the corridor of cells, walking arm in arm toward his desk, followed by Lehman and Elmer.

SLOCUM: Now, uh, Susie, I want you to tell the truth, you understand? You'll never get into trouble . . . I notice you're limping there. Suppose you got shot in one of them stickups.

SUSAN: No, I lost my heel.

SLOCUM: Well, don't bother about him. Just sit right down there. *(Susan sits on a corner of a table.)* Come on, Doc, grab this chair. *(Lehman sits, holding his notepad.)* Here, Elmer, grab a hold of that typewriter. *(Elmer lifts a heavy typewriter off a cabinet.)* Want to get this whole thing now in affidavit form. Now look here, young lady. I want you to talk and I want you to talk fast.

SUSAN *(overlapping)*: Cigarette me, then I'll talk.

SLOCUM: I don't smoke cigareets.

566. MCU: *Susan sitting on the desk, bounded by Lehman and Slocum.*

SUSAN: Well, I guess this'll have to do. *(Takes a cigar from Slocum's pocket and sniffs it.)*

SLOCUM: Huh?

SUSAN: Oh, it's a two-fer.

SLOCUM: What's that?

SUSAN: Two fer a nickel. Gimme a match.

SLOCUM: Here.

Susan bites off end of cigar, spits it out, and puts the cigar in her mouth.

SLOCUM: Uh . . .

567. MS: *Susan, Slocum, and Lehman, windows behind.*

SLOCUM: Now look here, I'm not gonna stand for that in this jail. *(Draws cigar from her mouth and returns it to his pocket.)*

SUSAN: No smokey, no talkey. *(Rises.)* Put me back in the cell, wrap me up again.

Lehman takes out his cigarette case.

SLOCUM: Uh, uh, uh . . .

SUSAN: Ain't gonna talk unless I have a cigarette.

SLOCUM: Now, now, now hold on here. Just, just sit down, now, sit down. She won't talk without a . . . Here, Doc, give her one of them cigareets. *(Handing Lehman's cigarette case to Susan.)*

Susan puts a cigarette in her mouth, then hands a cigarette to Lehman.

SLOCUM: Now, then, if you just, uh, tell the truth, why we'll make it as easy as we can.

Susan starts to slip the cigarette case into her pocket when Lehman notices that he is about to put a cigarette, not his case, into his pocket.

LEHMAN: Hey! My case, if you please.
SUSAN: Oh, well, well, well. Now there I go again! Sorry, boys, force of habit. Forgot where I was for a minute. *(She polishes the case and hands it to Lehman, then strikes the match on the table.)*

568. MCU: *as in 566.*

SLOCUM: Hey! *(Points to desk, clears his throat.)*
SUSAN *(lighting her cigarette, looking to her left)*: How 'bout a little fresh air. It's kinda hot in here.
SLOCUM: Yes, 'tis a little bit muggy, isn't it? Always that way around here this time of the year. *(Leaves the frame, as Lehman fans away Susan's smoke.)*

569. MS: *Slocum opens the window, with Elmer in the foreground.*

SLOCUM: The humidity. Now, uh, what about the Cleghorn jewels? *(He crosses back to Susan as the camera pans with him.)*
SUSAN: Aaah! That's hot ice, mister. We're waitin' for it to cool off.
SLOCUM: We're waiting for it to cool . . . We're? What do you mean "we"?
SUSAN: The gang. The gang! All of us.
SLOCUM: You mean to say you all belong to the same gang?
SUSAN: Sure. The "Leopard Gang." Organized in Buffalo.

570. MCU: *Slocum, flanked by Susan and Lehman, with Elmer at the typewriter behind.*

SLOCUM: The Leopard Gang! That's what I'm after, Doc. We'll round 'em all up in one fell swoop! You got that down? *(Leans over Lehman.)*

LEHMAN: I got it.

SLOCUM: Fine. How 'bout you, Elmer?

ELMER: Not so fast, Ed. This is new to me.

Slocum steps to Elmer and looks over his shoulder at the sheet in the typewriter. Susan slides off the table and strolls toward Slocum and Elmer.

SLOCUM: Say, hold on, you fool. You can't spell leopard with a "u."

ELMER: How do you spell it?

SUSAN: Double "u."

SLOCUM: Double "u." What about that bank robbery?

571. MCU: *Susan and Slocum.*

SUSAN: Boy, oh boy, oh boy. Wasn't that a honey? Wasn't that a pip? *(She turns and strolls to the open window.)* A neater job has never been pulled in this neck of the woods. *(She sits on the window sill.)* Jerry was the inside man on that job.

SLOCUM: Oh, he was, was he? Were you there, too?

SUSAN: Sure. What do you think? I'm a one-man woman. Where my man goes, I go. And if I don't, he knocks my block off.[60]

572. LS: *Susan, perched on the windowsill, Slocum, Lehman taking notes, and Elmer at the typewriter.*

SUSAN: Applegate, Baby-Face Horace, he's the triggerman that . . .

ELMER: Wait a minute. You're talking too fast.

SLOCUM *(crossing toward Elmer)*: Huh? Huh? What's that?

LEHMAN *(rising with his notepad)*: I only got as far as . . .

In the rearground, Susan ducks out the open window and disappears from view.

SLOCUM: Confound it, Doc. Look at there. You only got as far as the Cleghorn jewels.

573. MS: *Slocum, Lehman, Elmer, and the Cop.*

SLOCUM: Now we gotta start all over again. Now, young lady . . .
(Stops and does a take.) Say!

The camera pans as they all rush to the window to look out. Sound of a car driving off.

SLOCUM: There she goes.
LEHMAN: She's got my car again! *(He dashes off to the right.)*
SLOCUM: Go on, boys, after her. Hurry up! Get her! Get her!

They rush off to the right.

574. LS: *Slocum, Lehman, Elmer, and the Cop come running out of the jail. Lehman points to his right.*

COP: There she goes!

Elmer and the Cop jump in a police car parked at the curb.

SLOCUM: Go get her, boys! Go get her! If you don't bring her back, there's going to be a shakeup in this department! Elmer, go get her! *(Elmer drives the car off to the left.)* By jingo, if I get my hands on her, I'll lock her up so tight . . .

Mr. Peabody and Alice Swallow enter from the right foreground and walk up to Slocum and Lehman.

PEABODY: Are you the constable here?

575. MS: *Lehman, Slocum, Peabody, and Alice.*

SLOCUM: Yes, I am. What do you want?
PEABODY: I'm looking for Mrs. . . .
SLOCUM: Now don't tell me that you're looking for a leopard or, by jingo . . . *(Pounds his fist in his palm.)* . . . I'll lock you up!

PEABODY: I'm looking for Mrs. Carleton Random.

SLOCUM *(take)*: Eh? Hm? Well, so is everybody else. Let me tell you, she's not here!

PEABODY: I have reason to believe she is here.

SLOCUM: Say, who are you?

576. MCU: *the foursome, with Peabody center.*

PEABODY: I'm her attorney, Alexander Peabody.

ALICE: And I'm Miss Swallow. I'm looking for a man by the name of Dr. Huxley—Dr. David Huxley. Is he here with Mrs. Random?

577. MCU: *the foursome, Slocum center.*

SLOCUM: Oh, now, lady, look here. The only folks we got here is an old woman who keeps saying that she's Mrs. Random. Then we got a gangster here by the name of Bone. *(Lehman taps Slocum on the shoulder.)* Then we have Baby-Face Horace. *(Lehman touches Slocum's arm and shoulder.)* Stop it. Then we have . . . Stop . . . What is it you want?

LEHMAN: I can identify this gentleman. You may remember, Mr. Peabody, I testified for you during the breaking of the Borden will.

PEABODY: Yes, I remember. I demand to see my client at once.

LEHMAN: Slocum, you may have made a mistake.

578. MCU: *as in 576.*

PEABODY: And if you have made a mistake, your position as constable in this county will be in serious jeopardy.[61]

579. MCU: *as in 577.*

SLOCUM: Are you sure that he's the old lady's attorney?

LEHMAN: Positively.

SLOCUM *(whistles, clears his throat)*: Election next week, too. *(Clears his throat again.) (Slocum leads Peabody toward the jail door.)* Uh, Mr. Peabody, you'll just step inside, now, and we'll straighten this thing out. As a matter of fact, we don't make mistakes . . .

The foursome moves toward the door.

Dissolve

Westlake Jail, night

580. LS: *the corridor of cells. Slocum leads Peabody, Lehman, and Alice toward Aunt Elizabeth's cell. Alice leaves the frame to the left.*

> SLOCUM: Well, here you are. Now is she or ain't she Mrs. Random?
> AUNT: Well, Alex, it's just about time you came!
> PEABODY: Of course she's Mrs. Random. This is absurd! Open that door at once!
> SLOCUM: Well, all right. *(Starts to open cell door.)* What about him?
> AUNT *(overlapping)*: I told you . . .[62]

581. MCU: *Alice at David's cell, the angry voice of Aunt Elizabeth off-frame, loudly.*

> ALICE: But, David, I don't understand. You said . . .
> DAVID: Well, Alice, it's just one of those things. I can't explain it. It happened, and here I am. I . . .
> ALICE: Yes, and in the last place in the world I expected to find you.
> DAVID: Yes, well, oh, I don't like it any better than you do.[63]
> ALICE: Oh, really, David . . .

582. LS: *as in 580.*

> AUNT: And let that young man out, too!
> SLOCUM: Oh, shucks! Looks like I got the whole thing fuddled up. *(Starts toward David's cell.)* Well, sorry. That's all I can say about it.
> PEABODY: And you haven't heard the end of this either.

583. MS: *Slocum opens the door of David's cell as David steps out.*

> PEABODY *(off)*: Huxley! *(He enters the frame from the right, followed by Aunt Elizabeth. He taps David with his cane.)* What did you mean by throwing rocks at me last night?

DAVID: Well, you see, I . . .

AUNT *(entering the frame)*: Well, you mean to tell me that this is the young man you wanted me to donate a million dollars to for his museum?

PEABODY: Yes, yes. Oh, no! No! No! No! No, I did but I've changed my mind! I'm . . . . I'm . . .

ALICE *(overlapping)*: Oh, David, what have you done?

DAVID: Oh, just name anything and I've done it.[64]

584. MLS: *Joe and Mac get out of the circus truck, slamming the doors. Camera pans with them as they walk toward the jail door.*

MAC: Hey, Joe, what're you gonna tell 'em?

JOE: Tell 'em the truth. We lost a leopard.

As they go through the door, Baby trots into the frame from the right rearground. Behind Baby trots George. The animals follow Joe and Mac through the jail door.

585. MLS: *Joe and Mac enter from the right. Camera pans with them as they cross to the cell corridor, where Slocum stands with his released prisoners.*

JOE: Say! Hey! You the constable around here?

SLOCUM: Well, I am until the next election anyway. What is it you want?

JOE: Well, we need some help.

SLOCUM: Well, that's what I'm here for. To serve the public.

586. MS: *Slocum, Mac, and Joe observed by the group.*

SLOCUM: What is it?

JOE: Well, we're looking for . . . Well, we're looking for . . .

SLOCUM: Nah, nah, nah. Don't tell me that you're looking for a leopard.

JOE: How did you know that?

SLOCUM: Eh? . . . Huh? Know what?

JOE: That we're looking for a leopard.

SLOCUM: Eh . . . Now look here! This has gone far enough! There are no leopards in the State of Con . . . *(Five barks off interrupt Slocum.)*

587. MS: *Baby leaps up on a table in the outer office. George stands at the foot of the table, barking lustily.*

588. MLS: *Slocum, Mac, and Joe.*

> SLOCUM *(dropping his keys)*: Look out! Look out everybody! *(He climbs up the bars of a cell, where Gogarty retreats for protection.)*

> JOE: That's a bad cat! Somebody get a gun! He's a killer!

> *David steps forward to take charge.*

> DAVID: Oh, now, don't be alarmed, Alice. There's no need to be frightened, gentlemen. Everything's gonna be all right. *(He walks toward camera.)*

589. MS: *David walks over to Baby.*

> DAVID: Hello, Baby. *(Reaches out to stroke the animal.)*

590. MLS: *the group amazed as Aunt Elizabeth begins to walk forward.*

591. MS: *Aunt, David, and Baby.*

> DAVID: Oh dear.
> AUNT *(crossing to David, and Baby on the table)*: Is this my leopard?
> DAVID: Yes, that's Baby.
> AUNT: Oh.[65]

592. MLS: *in the cell corridor. Gogarty stands beside Applegate, shaking his head.*

> APPLEGATE: He didn't do . . . He didn't act that way with me.
> JOE *(moving forward)*: Say, wait a minute. That ain't my leopard.

593. MS: *as in 591.*

> DAVID: Well, of course it isn't. That's why I took it out of the truck.

594. MS: *Joe, Mac, and the group.*

> JOE: You never let that one out of the truck. You couldn't touch our cat with a ten-foot pole.

595. MS: *as in 591.*

> DAVID: You . . . You mean to say there's another leopard?

596. MS: *as in 594.*

> JOE: That's what I'm trying to tell you. Our cat came from the circus. He just clawed a man.

597. MS: *as in 591.*

> JOE *(off)*: He's bad!
> DAVID: Oh, my goodness. Susan's out trying to catch the wrong leopard! Oh, poor darling Susan. She's in danger and she's helpless without me.

598. MLS: *Susan walks toward the jail door, holding a long rope. She stops and jerks backward as a leopard snarls off-frame. Susan tugs on the rope.*

> SUSAN: Hey! Oh, what's the matter with you? *(Snarling continues off-frame.)* Now, come on. *(Mutters.)* If I have to drag you. I'm gonna get me out of this place. *(She drags the leopard into the frame, who balks by rolling on his back.)*

599. MCU: *Susan, dragging rope.*

> SUSAN: Oh, what's the matter with you? You've been slapping at me the whole way. Now, come on. We've got to get in here. And you might as well come . . .

600. MCU: *the leopard, resisting, on the pavement.*

> SUSAN *(off)*: . . . without being stubborn.

601. MCU: *as in 599.*

> SUSAN: Now listen. I'm just as determined as you are. So you might just
> as well come with me. Because . . .

602. MCU: *as in 600.*

> SUSAN *(off)*: I'm going to drag you! *(Leopard snarls.)*

603. MS: *the outer office of the jail.*

> SUSAN: I don't like it here any more than you do. But this is where
> we've got to be. *(She drags the leopard into the office.)* Hey, David!

604. MS: *Aunt and David standing beside Baby on the table. David looks
astonished. Aunt Elizabeth screams and rushes toward the corridor of
cells.*[66]

> DAVID: Susan!

The camera pans with Aunt Elizabeth as she dashes toward the corridor.

> JOE: There's the killer! Let's get out of here.

Noisy confusion as they all rush for the cells.

605. MS: *Susan with the leopard on a rope, sounds of confusion off-frame.*

> SUSAN: Well, did I fool you this time. You thought I was doing the
> wrong thing. But I've got him.

606. MS: *David, looking off toward the left, with Baby on the table and
George on the floor.*

> DAVID: No, you haven't, Susan. Look! *(Points at Baby on the table, twice.)*

*George, with a bark, rushes off to the left, toward the cells. Baby leaps
off the table to follow George.*[67]

607. MS: *George, barking, runs into the first open cell, followed by Baby.*

608. MLS: *Applegate lets out a howl and quickly leaps out of the cell, followed by Gogarty. Gogarty hastily slams the door shut and the two of them dash up the corridor into another cell. Slocum, who has climbed up the bars of the cell, remains with Baby and George.*

SLOCUM: Boys! Boys! Don't leave me in here. Don't leave me in here!

609. CU: *Susan looks right, then left, then right again—as Slocum and George continue to squeal off-frame.*

610. CU: *leopard, at the end of a rope, snarls.*

611. LS: *Susan and the leopard.*

SUSAN *(dropping rope, screams)*: Oh-h-h—David—Oh-h-h.

612. CU: *David.*

DAVID: Susan! *(He rushes off to the right.)*

613. LS: *David rushes into the frame, pushes Susan to his right, grabs a chair, and holds it between himself and the leopard.*

DAVID: Susan, run. Run.

614. CU: *leopard snarling.*

615. LS: *Susan and David back away toward the cell corridor, David holding the chair up in front of him for protection against the leopard, who follows them. Snarls and screams continue.*

616. MCU: *camera pans with Susan and David, as they back to the left.*

DAVID: Run, Susan.
SUSAN: No!
DAVID: Run while you have the chance.

SUSAN: No. I won't leave you. I love you.
DAVID: What?

617. CU: *leopard paws at the legs of the chair, snarls.*

618. MS: *Susan and David backing to the left.*

619. LS: *David and Susan back through the gate leading to the cell corridor. George yaps off-frame.*

DAVID *(thrusting chair)*: Shoo! *(David makes a grab for the gate.)*

620. CU: *leopard snarls.*

621. LS: *David with the chair, Susan behind him, continue backing away from the leopard into the cell corridor.*

DAVID: Oh!⁶⁸

622. MS: *David and Susan, in front of a row of cells, observed by Alice, Peabody, and Aunt Elizabeth in the cells.*

SUSAN: Poke him, David. Poke him. *(Holding him from behind.)*
DAVID: Oh, let go, Susan! Please!
SUSAN: No, no.⁶⁹

623. CU: *leopard slashing with left forepaw at the legs of the chair. The off-frame sounds of panic continue.*

624. MCU: *David and Susan.*

DAVID *(busy with the chair)*: Susan, please run back there. Can't you see I'm trying to get him into a cell?
SUSAN: Oh . . .

Susan, standing behind David, looks to her left, then makes a sweeping gesture with her left arm.

625. CU: *the leopard, prodded by the chair, walks into the cell on his right.*

DAVID *(off)*: Get in. Get in.

626. MS: *David with the chair, Susan observing.*

DAVID: Get in there. Get in. *(He slams the cell door and holds it closed.)* Get the key, Susan.
SUSAN: Oh.

Susan runs off-frame as David holds the cell door. She returns with the key but can't get it into the lock.

DAVID: Oh, give it to me. *(He takes the keys out of her hands and locks the cell door himself.)*

They pause for a breath of relief.

SUSAN: Oh, oh, David. Oh, you're wonderful! Oh, you're wonderful. You're absolutely wonderful!

David, still stunned, leans on the chair for support, turns toward Susan, raises his right index finger, and tries to speak.

SUSAN: You're a hero. You saved my life. Oh, you'll go down in history. I've never seen such bravery in the . . . *(She notices his upraised finger.)* Did you want to say something, David?

David opens his mouth to speak, but only stammers inarticulately.

SUSAN: What? Yes? Yes?
DAVID: Uh . . .
SUSAN: What was it?

David collapses in a faint in Susan's arms.

SUSAN: Oh!

Joe and Mac rush in to help.

JOE: Hey, Mac!
SUSAN: David, you fainted. David.[70]

Dissolve

The Brontosaurus Hall, day

627. MCU: *Alice is wearing street clothes, David, his scientist's smock. His chin rests in his right hand.*

   ALICE: Well, there's nothing I can say. Except that I'm glad that before our marriage, you showed yourself up in your true colors. You're just a butterfly. *(She turns to her right and leaves the frame.)*
   DAVID: Oh, now I'm a butterfly. *(He looks to his right.)*

628. MLS: *Alice walks toward the heavy iron door, opens it, and leaves without a glance in David's direction.*

629. MLS: *David, standing alone, flanked by the cases of zoological exhibits. Off-frame the sound of a closing door. David looks down and walks over toward the dinosaur's legs, as the camera pans. He sits beside a miniature model of a dinosaur.*

   SUSAN *(off)*: David! David!

630. LS: *from between the brontosaurus's huge legs. The door bursts open and Susan hurries in.*

   SUSAN: David!

631. MLS: *David, seated at the base of the brontosaurus, looks off toward his right. He quickly starts up the ladder to his working platform, high above the floor, as the camera tilts.*

   DAVID: Oh. Oh.

632. LS: *as in 630. Susan rushes in to the room.*

   SUSAN: Oh. Hey. Oh, where you going, David?

633. MCU: *Susan.*

   SUSAN: Well, don't go up there. I want to talk to you. See, I've got it. But, David, I can't even see you. Now, where are you?

634. MLS: *low angle. Susan stands below with David high above.*

   SUSAN: Oh, there you are. David, I followed George around for three days. And I dug holes with him and he dug holes with me.

635. MS: *Susan.*

   SUSAN: And then he came and put it in my shoe. *(She extracts the intercostal clavicle from her purse and holds it up.)* Darling, look.

636. MS: *David on top of platform.*

   DAVID: Oh.

637. MS: *as in 635.*

   SUSAN *(lowering the bone)*: Oh, well, David, don't be mad at me.

638. MS: *as in 636.*

   DAVID: Thank you very much, Susan. Put it down there on the table and go away.

639. MS: *as in 635. Susan smiling. She moves to her right, then stops.*

   SUSAN: Hey, but wait a minute, I don't want to go away. I want to talk to you.

640. LS: *Susan sees the ladder beside the brontosaurus and starts up it.*[71]

DAVID: Write me a letter. Don't . . . oh, oh, oh . . . Go . . . go, go back, Susan. Don't . . .

Susan arrives at the top of the ladder.

SUSAN: Huh! Jeepers, it's high up here. Oooh![72]

641. MS: *David looking down, over the brontosaurus's backbone, at Susan on the ladder.*

DAVID: Susan. Now, look, please. Go back down the ladder. Quietly.
SUSAN: Well, when I go down, I'll go down quietly, David. But . . .

642. MCU: *Susan on ladder.*

SUSAN: . . . I want to find out something first. Why did you run up that ladder when I came in here?[73]

643. MS: *David from a low angle.*

DAVID: Well, if you must know, I'm afraid of you, an . . .

644. MLS: *David and Susan, the camera high above them, looking down.*

SUSAN: But, David, if you're afraid of me, well, then, that's the same as if . . . admitting . . . *(She shifts position on ladder, it teeters; she slips.)*
DAVID *(pointing at the ladder)*: Uh! Uh!
SUSAN: Oh! Oh! *(She steadies herself on the ladder, giggles.)* Well, don't worry, David. Everything's going to be all right. I'll see to . . .
DAVID: Uh, uh, every time you say that, something happens. Now, now, please go down. Because you've already cost the museum a million dollars.

645. MS: *at David's shoulder level, observing Susan.*

SUSAN: Oh, no, I haven't, David. I've got the million dollars. Aunt

Elizabeth gave it to me. And I'm going to give it to you for the museum.

646. MS: *reverse shot, behind Susan's shoulder, observing David.*

DAVID: Oh . . . Well, I . . . I'm sure they'll be very pleased.

647. MCU: *Susan.*

SUSAN: Aren't you pleased, David?

648. MS: *David.*

DAVID: Yes, I suppose so, dear. It's . . .

649. MCU: *as in 647.*

SUSAN: It's too late, isn't it? I've made a mess of everything, haven't I?

650. MS: *as in 648.*

DAVID: Oh, no.
SUSAN *(overlapping, off)*: Oh, I was so happy when I found the bone this morning.

651. MCU: *as in 647.*

SUSAN: Oh, David, if I could only make you understand. You see, all that happened happened because I was trying to keep you near me, and I just did anything that came into my head. I'm so sorry.[74]

652. MS: *as in 648.*

DAVID: But . . . I ought to thank you.

653. MCU: *as in 647.*

SUSAN: Thank me?

654. MCU: *as in 648.*

DAVID: Yes.
SUSAN *(off)*: Well, why?
DAVID: You see, well, I've just discovered that was the best day I ever had in my whole life.

655. MCU: *as in 647.*

SUSAN: David, you don't mean that.

656. MS: *as in 648.*

DAVID: I never had a better time.

657. MCU: *as in 647.*

SUSAN *(laughs)*: But, but I was there.

658. MS: *as in 648.*

DAVID: Well, that's what made it so good.

659. MS: *as in 641, behind David's back, looking at Susan over the brontosaurus' backbone.*

SUSAN: Oh, did you really have a good time? *(She starts to sway happily from side to side on the ladder.)*
DAVID: Yes, I did.
SUSAN: Oh, that's . . . But that's wonderful. Do you realize what that means? That means you must like me a little bit. *(The arc of her swinging ladder gets wider.)*

660. MS: *behind Susan's back, swaying on the ladder, looking at David on the other side of the brontosaurus' backbone.*

DAVID: Oh, Susan! it's more than that. *(David sways with her, in her rhythm.)*
SUSAN: Is it?
DAVID: Yes. I love you, I think. *(Both are energetically swaying.)*
SUSAN: Oh!

661. MS: *as in 641, Susan swaying on the ladder.*

SUSAN: That's wonderful. Because I love you too. *(Laughs.)* Stop rocking, Da . . .

662. MCU: *David.*

DAVID: Oh, I'm not rocking. I . . . I . . . I . . . *(His face falls.)*

663. MCU: *Susan struggles to stay aboard the furiously rocking ladder.*

SUSAN: Oh! Oh! OH!!!

664. MCU: *David.*

DAVID: OH!!!

665. MCU: *Susan rocking, screaming Oh!, holding onto the ladder for dear life.*

DAVID *(off)*: Susan! No, no, Susan!

666. MS: *Susan rocking in the foreground, screaming, as David pleads from the scaffolding.*

DAVID: No, Susan, please. The brontosaur . . . Oh, my good . . . Four years went into this!
SUSAN *(overlapping)*: Oh, I can't help it! Whoa! David . . .[75]

667. MCU: *Susan swaying on the ladder, clutching the clavicle in her right hand, her purse in the left, trying to stay aboard.*

SUSAN *(screaming)*: Oh!

668. MLS: *David on top of platform, watches Susan sway in wide arcs on the ladder.*

SUSAN: Oh! Oh, David. *(She drops her purse.)*
DAVID *(overlapping)*: Susan! Susan!
SUSAN: Oh! Oh! *(Susan climbs off the ladder onto the backbone of the skeleton, still holding the clavicle. The ladder falls with a crash off-frame.)* Oh! Oh! *(Susan crawls toward David, who stretches out a hand toward her.)*
DAVID *(overlapping)*: Susan, please! Look out, Susan. Oh, my good . . .

The back of the skeleton begins to sag with a groaning crunch.[76]

669. LS: *the huge backbone gives way and the brontosaurus crashes to the floor. Susan manages to catch David's outstretched hand and hangs suspended in his grasp. For a moment she dangles in the air. Her hat flies off.*

670. MS: *Susan dangles in David's grasp.*

DAVID: Hold on, Susan. Hold on! Don't let go! Don't let go! Uh . . .
SUSAN: Oh, David, look what I've done.

David lifts her up onto the platform. The camera tracks in as they begin to sit.

DAVID: Oh, oh, oh.
SUSAN: Oh, I'm so sorry.
DAVID: Oh, oh.

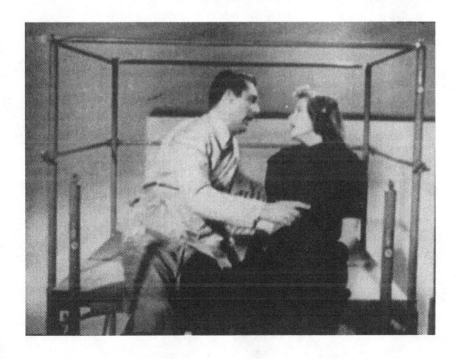

671. MCU: *David and Susan seated side by side on the platform.*

> SUSAN: Oh. *(Sighs.)* Oh. *(Sighs.)* David, can you ever forgive me?
> DAVID *(shaking his head, pointing downward)*: I . . . I . . . I
> SUSAN: You can? And you still love me?
> DAVID: Susan, that . . . that . . . that . . . *(Points and waves his finger.)*
> SUSAN: You do! Oh, David. *(She puts her arms around him and rests
>   her head contentedly on his shoulder.)*
> DAVID: Oh, dear. *(He wraps his arms around her.)* Oh, my. Hmm.

*"I Can't Give You Anything but Love, Baby," in a bouncy orchestral
version, invades the soundtrack.*

672. LS: *David and Susan embrace on the platform high above the floor, the
ruins of the brontosaurus below, as the music continues. "The End" in
RKO corporate script dissolves into the image.*

Script Variations

The following passages were shot, included in the film's initial cut, then deleted in the final editing of the film from 10,150 to 9,204 feet. The passages come from the studio's continuity script of March 23, 1938, prepared for legal and copyright purposes by an RKO employee, M. Kent.

1. *During the above, David has managed to break away and is now moving off into the b.g. Susan spies him and follows. Louis steps up to Lehman.*

   LOUIS: I know the young lady very well, sir. I think perhaps it might be well to drop the matter—if you don't mind, sir.
   LEHMAN *(turns to Mrs. Lehman, who has sat down at their table)*: You have the purse?
   MRS. LEHMAN: Yes.
   LEHMAN *(to Louis)*: Thank you.
   LOUIS *(bows)*: Thank you.
   Louis exits. Lehman joins Mrs. Lehman at the table.

2. DAVID: Oh!
   SUSAN: Hey, who was that?
   DAVID: That was Mr. Peabody.

SUSAN: What happened to him?
DAVID: You conked him.

3. DAVID: Yeh—yeh—yes, Alice—no—no—well, yes—you see, there are some things that are very hard to explain and as soon as I—
   MS: *Alice, seated at desk, talking over phone.*
   ALICE: But David—I don't understand. Did you see him or didn't you?

4. MS: *David on phone.*
   DAVID: I realize it's all rather confusing.
   MS: *Alice on phone.*
   ALICE: Yes, but are you going to see him again today?
   MS: *David on phone.*
   DAVID: No—I don't think I'll make an appointment with him today . . . no . . . well, because I think he has a slight headache.

5. MS: *David on phone.*
   DAVID: You say this leopard's in the bathroom?
   MS: *Susan leaning against door to bathroom.*
   SUSAN *(into phone)*: Yes, David.
   MS: *David.*
   DAVID: Is the bathroom door closed?
   MS: *Susan.*
   SUSAN: Yes, David.

6. MS: *at door to bedroom. The door opens slowly and Susan's maid peeps out. She spies Susan lying on the floor.*
   MAID *(frightened)*: Miss Susan—are you all right?
   LS: *Susan contentedly stretched out on the floor in front of fireplace.*
   SUSAN *(dreamily)*: Oh, Carrie, I'm in love and he's the most wonderful . . .
   MAID *(off)*: I think you're crazy!
   SUSAN: So does he—*(Sits up.)*—but it doesn't matter. . . . *(Comes out of the fog.)* What are you standing there for? He's coming here—*(Gets to her feet.)*—and I've got to hurry—I've got to hurry—or I'll catch it. *(She rushes off in direction of bedroom.)*

7. SUSAN *(talking faster)*: Wait! Did I hesitate last night when you were in trouble?

DAVID: Susan . . .

SUSAN: No. Do you think there is anything I'd hesitate to do for you?

DAVID *(trying to shut her up)*: Susan!

SUSAN: No. That makes it an obligation, David.

DAVID: SUSAN! SHUT UP!

SUSAN *(the wind out of her sails)*: It's only twenty miles to Westlake.

DAVID *(doggedly)*: Susan, I'm a zoologist. I'm going to marry a zoologist. That makes me happy. This makes me unhappy. I have only one desire. That is to go and finish my brontosaurus—now! *(He turns away.)*

8. SUSAN: You look silly, David.

DAVID: Susan, go 'way!

SUSAN: David—have you ever been arrested?

DAVID: No—and I'm not likely to be, either.

9. SUSAN: Do you want a cigarette, David?

DAVID: No.

SUSAN: Match?

DAVID: No.

SUSAN: Chewing gum?

DAVID: No.

SUSAN: Peanuts, popcorn, soft drinks?

DAVID *(peevishly)*: Oh, stop it—*(He sinks back into seat corner to look at Baby in rear of car.)*

SUSAN: David, if you're going to be grouchy, I don't know why you bothered to come. I didn't ask you to—you insisted. All I was doing was driving peacefully—

DAVID *(sharply)*: All you were doing was leaving me in the middle of Park Avenue with a leopard.

10. SUSAN: David, you take things so seriously. If you hadn't interfered, I'd have talked us out of it. I could have wound that man around my little finger.

DAVID: Well, I still maintain that it's going too far to tell a man we're part

of a circus. Of course, I don't deny that you might be a trapeze artist,
but by any stretch of the imagination do I look like a knife-thrower? *(He
turns to her.)*
SUSAN *(studying him a moment)*: Well, I don't know—*(Indicates the
rearview mirror.)* Have a look—what do you think?
*David looks—isn't pleased with what he sees, and with a disgusted grunt
settles down in his seat.*

11. DAVID: I—I—I—oh, isn't that terrible? I've forgotten what I want—
    CLERK *(trying to help)*: Bacon? *(No reaction from David.)* Ham? *(Still no
    reaction.)* Steak?
    DAVID: Yes—steak.

12. *Clerk, carrying a couple of dressed chickens and a bag of groceries, enters
    from market and crosses through in b.g. to place them in limousine parked
    beside the station wagon.*
    SUSAN: Oh, we could all get to the fire in time if we were polite about it.
    SLOCUM: Now look here—the firemen have to get to the plug, lady. We
        don't care whether you get to the fire or not.
    SUSAN: Is there a fire?
    SLOCUM: No.
    SUSAN: Then why are we discussing it?
    SLOCUM *(swallowing his anger)*: Because you're parked in front of a
        fireplug.
    Clerk crosses through in b.g. from limousine to market.
    SUSAN: You said that before.
    SLOCUM: I'm not going to say it again.
    SUSAN: Oh, good.

13. MS: *Aunt and Hannah at stairway, looking toward guest room.*
    AUNT: Could you make any sense out of all that?
    HANNAH: No, ma'am.
    AUNT: Well, maybe I'm crazy—*(Starts toward stairs.)*
    HANNAH: Yes, ma'am—*(Catches herself.)*
    AUNT *(quickly turns to Hannah)*: Get the things out of the car and bring
        them upstairs—

HANNAH *(meekly)*: Yes, ma'am—
Aunt goes upstairs—Hannah starts toward entry door.

14. CU: *a hole in another part of the garden. Camera slowly pans away from the hole and past a series of similar holes, beside which are lying various old articles. Camera stops on a hole. A spade comes into scene and empties a clump of soil into hole. A hand comes into scene and lifts up an old hot-water bag. Camera pans up with the hand, revealing Gogarty, the gardener, as belonging to the hand.*
GOGARTY *(surveying the hot-water bag with disgust)*: Oh, give me patience.
He throws the bag behind him into a wheelbarrow which is filled with unearthed boots, boxing-gloves, etc. He returns to filling up the hole.
MLS: *Aunt enters from direction of the house. Camera pans with her as she walks toward Gogarty.*
AUNT: Good afternoon, Gogarty.
GOGARTY *(off)*: Good afternoon, ma'am.
AUNT *(reaching Gogarty's side)*: Isn't it a beautiful day? *(Notices the holes.)* What's all this? What are you planting?
GOGARTY *(irritably)*: Don't you see very well, ma'am? I'm not planting anything.
AUNT: Then what are you digging the holes for?
GOGARTY: I'm not digging the holes. I'm filling the holes.
AUNT: But you can't fill up the holes until after they've been dug. You must have dug them first.
GOGARTY: Oh, give me patience! I didn't dig them—I'm merely filling them up. Might I ask you one little favor—just one little favor?
AUNT: Certainly. What is it?
GOGARTY *(exploding)*: If Miss Susan must dig, why don't you get her a sand pile?
AUNT: What has Miss Susan to do with it?
GOGARTY: Everything. Miss Susan and that young man and your dog are careening around this garden just digging wherever they see fit.
AUNT: Miss Susan, the young man, and the dog? Where are they?
GOGARTY *(indicating)*: Do you see those holes all over your beautiful lawn? Follow them and you'll find them. *(As Aunt starts off.)* And when

you do, would it be too much to ask that you use your influence and stop her digging up my garden!

Aunt exits. Gogarty viciously returns to his spade.

MLS: *Aunt enters, looking about for Susan. Camera pans with her.*

AUNT *(calling)*: Susan—Susan! . . . *(She exits.)*

15. AUNT *(calling)*: George! Come here this minute! George! George!

SUSAN *(as Aunt continues to call George)*: Oh, Auntie, don't do that— please don't do that—that's the meanest thing I ever heard of anyone doing!

MLS: *at hedge. Aunt's voice comes over, calling George. George trots in from behind the hedge, with David still following him. He dashes off toward Aunt's voice. David makes a quick grab at him, but misses and sprawls.*

MLS: *Aunt and Susan.*

AUNT: You keep that lunatic away from me—and if you have any sense, you'll stay away from him yourself. First thing you know he'll cut your throat.

16. *Dissolve*

MLS: *a romantic spot beside a stream. David is seated on a log, staring dully before him. Susan is seated at his feet.*

SUSAN: My, how quiet it is. Isn't it nice, David, just to be quiet and alone like this . . . *(Camera moves slowly up to a closer shot as Susan edges up closer to David's knees.)* . . . without a lot of people talking to us, I mean.

DAVID *(gloomily)*: I can't understand how he could have found a place where we didn't dig. We've dug up almost twenty-six acres.

SUSAN: Now, David, everything is going to be all right. *(Moves up still closer to him.)* The bone's here somewhere. George knows where. There's no point in our digging without George—and we can't have George because Aunt Elizabeth won't let him out of the house. *(She lays her head on his knee.)* Wouldn't it be nice if we could just sit here forever and ever?

DAVID *(glumly)*: But she has to let him out of the house sooner or later.

SUSAN: You know, I always say that people in the city don't have time to fall in love. Now what could be nicer than just spending months and months getting acquainted—with somebody you like—and maybe could fall in love with.

Another angle.

DAVID *(hopelessly)*: It's just possible—

SUSAN *(a ray of hope)*: What's possible?

DAVID: It's just possible that he didn't bring it out of the house at all. *(He rises abruptly.)*

SUSAN: Don't you relax for even a minute, David? *(Susan gets to her feet and follows David to foot of steps that lead to the road.)*

DAVID *(pausing and turning to her)*: Do you realize that I can't get married until I find that bone? . . . Oh, the shovel—*(He steps past her to the log, picks up shovel, and returns.)*

SUSAN: It must be terrible for a girl to realize that a bone is more important than she is.

DAVID: Oh, it isn't that. I wouldn't dare tell Miss Swallow I've lost the intercostal clavicle. I don't know what the shock would do to her.

SUSAN: David, don't tell her. What I want to suggest is that you tell her you'll be married at the same time next week—*(As David starts up the steps and she follows.)* That will give you a week here. We're sure to find it in a week.

DAVID: Oh, Susan, stop suggesting things . . .

By this time they have reached the road and are walking up it, away from camera, David dragging the shovel behind him. Susan, trying to keep up with his long stride, steps on the shovel and falls into him.

DAVID: And get off the shovel.

SUSAN: I'm sorry—

They continue up the road.

Dissolve

LS: *The Vance living room at night. The camera pans as Susan, in dinner dress, excitedly flies down the stairway, across the living room to the door to Mark's room, and knocks on the door.*

SUSAN *(in loud whisper)*: David—*(Tries the door; finds it locked; jiggles the knob.)*

17. SUSAN *(off)*: I know, but listen to me.

DAVID *(into phone)*: Hello, Alice . . .

MS: *Susan at door.*

SUSAN *(in loud whisper)*: David, let me in.

MS: *David.*

DAVID *(cupping hand over phone)*: Susan, I can't hear you—I'm talking—go 'way—I'll be with you as soon as I'm finished.

MS: *Susan at door.*

SUSAN: David, you have to let me in. This is important—it's about the leopard—we haven't fed him—he's yelling—*(Jiggles the door.)* David—please—

18. MS: *Alice on phone.*
    ALICE: Hello—David? Who is that? . . . Hello—hello—hello—can you hear me? Who is that with you? . . .

19. MS: *Alice on phone.*
    ALICE: I said, who is that with you? . . . Hello . . .

20. MS: *Alice on phone.*
    ALICE: Hello, David. . . . What I'm trying to understand is why you can't leave. . . . Yes, why do you have to stay? . . .

21. MS: *Susan again bongs the ashtray.*
    SUSAN: When you hear the tone, the time will be 7:37 and one-half.
    MS: *David on phone.*
    DAVID: Oh, Susan, please get off the line—Alice—I'm—I'm—I'm awfully sorry about this . . .
    MS: *Susan again bongs ashtray.*
    SUSAN *(into phone)*: When you hear the tone, the time will be 7:38.
    MS: *David, on phone, is nearly out of his mind.*
    DAVID: Susan, get off the line! Alice—I'm trying—Alice—I—Su—*(He takes a deep breath for the final plunge.)* Well, Alice, I might just as well tell you—I've lost the intercostal clavicle—
    MS: *Alice on phone.*
    ALICE: YOU'VE LOST THE—*(She drops the phone and falls in a dead faint.)*
    MS: *David on phone.*
    DAVID: Alice . . . Alice . . . Alice . . . *(He jiggles the phone, then hangs up.)*

22. APPLEGATE: Once I start on him he'll be talking ten to the dozen—or twelve to the gross—or whatever the saying is. How fortunate. Big game, eh? Well, well, well—*(Indicates the tray.)* Won't you have a drink?
    AUNT: No, thank you—not for me.

23. DAVID: I can't afford to lose George. If I do, I'll never find my bone.
    SUSAN: Well, one thing, anyway—you've got perfect control over him.
    DAVID: What makes you think so?
    SUSAN: He hasn't growled once since you picked him up.
    DAVID: He can't. His mouth is full of my hand!
    SUSAN: Oh—does it hurt?
    DAVID *(sarcastically)*: Does it hurt!
    They continue on toward house.

24. SUSAN *(gazing lovingly after David)*: Isn't he sweet! Did you ever see
    such shoulders?
    APPLEGATE *(acidly)*: And what legs! He'd make a splendid messenger
    boy.
    SUSAN: Yes.

25. GOGARTY *(starting toward stables)*: I'll be a nervous wreck. I can't
    stand it.
    MLS: *Gogarty comes through stable door, slams the door shut, and walks
    toward the stall, mumbling unintelligibly.*
    GOGARTY *(pausing)*: No—there's a limit—there's a limit to everything—
    (Takes a few steps and again pauses.) I'm a sensitive man—I'm nervous—
    I'm highly strung. If one more thing happens to upset me, I'll go crazy!
    *Camera dollies ahead and pans as he continues toward the stall, revealing
    a hoop-skirted dressmaker's form standing close to the stall.*
    GOGARTY: Digging trenches in the garden! I know what I'll do. I'll leave
    the place. I'll walk up to her quietly and say—*(Takes off his hat and ad-
    dresses the form.)* Mrs. Random, I resign . . . and likewise I quit. Mrs.
    Random, I'll say, you're crazy—your dog is crazy—your niece is crazy—
    you're all crazy—and if I don't have a drink for meself *I'll* be crazy. *(He
    turns to the stall door, opens it and exits, muttering.)* Digging trenches—
    MLS: *Gogarty walks through the door and ambles toward a haybox at
    back of the stall.*
    GOGARTY *(grumbling)*: —spying on an innocent dog—*(Reaches into
    haybox.)*—anyone ever hear such nonsense—*(Comes up with bottle.)*—
    it's enough to make a man crazy—*(Returns to doorway.)*—and then
    they say, "Don't drink"—*(Pauses in doorway and removes cork from
    bottle.)*—not even a wee drop to steady a man's nerves—*(Takes a

drink.) If one more thing happens, I'll quit—I'll quit—*(Walks away from the stall toward door leading to exterior.)*—and where Aloysius Gogarty goes, Mrs. Aloysius Gogarty goes, too.
He exits, and as his footsteps die away, Baby comes through stall door and exits in Gogarty's direction.
MLS: *Gogarty comes out of stable, with the bottle.*
GOGARTY *(mumbling)*: Going through a garden—a man chasing after a dog . . .
He slides the bottle under his vest and exits toward the house. Baby ambles through the open stable door, looks off toward Gogarty and then exits in opposite direction.

26. APPLEGATE: That's the strangest thing I've ever heard—leopards in Connecticut!
    SUSAN: Yes—leopards in Connecticut!

27. AUNT *(off)*: Don't be ridiculous!
    HANNAH *(off)*: That's what I said, ma'am.
    GOGARTY *(off)*: Aye—it came up and breathed in my face!
    MS: *Aunt, Gogarty, and Hannah in center of kitchen.*
    AUNT: Gogarty, you've been drinking.
    GOGARTY: Nary a drop have I had—as I live and breathe.
    AUNT: Don't argue the point. I know you. Now be quiet—be quiet.
    Gogarty quiets down.

28. HANNAH *(indicating the floor)*: There's the next course, ma'am.
    AUNT: Then serve the dessert.

29. *In the kitchen, Aunt is moving toward Applegate who stands in the doorway, looking after David and Susan.*
    APPLEGATE: What? What are you—
    GOGARTY *(off)*: Where's me gun? I must have me gun!
    HANNAH *(off)*: Don't be talkin' about your gun! Help me clean up this mess!
    AUNT: I'm going to finish my dinner—I know that!
    Aunt has reached Applegate's side and looked around to find Susan and David have disappeared.

AUNT: Well, now where are they?

APPLEGATE: They've gone again.

AUNT: Well, I suppose it's too much to expect, but would you mind staying through the meal?

APPLEGATE: Oh, no, I wouldn't mind at all. In fact, I was planning on it. *(As they walk to the table.)* Now, to get back to the jungle, Elizabeth . . .

30. DAVID: We've lost a leopard. We're responsible and we've got to tell people.

SUSAN: Yes, but how do you tell people you've lost a leopard?

DAVID: Oh, I suppose you just say you saw a leopard.

SUSAN: No, that's too simple. They won't believe you.

31. MLS: *Susan and David hurry toward the house. Susan pauses abruptly and turns to David. They talk in loud whispers.*

SUSAN: Oh, now, wait a minute! What am I supposed to do?

DAVID: Just go back in to dinner.

SUSAN: Wouldn't it be better if I came in and helped you?

DAVID: No, Susan. It's better if I telephone the zoo alone. You go in and chatter loudly and brightly and keep an eye on George. Can you remember that, Susan?

SUSAN: Chatter and George.

DAVID: Chatter and George.

32. AUNT *(to Applegate)*: I know it's too much to expect, but would you mind staying through this meal?

APPLEGATE: No—I'd like to, Elizabeth—I was planning on it, really.

33. MLS: *The door to the living room opens and Aunt is forced through it into the room by Applegate, who hastily closes the door behind them.*

AUNT *(protesting)*: Don't do that.

APPLEGATE: There we are. Don't you feel better?

AUNT: No. It's a lovely, balmy evening.

APPLEGATE: It's much healthier for you indoors.

AUNT: Don't be silly.

APPLEGATE: Quiet. Let me ask you something. Elizabeth, have you a gun?

AUNT: Of course not.

APPLEGATE: Gogarty has one, hasn't he?

AUNT: You ought to know. He poked it at you a few minutes ago.

APPLEGATE: Yes, yes—that's right. Where can I find him?

AUNT: In the kitchen. Why?

Camera pans with Applegate as he trots through the dining room toward kitchen door.

APPLEGATE: Don't worry. I'll explain later, Elizabeth. Don't worry. Just leave it to Horace. Horace will take care of everything. He always does.

As he exits through the door, camera pans to open door in dining room which leads to the garden. Baby comes through the door, pauses, and looks off toward living room.

APPLEGATE *(off)*: Give me that gun.

GOGARTY *(off)*: That's my gun.

MLS: *the kitchen door opens and Applegate hurries out, carrying a shotgun. Gogarty follows on his heels, protesting. Camera pans as they trot past Baby without seeing him and continue on toward the living room.*

APPLEGATE: I'm better able to use it than you are.

GOGARTY: Do you mean to insinuate that Aloysius Gogarty can't fire a gun as well as you?

APPLEGATE: We won't argue about that. Follow me.

GOGARTY: That's my gun.

MS: *Aunt is standing where Applegate left her. Applegate enters with the gun. Gogarty follows.*

AUNT: What on earth are you doing?

APPLEGATE: Elizabeth.

AUNT: Don't point that thing at me!

APPLEGATE *(lowering the gun)*: I'm sorry, Elizabeth.

GOGARTY: You'd better let me have that gun.

APPLEGATE: Please—please—quiet!

GOGARTY: Will ye give me that gun?

APPLEGATE: Let me do the talking. Would you mind? *(He turns to Aunt.)* Now, Elizabeth, I want you to promise me to stay in the house and keep all the doors closed. And the windows. Definitely, the windows.

AUNT: But why? Why?

APPLEGATE *(crossing to a window to close it)*: Well, I don't know. I just have a feeling that this is the best thing to do.

GOGARTY *(following Applegate to window)*: Can I have me gun?

APPLEGATE: No, you can't have the gun. You close the windows in this room and I'll take care of the dining room.

GOGARTY: I won't budge a foot until I get me gun!

APPLEGATE: Wha—why—you've been drinking again, haven't you? *(Shoves Gogarty away.)* Go ahead. My goodness, what a stubborn man you are!

AUNT: Gogarty—have you been drinking again?

GOGARTY *(turning to her)*: I'll close the windows, Ma'am. *(He starts off.)*

APPLEGATE: Be sure and close them all. You see, Elizabeth we've got to keep everything out—we must be sure that nothing gets in.

AUNT *(sarcastically)*: No. Not even air, I suppose.

APPLEGATE: Oh, definitely. You never know what might come in with it . . . *(Hands gun to her.)* Here, hold this gun, Elizabeth. Don't worry—keep happy—you're in the hands of an expert.

MLS: *Applegate starts toward the dining room.*

AUNT: Of all the ridiculous child's play!

Camera pans with Applegate to dining room. He exits toward door leading to the rear garden, while camera centers on Baby still resting in front of door leading to the front garden. Baby's eyes follow Applegate for a moment, then he ambles off in Applegate's direction.

MLS: *camera pans with Applegate as he shuts the door, then crosses to window and closes it.*

APPLEGATE: It's a good thing, Elizabeth, that I'm around. *(As he crosses to another window, Baby enters and follows him.)* But of course, with the windows all closed, the situation will be entirely different.

He closes the second window and exits past fireplace to other side of room, Baby directly behind him.

MLS: *Applegate trots to the door.*

APPLEGATE: My goodness—got to close the door. *(He swings the top half of the door shut, then tackles the window beside the door. As he closes window.)* And the window—and everything will be hotsy-totsy.

He turns and looks directly down into the face of Baby who stands a few feet away from him, obviously enjoying the game of follow-the-master.

APPLEGATE *(with a yell)*: Oh—oh—the gun! the gun!—*(Dashes toward living room.)* Give me the gun! *(He exits.)*

CU: *Baby. He watches Applegate for a second, then trots through the open lower-half of the door and disappears into the garden.*

MLS: *camera pans with Applegate as he runs in from dining room to Aunt and Gogarty who, aroused by his yelling, are hurrying toward him.*
AUNT: What's the matter?
APPLEGATE *(taking the gun from her)*: Follow me. Follow me.
Camera pans with the three of them as they stalk toward dining room. Almost simultaneously:
APPLEGATE: Quiet. Quiet. Sh-h-h.
AUNT: Don't shush me.
GOGARTY: Give me the gun.
They reach dining room entrance. Applegate quickly leaps forward and levels the gun to shoot—but suddenly sees that there is nothing to shoot at.
APPLEGATE: Oh. *(Bends down to look under table.)* Oh—it's gone!
AUNT *(puzzled)*: What's gone?
APPLEGATE: Don't worry—I'll find it. Come with me, Gogarty.
Applegate and Gogarty move to the half-closed door.
AUNT *(irritably)*: Find what?
APPLEGATE *(crawling through lower part of doorway)*: Remember what I told you, Elizabeth. Don't forget.
AUNT: You haven't told me anything *(As she sees Gogarty follow Applegate through the door.)* Where are you going? Gogarty—come back here. Come back here.
But Applegate and Gogarty disappear in the garden.
AUNT *(thoroughly disgusted)*: Balmy! Balmy! *(Slams lower portion of door shut.)* The lot of you! Oh . . . I came down here for a nice, quiet rest—oh-h-h . . . *(She stalks off.)*

34. SUSAN: I'm doing all the work. I'll bet if Miss Swallow told you to, you'd sing—I'll bet if Miss Swallow told you to do anything, you'd do it.
    DAVID *(looking about for signs of George; now looks at Susan)*: I'd have to see her first, but I've a feeling I never will.

35. An alternative version of these two lines was also shot.
    DAVID: This is no time to be fooling around!
    SUSAN: I'm not fooling.

36. DAVID: Can you remember 'way back to this morning?
    SUSAN: Yes.

DAVID: That's where I'm supposed to be throwing knives and you're riding on a trapeze—and here we are—just loafing.

SUSAN: Well—you might as well put on your junk. *(She hands him his coat.)*

37. JOE *(to one of the group)*: Do you know where Bridgeport is?

MAN: Not me.

JOE: Come on, Mac.

They exit to get into truck.

38. *They get out. Mac walks up to the signpost.*

MAC: Doesn't say nothing about Bridgeport.

JOE *(joining him)*: We should've turned to the right.

MAC *(indicating)*: Bridgeport's that way.

JOE: No it ain't. *(Indicates opposite direction.)* It's that way.

MAC: All right—go that way, but you won't get to Bridgeport.

JOE: Come here. I'll show it to you on the roadmap.

Joe takes out the roadmap and they step closer to the headlights.

39. DAVID: I've been in the river—naturally I lost a couple. But to get back to our previous subject, gentlemen—of course, Bridgeport is a nice little town, but with a population of fifty thousand you can't expect to have much fun. On the other hand, New York, with a population of seven million, tends to have a bigger and better source of entertainment. So it's obvious you would have a much better time in New York . . . *(Half rises, feels bumper.)* This bumper isn't very soft, is it? Well, no matter.

40. DAVID: You see, gentlemen, years ago, where New York City now stands—and by years ago I mean, oh, even before the Dutch purchased the island from the Indians, there existed a peculiar kind of animal.

41. MAC: Hey, that feller knows something.

JOE: Yeah—but which way is Bridgeport?

MLS: *David and Susan rush in, looking about for the leopard.*

SUSAN: Don't you think I ought to sing, David?

DAVID: No.

The sound of a leopard's cry brings them to an abrupt stop.

SUSAN *(locating the sound)*: Over there.
They run off.

42. *Another location. Applegate, carrying the gun, and Gogarty enter and cautiously move toward the foreground, looking around. Applegate rests his gun against a tree, raises his hands, and emits a leopard cry. Gogarty jumps, startled, and turns on Applegate.*
   GOGARTY: Oh, I wish you wouldn't go on making those noises. They make me nervous.
   APPLEGATE: My dear young man, I've told you repeatedly . . . *(He is stopped by the sound of an answering leopard cry.)* Ah-hah—hear that? Follow me. *(He starts off around tree, momentarily forgetting the gun, but just as Gogarty eagerly reaches out for it, Applegate's hand appears, picks up the gun and exits.)*
   GOGARTY *(as he follows)*: I wish you'd give me that gun—I wish you'd give me that gun.

43. GOGARTY: Here—give me that gun.
   APPLEGATE: Quiet! Quiet!
   GOGARTY: You better give me the gun.
   APPLEGATE: Quiet!

44. APPLEGATE: Of course not. Isn't that strange—to think that—*(To Gogarty.)* I think he went *that* way. *(Indicating his original direction.)*
   GOGARTY: No—no—he went *that* way. *(Indicating opposite direction.)*
   APPLEGATE: I think he went that way.
   GOGARTY: Oh, no.
   They turn toward each other and bump.
   APPLEGATE: Do you want to catch this leopard?
   GOGARTY: Of course I do.
   APPLEGATE: Well, follow me—
   Applegate turns and starts off in the direction from which Susan and David had just come (the stone fence). Gogarty follows behind, reluctantly.
   GOGARTY: All right—certainly—with pleasure—but something tells me we're going the wrong way.
   MLS: *Aunt Elizabeth is standing in the doorway of her front porch, talking to a group of zoo officials. It is evident that the zoo officials have been here for some little time, trying to make themselves clear to Aunt.*

OFFICIAL: Lady—I'm trying to tell you we're from the zoo. We had a telephone call—it came from here—this house.

AUNT: And I'm trying to tell you that there must be some mistake. My leopard hasn't come yet.

OFFICIAL: I know that. That's why we're here.

AUNT: Who told you about the leopard?

OFFICIAL: We had a telephone call.

AUNT: But the leopard isn't here.

OFFICIAL: I know that.

AUNT: Can't you understand? The leopard hasn't come.

OFFICIAL: Do you expect it to walk up and in?

AUNT: No, but I do expect—*(Stutters with anger.)*—to—to get a notice or something from the freight office.

OFFICIAL: Sure, lady—now don't get excited.

AUNT *(on her high horse)*: Don't you tell me not to get excited.

OFFICIAL: Sure—you'll have a notice from the freight office. *(To man standing beside him.)* Won't she, Pat? *(Man nods.)*

AUNT: What you're looking for is a loon. *(She abruptly turns away from them and slams the door in their faces.)*

OFFICIAL *(to the closed door)*: Well, I don't have to look any farther. *(To the man.)* Daffy!

They exit.

45. GOGARTY: Major Applegate, I've a feelin' . . .

APPLEGATE: Now please, please, Gogarty—don't worry. As I told you before, it being a tame leopard makes the situation entirely different.

GOGARTY: Oh, I'm not worryin'.

46. *Applegate and Gogarty, pursued by the leopard.*

APPLEGATE AND GOGARTY: Get out of me way. The gun, man. What's the matter with the gun? Use the gun—the gun! Stand and face him.

47. *Tracking shot: David, carrying Susan piggyback.*

SUSAN: You know, David, I've been trying to figure out why you didn't kiss me back there. You almost did.

DAVID: We won't discuss that, Susan.

SUSAN: Well, there's nothing really wrong in kissing a girl. I mean, it's just that you have to get a point of view about it. Now if you were to

reach out and touch my face—*(Pats his cheek.)* like this, there wouldn't
be anything wrong about that, would there? I mean, you could even do it
accidentally, couldn't you?

DAVID *(setting Susan down on her feet)*: Susan, I couldn't kiss you
accidentally. If I were to kiss you, it would be quite deliberate. You see?
(Starts walking again. Susan follows.)

SUSAN: But there wouldn't be anything wrong in your touching my cheek
deliberately, would there?

DAVID *(trudging on)*: No, I don't suppose there would.

SUSAN: Then I don't see why it would be wrong for you to kiss me deliberately. It's the same thing really, isn't it?

DAVID: No—it's quite different.

SUSAN *(grabbing his arm to stop him)*: Well, anyway, I'd like to try it.
Well, I mean, I think we should try it just once—to see whether it is
different, I mean.

DAVID: Susan, I'm an engaged man. If I hadn't lost my intercostal
clavicle, I'd be a married man by now.

SUSAN: Oh, I wouldn't want to kiss you if you were a married man.
(Moves closer to him.)

DAVID *(backing away from her, into a bush)*: Oh, now look here, Susan—
I don't intend to kiss you. I intend to get back to New York and get married.

SUSAN: But, David . . .

The sound of George's barking makes them turn suddenly and look off.

DAVID: Oh, there they are.

He runs off, followed by Susan.

48. MS: *Mrs. Lehman talking over the phone.*

MRS. LEHMAN: Yes, yes, Constable, I wish you'd come right over. The
girl is obviously deranged. Dr. Lehman is working on her right now . . .
yes, mental cases are his specialty. You will? Thank you. *(She hangs up
and exits.)*

MLS: *David, carrying George, sneaks along front of the house to verandah, glances toward the door, then steps up to a window and looks in.*

MLS: *Lehman has Susan strapped in a chair under a strong light, and is
giving her a psychiatric examination. Susan is now quite calm.*

LEHMAN *(leaning over, close to her)*: It must be clear to you by now that
you are the victim of a love-fixation. Yesterday, when I talked to you at

the Ritz-Plaza, you thought you were pursued by a young man. Do you associate that young man with a leopard?

SUSAN: Oh, yes.

LEHMAN: Um-hum . . . You have transferred his image to a leopard. Now, you are pursuing the young man. Isn't that so?

SUSAN: No, I'm pursuing the leopard.

LEHMAN *(becoming excited)*: But the leopard is really the young man. You must understand that, my dear young lady.

SUSAN: All right. Don't get excited. He's a leopard.

LEHMAN: Now we're getting somewhere. Now, when you were a little girl your mother wouldn't allow you to have a cat, would she?

SUSAN: I never wanted a cat.

LEHMAN: That's the wrong answer.

SUSAN: I wanted a dog.

LEHMAN: Well, let's approach it from a different angle. One key to the subconscious is association. When I say a word I want you to tell me quickly the first thing that comes into your head. You understand?

SUSAN: I don't understand, but I'll do it.

LEHMAN: It isn't necessary for you to understand. Just tell me the first thing that comes into your mind.

SUSAN: Um-hum.

LEHMAN: Ready? *(He steps away from her as she nods—suddenly points at her.)* Leopard!

SUSAN: George!

LEHMAN: Ah—you're in love with George.

SUSAN *(laughs)*: Don't be silly.

LEHMAN *(angrily)*: Who are you to call me silly!

SUSAN: Well, really, you don't understand.

LEHMAN: Well, just confine yourself to answering my questions. *(Resumes the questioning.)* Money!

SUSAN: Baby!

LEHMAN: Ah, now we have it. You wish to become a mother!

SUSAN: Well, really—I only met David yesterday.

LEHMAN *(half to himself)*: Let's see—David and George—*(Back to the questioning.)* Man!

SUSAN: David!

LEHMAN: David!

SUSAN: George!
LEHMAN: George!
SUSAN: Baby!
LEHMAN: Baby!
SUSAN: Loon!
LEHMAN: Loon!
SUSAN: You!
LEHMAN: Me!?
SUSAN: Nut!
LEHMAN *(ready to tear his hair)*: We're not getting anywhere.
SUSAN: Look—don't you think you ought to go to a sanitorium for a nice long rest?
LEHMAN: Yes—NO!—*(Tears in his voice.)* Please, just concentrate and answer my questions.

49. MS: *Lehman questioning Susan who is still strapped in chair.*
LEHMAN *(exhausted)*: Will you please concentrate?
SUSAN: I'll concentrate.
LEHMAN: We'll start all over again.
SUSAN *(discouraged)*: Oh.
LEHMAN: All right. *(On with the questioning.)* Money!
SUSAN *(lifelessly)*: Aunt Elizabeth.
LEHMAN: Aunt Elizabeth.
SUSAN: Applegate!
LEHMAN: Applegate!
SUSAN: Gogarty!
LEHMAN: Gogarty!
SUSAN: Gun!
LEHMAN: Gun!
SUSAN: Leopard!
LEHMAN: Leopard!
SUSAN: Dog!
LEHMAN: Dog!
SUSAN: Bone!
LS: *The door suddenly opens. Elmer struggling with David, forces him into the room. Slocum follows. They walk to entrance to study, looking off toward Lehman and Susan.*

LEHMAN *(off)*: Bone!
SUSAN *(off)*: Intercostal clavicle!
DAVID *(pricks up his ears and shouts)*: WHERE!!!!
MS: *Susan and Lehman. They quickly look toward foyer.*
LEHMAN *(to David)*: YOU!
SUSAN *(joyously)*: DAVID!
MLS
SLOCUM: Doc, I caught this feller prowling around your porch.
LEHMAN: Constable, take these two people and lock them up. He's a thief and she's his accomplice.
SUSAN *(gets an idea and quickly turns the tables on Lehman; using his terse manner of questioning)*: Accomplice!
LEHMAN *(unwittingly falling in)*: Accomplice!
SUSAN: Thief!
LEHMAN: Thief!
SUSAN: Who?
LEHMAN: You!
SUSAN: You!
LEHMAN: Me?
SUSAN: Yes!
LEHMAN *(reaching the breaking point and shouting)*: No—yes—no— Oh, take them away! I can't stand any more!
LS: *The Vance house at night. A series of weird "Halloos" break the stillness. The door opens, and Aunt comes out. She slowly moves to edge of verandah in a listening attitude, then moves off in direction from which the sounds are coming.*
LS: *Applegate and Gogarty have taken refuge in the upper limbs of a large tree, and are sending forth their weird cries in all directions.*
MS: *Dolly ahead of Aunt as she walks along, trying to locate the origin of the cries. She sees Gogarty's gun lying on the ground—picks it up and continues walking. Suddenly pauses and looks up.*
AUNT: Why, Horace Applegate!
LS: *Applegate and Gogarty astride limbs of tree, see Aunt approaching, carrying the gun.*
APPLEGATE: Peekaboo, Elizabeth. Here we are.
AUNT: What on earth are you doing in that tree?
APPLEGATE: Well, it seemed like a good idea at the time . . .

(ALTERNATE)
In the light of all preceding incidents, I don't quite know.
AUNT: Come down at once! Both of you! *(Applegate starts down. Gogarty doesn't budge.)* Gogarty!
GOGARTY: If you don't mind, ma'am—I'm kind of comfortable here—
AUNT: Come right down. *(To Applegate.)* Look out—you'll break your leg.
MLS: *Aunt standing near foot of tree. Applegate drops to the ground. Gogarty climbs down.*
AUNT: Why, Horace, I'm surprised at you.
APPLEGATE: I'm not surprised that you're surprised. Elizabeth, let's go back to the house. . . . *(Starts leading her.)* Shall we run again? *(Takes gun from her.)* I'll take the gun.
They all move off in direction from which Aunt has come.

50. MS: *Slocum on phone.*
    SLOCUM: Are you sure?
    MS: *Aunt on the phone.*
    AUNT: Of course I'm sure.

51. AUNT *(continuing)*: Now see here. If you've picked up a feebleminded girl who claims she's my niece, it's no affair of mine . . .

52. MS: *Aunt and Applegate.*
    APPLEGATE: But Elizabeth, I think there's something you should know.
    AUNT: Well, what is it?
    APPLEGATE: I have a feeling that that is Susan.
    AUNT: What do you mean?
    APPLEGATE: Susan is the one the man is talking about.
    AUNT: Can you give me one good reason why Susan should be singing around under windows?
    APPLEGATE: Yeah—no—no, I can't give you a good reason, but I saw her singing under a tree.
    AUNT: Singing under a tree?
    APPLEGATE: Yes—there was a leopard in the tree—a four-legged leopard—your leopard—your leopard has arrived, Elizabeth—in all its glory.

AUNT *(relieved)*: That explains everything, doesn't it?
APPLEGATE: Well—yes—er—no—er—I—
AUNT: Don't stand there looking like an idiot! Can't you do something?
APPLEGATE: Well—er—yes—I can have a drink, thank you.
He starts off toward bar. Aunt follows.

53. GOGARTY: How do you know?
    SLOCUM: Well I just telephon . . . *(Catches himself.)* Confound it! I told you she hasn't got an aunt!
    GOGARTY: Then who have I been working for for the last twenty years?
    MS: *Susan in her cell.*
    SUSAN: My aunt! *(She turns away from the door of the cell and sits down on the cot.)*

54. SLOCUM: I'm going to ask a few questions and I want absolute quiet.
    The people in their cells take this as their cue to send forth an ear-splitting racket.
    MCU: *Aunt and Applegate in their cell.*
    AUNT AND APPLEGATE: Now you open this door! You can't do this to us. The idea! I'm sure we can explain the whole thing! Now look here, Constable, there's no necessity to incarcerate us this way! If you'll let us out we can explain the whole thing!

55. DAVID: Al Smith and Jim Farley.
    SLOCUM: Al Smith and Jim Farley. Put those names down, Doc.

56. MCU: *Aunt and Applegate in their cell as they stare off toward Susan, wide-eyed. They look at each other questioningly, then off at Susan again.*

57. MCU: *Aunt and Applegate in their cell, as they protest.*
    AUNT AND APPLEGATE: Here—you can't do that! You've no right! Let us explain—we'd feel happier about it! I never heard of such indignity!

58. MCU: *Aunt and Applegate, staring off at Susan, completely bewildered.*
    AUNT *(in a loud whisper)*: Horace, what does that mean?
    APPLEGATE: I don't know, but some of the words sound like English.

59. SUSAN: Oh—oh—just a minute. I forgot something.
    SLOCUM: What?
    SUSAN: Do you mind if I say goodbye to hot-lips before I go?
    SLOCUM: Well, hurry up—hurry up—
    SUSAN *(stepping to David's cell)*: Hello, hot-lips—*(David turns to her.)*
      Well, Jerry, this may be the last time we ever see each other—
    DAVID *(burning)*: I hope it is!
    SUSAN *(to Slocum)*: A sentimentalist . . . *(To David.)* Aren't you going to
      kiss me goodbye?
    DAVID *(in no uncertain terms)*: NO!
    SUSAN *(wheedling)*: Aw, come on, Babe—pucker up—
    DAVID *(thoroughly disgusted)*: AWWW . . . GO 'WAY—*(He turns his
      back to her.)*
    SUSAN *(turns to Slocum)*: Now there's a cold man—frappéed from the
      ankles up—
    *She flips a gesture in David's direction, then joins Slocum and Lehman and
    they start toward gate in b.g. David jumps up to bars of his cell.*
    DAVID *(yelling)*: Constable—you don't know what you're letting yourself
      in for! She'll set fire to your jail!
    SUSAN *(pausing and turning to David)*: Aw, can it, Romeo.

60. SLOCUM: What about the old lady?
    SUSAN: Who? Liz? She's the brains of the mob. *(Talking fast.)* She picks
      out the soft spots and gives us our orders.

61. PEABODY: And if you have made a mistake, your position as constable of
      this county will be seriously jeopardized!
    SLOCUM: Leopardized! I've heard all I want to hear about leopards! Say,
      hold on here.

62. SLOCUM *(indicating Applegate)*: What about this feller?
    AUNT: That's Major Applegate—*(Slocum unlocks cell door.)* I told you
      that.
    PEABODY: Let them both out.

63. ALICE: Have you found the intercostal clavicle?
    DAVID: Excuse me?

ALICE: Have you found the intercostal clavicle?
DAVID: No, I haven't.
ALICE: Oh, really, David.

64. *Gogarty in his cell off, begins to rattle his door and protest. All turn and look off at him.*
   AUNT: Let him out, too. That's my gardener.
   Slocum exits toward Gogarty.

65. AUNT: Isn't it sweet.
   DAVID: Oh, sure.
   AUNT: It'll make a lovely pet.
   DAVID: Oh, sure.

66. DAVID *(worried)*: Oh, I wish I knew where she was, because . . . *(His attention is attracted to the door.)*

67. MLS: *Susan at door, tugging on rope.*
   SUSAN: Come on Baby—come on—What did you say, David, I didn't hear.

68. MS: *Applegate and Gogarty in cell as they watch David and Susan backing away from the leopard.*
   APPLEGATE AND GOGARTY *(ad lib)*: Take care! Take care! Easy— easy—Keep that chair up! Stare him in the eye, man, stare him in the eye! Back him into the cell! Careful—careful!
   MS: *Aunt and Peabody in cell as they, too, follow David and Susan's progress.*
   AUNT AND PEABODY *(ad lib)*: Susan! Susan! Get away from there! Run—run—run—this way—quick! Susan! go 'way—go 'way, Susan!
   MCU: *Slocum perched on wall of cell, staring at Baby in his cell, and the leopard in the corridor.*
   SLOCUM: Oh—who said there were no leopards in the State of Connecticut! Oh—puss—puss—puss—kitty—kitty—kitty—go 'way—oh, oh, help—help—help—Elmer!

69. DAVID: Please go 'way—run back there!
   SUSAN: No, I won't leave you.

DAVID *(poking at the leopard)*: Susan, please let go—I'm trying to get it into the cell—*(To leopard.)* Go in there.

ALICE *(watching from adjoining cell)*: David, be careful.

70. *The others have slowly come out of their cells. Lehman, Joe, and Mac now quickly run to Susan, to help her with David.*

SUSAN *(wanting the unconscious David to herself)*: Go 'way—I'm holding him up—you get some water and pour it on him.

Fade out

Fade in. MLS: *David in his working clothes is seated on a wooden horse in the Brontosaurus Hall, listening to Alice, who stands in front of him. He is dreadfully subdued. Alice is cold, but calm.*

ALICE: I'm sorry to say this, David, . . . *(Starts to take off her engagement ring.)* . . . but under the circumstances I can never marry you.

DAVID: I'm sorry too, Alice.

ALICE *(handing him the ring)*: I don't believe you are. I've been watching you for the last three days and since your experience with that girl you've been a changed person. And I don't appreciate the change. Oh, I realize men must sow their wild oats, but while they're sowing them they needn't lose an intercostal clavicle!

DAVID: Yes, Alice.

ALICE: I suppose you're going to marry her now and give up research entirely.

DAVID: No—I couldn't marry her. Multiply one day with her by three hundred and sixty-five and the result is unthinkable.

ALICE: Well, it's a relief to know that you're not going to rush into marriage with a woman who can't be trusted with an intercostal clavicle!

DAVID *(the thrust hurts)*: Oh, Alice, I do wish you'd stop bringing that up *(He rises and paces.)* . . . I didn't want to lose it—I didn't mean to lose it—*(Turns to her.)*—but I lost it. And the funny thing is, I don't care.

ALICE *(unbelievingly)*: You don't care?

DAVID: No. Somehow . . . *(Looks up at the brontosaurus which looms up behind them.)* . . . all these little friends don't seem nearly as poetic as they did.

ALICE: I suppose true poetry is chasing a leopard around the country.

DAVID: No, it isn't. But I had fun.

ALICE: You had fun.

DAVID *(brightening)*: Yes, I had a good time. And it's the first time in my existence I haven't been thinking about work. Except for that, my life has been just one bone after another.

ALICE *(coldly)*: Oh, it has. Well, I don't think there's anything else to say. *(Holds out her hand.)* Goodbye, David.

DAVID: Oh—goodbye, Alice.

They shake hands. Alice turns and exits toward doorway. David thoughtfully walks up to foot of brontosaurus and sits down.

71. DAVID *(off)*: Don't come up here.

     SUSAN: I have something important to discuss with you. *(She continues up toward the top.)*

72. DAVID: Susan, please.

     SUSAN *(surveying the skeleton)*: So this is your brontosaurus—I don't know much about them, but it seems like a lovely one—*(Stretches out her hand to touch it.)* What do you do, David? String them up?

     The ladder teeters slightly. David gasps.

     SUSAN *(as she straightens it up)*: Oh—this ladder's tipsy.

73. DAVID: Oh, I don't know, Susan. I'm all confused.

     SUSAN: Confused? About what?

73. DAVID: Don't apologize, Susan.

     SUSAN: Oh, please forgive me, David.

75. INSERT: *bottom of ladder as it rests on one end and then on the other.*

76. INSERT: *two front legs of the brontosaurus—they sway, break away, and fall.*

"Bringing Up Baby"

Hagar Wilde

David was surprised when Suzan's call was announced. They'd had a row the
night before and it was Suzan's custom to punish the people who quarreled
with her by making them call first, thereby placing them at a disadvantage.
David reflected that Suzan must want something. For a brief moment he considered having Ching tell her that he had gone out with a "velly plitty lady" but
Suzan was smart and she'd know that he was skulking there listening to every
word. No, the thing to do was take this call and make Suzan feel that she'd been
something of a weakling to ring him up.

He said, "Hello, Suzan." In brighter moments she was Suzy.

Suzan's voice was vague and far away as though she were lighting a cigarette,
which she was. "Do you want a panther?"

"Do I want a *panther?*" David said. He untwisted the telephone cord, a fu-
tile gesture, but instinctive. "I can't hear you very well. Come closer to the
transmitter."

Her voice came, cupped and resounding, even scratching a little along the
sides of the wires. "I said, do you want a panther?"

"No," David said. "Why should I?"

"Well, for that matter," Suzan said peevishly, "why should I? But I've
got one."

"Where would you get a panther?"

"Mark."

From *Collier's* magazine (April 10, 1937).

Mark was her brother. He'd been away for two months, nobody knew quite where except that he was below the equator. An important point presented itself to David. "How big?" he said.

"Big," said Suzan. "He just fits into the bathroom. Aunt Elizabeth is coming and I have to farm the beast out somewhere."

"Suzan Vance, you get right out of that apartment."

"Nonsense," said Suzan. "I have a lease. Maybe Tommy—"

"Tommy's out of town."

"Rats," Suzan said.

Suzan's maid had taken her stand in the corridor but she had retained a key. This she delivered to David, who arrived breathless, with an oration. "It's not me that's putting any wild beast into any bathroom. If she wants it in the bathroom she can put it in the bathroom and I wish her good luck."

At this point, Suzan, a bit disheveled, popped her head out at them. "You can come in now, lionheart. I've stowed him away. Oh, hello, David."

David followed her inside. His hands were a bit clammy and perspiration was starting around his hairline. "Suzan," he said, "I will not allow—"

"Don't stand there yapping about what you'll allow. Try to think of some nice, responsible person you know who likes panthers."

"No responsible person likes panthers!" David yelled.

A familiar gleam entered Suzan's eye. "My brother Mark likes panthers and you wouldn't tell Mark to his face that he wasn't responsible."

David kept his temper because losing it never got him anywhere, "Darling—"

She said sharply, "Don't wheedle. If you're going to try and get your own way come out in the open and fight like a man."

"I was about to say, we'll get somebody from a zoo to—"

Suzan said stubbornly, "Mark says I'm to keep him, so I'm going to keep him." It had a note of finality. "I've other things on my mind. Listen." Producing two documents from a pile of mail on the table, she waved them at him and then read the first, prefacing the reading by saying, "From Mark. From Brazil":

"Dear Suzy:
"I'm sending you Baby, a panther I picked up. He's three years old, gentle as a kitten and he likes dogs."

Suzan paused, frowned a little and then smiled apologetically. "I don't know whether Mark means he eats dogs or is fond of them," she said. "Mark's so vague at times." She continued reading:

"He also likes music, particularly that song, 'I Can't Give You Anything but Love, Baby.' It may be because his name is in the lyric but, anyway, it enchants him. Try getting records with the word baby in them. That shouldn't be hard if music is what it was when I left. Guard him with your life. I am leaving Brazil tomorrow. Will communicate with you from the next port. Don't feed Baby potatoes. He gets sick as a dog.'"

"I wish he'd get sick as a panther and die," said David.

"Don't interrupt. Mark adds a postscript. Wouldn't Mark put a thing like this in a postscript! 'Aunt Elizabeth's changed her will in our favor again. Give the old girl my love when she arrives.'" Suzan put the letter down and stared at it angrily. "When she arrives! As though he didn't know that I never open Aunt Elizabeth's letters except on the first of the month!"

"I don't follow you," David said.

"Mark's probably known for weeks that she was coming, but I didn't. She writes four times a month, once with a check and three times with lectures, so naturally I skip the lectures. Fortunately I save them in neat little piles. Here's her last. I opened it after I read Mark's. Aunt Elizabeth says in it that she is arriving in America on the twelfth."

"That's tomorrow," said David.

"I know it," Suzan said, glaring. She went on reading:

"Why have you not replied to my last letter? I intend leaving my erstwhile friend Drusilla Maretti for good this time. Nobody could get on with her, what with her overweaning conceit about a voice that might have been good once but certainly is nothing to listen to now and that moth-eaten cheetah she's always lugging about. I am thoroughly out of patience.

"I will expect you to move out to the Connecticut house for the length of my stay.

"I understand that you are engaged. You might have apprised me of this fact but I suppose I can expect very little from you and Mark in the way of acting like human beings. However, I want your fiancé to come to Connecticut with us. It's a good idea, in the country, to have a man in the house.

"Drusilla and I, at the moment, are not speaking. It makes things very difficult, living in the same house. I look forward, in America, to peace and quiet.

"Your affectionate aunt,
"ELIZABETH REARDON."

Suzan stared into space, two frown wrinkles deeply embedded over her nose.

"So she comes to America to get away from a cheetah," she said, "and runs smack into a panther. Just after she's changed her will. It doesn't make sense."

"Drusilla Maretti's the opera singer, isn't she?"

"The ex–opera singer. They've lived together for years. They should both be packed away in woollies, knitting. But, no, they give the most ghastly dinner parties and wear feathers in their hair and serve champagne and Drusilla sings after dinner and Aunt Elizabeth sits in the corner and sneers."

"I've always wanted to make faces back at singers, too," said David.

"Then one of them packs up in a huff and makes a dramatic exit, saying she hopes she'll never set eyes on the other again. Two months later they're back together again, thick as thieves. Well, anyway—" Suzan sat briskly erect. This meant that she was now prepared to deal with the matter in hand. "Aunt Elizabeth can't know that we have Baby."

"Can Baby know that we have Aunt Elizabeth?"

"Don't be tiresome. We'll take him up to Connecticut in the station wagon. Two of the tenant houses are empty. We'll tie him in one and sneak food out to him nights."

"You mean I'll sneak food out to him nights," said David.

"Well, what do you think of it?"

"I think it's lousy," David said, his head in his hands, "but I don't suppose that makes any difference."

"How would you like me not to have any money if I ever decide to marry you?" Suzan demanded.

"I shouldn't like it. I've only got just enough to live on in luxury and entertain you. I certainly can't keep you."

"Precisely. So you help or I won't marry you."

"You broke our engagement last night," David said.

"Oh, that," said Suzan airily.

Hauling a panther seventy miles in a station wagon without bars between you and the panther is no joke. Suzan kept referring to Baby as a lamb because he was quiet but David was aware at all moments during the drive that Baby was no lamb. Those few hours marked a turning point in David's life. He realized that life was not all fun and that it might end in death by drowning or perhaps, through no fault of your own, by having a panther who was in a position of advantage take a dislike to you. He marveled at Suzan, who seemed perfectly cool and unaware of the fact that chance plays such an important part in whether one lives or dies and the manner of the latter.

He was still regarding Suzan with wonder at three o'clock the following afternoon. They sat in the drawing room of the Connecticut house. Suzan was pensively staring at the arrangement of a bowl of heather as though she hadn't another care in the world. She in no way resembled the girl who had pushed Baby into a deserted house a stone's throw away and secured him with what she optimistically called a sailor's knot.

She looked like a normal, exceptionally pretty girl of twenty-two, wearing a most attractive print dress and awaiting an aunt who was, if not beloved, at least highly respected. But there was an expression about her mouth that David had come to know. She wore it when she'd outwitted somebody.

Elizabeth Reardon was the biggest woman David had ever seen outside a circus tent. She was accompanied by a personal maid named Marie, a chauffeur named Anthony and a fox terrier named George.

When Suzan said, "I'm glad to see you, Aunt Elizabeth," she replied, "I've always said you'd grow up to be an accomplished liar." Then she looked at David. "Is this the man you're going to marry?" She implied that if Suzan had been a better specimen she might have expected better luck.

George, the fox terrier, and Aunt Elizabeth had lived together so long that each knew, without consulting the other, what had to be done first. Their first duty was an inspection of the premises.

An awkward moment arose when Aunt Elizabeth came face to face with Baby's rations. As David pointed out later, one look at Aunt Elizabeth should have told them that she'd go straight as a homing pigeon to the source of life. She yanked open the refrigerator door and there reposed what in its most elegant terminology could only be called a hunk of meat.

"What," said Aunt Elizabeth with loathing, "is that?"

Suzan stammered. "Meat."

"For what?" said her aunt.

David jumped into the breach with, "For George."

"George doesn't eat muck like that. Throw it away."

Under her and George's eagle eyes they chucked it into a garbage receptacle. Then Aunt Elizabeth unpacked.

The day wore on. It wore on everybody. When Aunt Elizabeth retired at nine o'clock Suzan and David dived quietly out the back door and rummaged for Baby's supper. "Got it," said Suzan finally and inelegantly.

Baby was pathetically glad to see them. Not only had he been feeling the pangs of the inner panther but he'd been lonely. He rolled over on his back and Suzan scratched his stomach. "Cute," Suzan said.

"Very cute," said David at a safe distance.

Suddenly Suzan jumped, listened and came over to clutch his arm, hissing, "What was that?" Baby had pricked up his ears and abandoned his supper momentarily.

What she'd heard was a sniffing sound. It grew in volume. It finally stood in the doorway. It was George, spying as usual.

"Grab him," said Suzan.

"You grab him," said David. "You know him better."

"That's why I won't grab him," Suzan said, dancing agitatedly.

David advanced, saying, "Nice George." George growled.

"He knows better than that," Suzan said, still dancing.

She panted, as they plunged toward the house with George in David's arms. "He must like you. He hasn't growled once since you picked him up."

"He can't," David said bitterly. "His mouth is full of my hand."

They persuaded George to relinquish David's hand and shut him up in Suzan's bedroom.

The following morning at ten o'clock a great uproar started, made its way down the corridor and turned out to be Aunt Elizabeth rousing the house. She stood in Suzan's doorway and said, "Get up."

Suzan stirred sleepily and sat up. She hadn't had much sleep.

"What's George doing under your bed?"

"Growling the first part of the night and snoring the last," said Suzan.

"Well, get up. Get that young man—what's his name?—David. Get him up, too."

Suzan sighed.

Suzan's devotion to George that day was a thing of beauty. The fact that it awoke in George no answering loyalty proved rather conclusively that he had a nasty character.

Suzan took him into the kitchen and gave him his breakfast with her own hands, standing guard while he ate it. When he went outside for his morning constitutional, Suzan was at his heels. George was all for heading straight toward the tenant cottage but at the risk of life and limb Suzan carried him in the other direction. She did everything but follow him into a hollow tree. After maneuvering him back into the house she sank exhausted upon the divan, her eyes glued upon his hideous form.

George stretched out on the drawing-room threshold and snoozed peacefully, his snores mounting in volume as he drew farther and farther away from a waking world. Suzan began to understand the principle of hypnotism. The object held in front of the eyes needn't be bright. It can be just a dog who is intent upon visiting a panther against your wishes.

David came in and found her, fast asleep, her arm tucked under her head. He joined Aunt Elizabeth in a game of double solitaire in the sunroom.

At three o'clock Suzan started up like a frightened doe. Asleep at the switch. Asleep on sentry duty. George was gone. Suzan started a systematic search of the house. She ended up in the sunroom gesturing wildly behind her aunt's back, making a pretense of barking and pointing toward the tenant cottage. David stared. "George is such a *nice* dog," Suzan said desperately.

"Nonsense," Aunt Elizabeth said, without turning, "George is a fiend and you well know it."

"He's gone for a walk *all by himself,*" said Suzan.

"That's because nobody with any sense would go with him," her aunt said.

David said, rising, "Excuse me, I just thought of something."

"Finish the hand," barked Aunt Elizabeth.

Suzan snatched David's cards. "I'll finish it."

She finished it and then she, too, bolted. Aunt Elizabeth could hear her little rubber heels thudding down the front steps at a terrific rate.

"Mad," said the old lady. "Balmy, the lot of them." She went on playing.

Suzan lunged around the corner of the tenant cottage. David was sitting on the top step. Suzan stood, quivering like an anguished pointer. "Were you in time?"

"Oh, plenty," said David. He displayed a frayed end of rope.

Suzan gasped and sank weakly beside him. "What do we do now?"

"I wonder," David said, "how one goes about telling people there's a panther at large without telling how he got at large."

"They j-just say they s-saw a panther."

"We might try it," David said.

Suzan didn't reply.

David made his plan on the way back. "I'll just call a zoo and tell them I've seen a panther. Then they'll come and catch him."

"It's too simple," said Suzan.

Aunt Elizabeth was still engrossed in her solitaire when Suzan came in. She slipped a ten into a king space and said, "Where's David?"

"Telephoning a friend," said Suzan.

David's opponent on the telephone was saying, "Yeah, I heard you. You saw a panther. In Connecticut."

"Well, aren't you going to do something about it?"

"You do something about it. You had the fun. Go to bed and sleep it off."

David clutched the instrument desperately and sank his mouth into the transmitter. "I tell you this is a bona fide *panther!*"

"Listen, I know every species of panther and that isn't one of them."

"He must be having a fight with his friend," said Aunt Elizabeth, slipping a queen into a king space.

The doorbell rang. Suzan went to answer it. Aunt Elizabeth took advantage of her absence to cheat on a large scale. She'd practically run her cards out when Suzan returned, flourishing a cablegram.

Aunt Elizabeth opened it, saying, "It's from Mark," and then, sharply, "Don't play until I've read it. It's not fair."

Upstairs, David was saying despairingly, "Let me talk to the man in charge. The man in charge of *everything.*"

Aunt Elizabeth adjusted her spectacles and read in a monotone, "Welcome America are you pleased with Baby Love Mark."

She put the cablegram down and stared at it. "Baby?"

"He means me," Suzan bleated.

"You're no baby," said Aunt Elizabeth, "and he doesn't say a word about my panther. You might know. Mark's always been highly unreliable. Cable him at once and say I want to know whether he's going to keep his promise."

Suzan had risen, disarranging her cards by clutching motions. "Panther?" said Suzan. "Promise?"

"Mark promised me a panther and I mean to get it. I'm not going to have Drusilla Maretti lording it over me any longer with her cheetah. I've given that young scoundrel enough money to run the White House—I've changed my will in his favor—and yours, I might add, though why I don't know—and all I asked was a panther. Then he cables me asking if I'm pleased with you. That's the way Mark does things."

"Excuse me," Suzan said faintly.

As she staggered from the room she heard her aunt booming, "I'll get a panther if I have to rob a zoo! Why I should have to pay a stranger to go out and hunt for me when I have a nephew—"

Suzan skidded across the waxed floors of the bedroom and landed at David's feet, saying, "Don't call the zoo! That Mark! He couldn't tell me! Don't call the zoo, David!"

David hung up, "I've called the zoo. It's all fixed."

"Call them back and unfix it. Don't ask questions. Call them back."

"I will not," David said indignantly. "I offered the man two hundred dollars and the panther, if he'd come over. And he's coming, with some helpers."

"You gave him Baby!" she raged. "You gave away my life's happiness, my brother's trust in me, my brother's inheritance—"

"Stop flinging your arms about," said David. "Explain."

Suzan explained but when David called back the zoo somebody said that everybody except himself and the night watchman had gone hunting a panther that was loose.

Suzan drew a deep, determined breath. "Then there's only one hope left. We must find him before they do. Have you any idea how to catch a panther?"

"No," said David simply.

"Start thinking about it," said Suzan. "If those men from the zoo ring the doorbell one of us must answer and get rid of them."

"How?" David said, but she was already on her way downstairs. He followed.

While they were at dinner there was a loud and insistent pealing of the doorbell.

Suzan drifted from the room and flew down the corridor. Opening the door a crack she slid out, closing it behind her. The man who stood outside was rubbing his chin as though by so doing he could free it of a two days' growth of beard. "You the party that called us about a panther?"

"Oh, no, indeed," said Suzan.

"Man live around here by the name of Melton?"

"Never heard of him," said Suzan.

"I've asked everybody on this road so far."

"Well, there are still five miles of this road. If you're going west, that is. Seven, if you're going east."

He hesitated, looking east. "Better lock up your chickens tonight, lady. There's a panther loose around somewhere."

"Haven't got any chickens," Suzan said, as though she'd just played an ace on his king. She went back to her dinner.

Seeing the expression around her mouth, David knew that she had been successful. He envisioned all the men from the zoo locked in the back of their truck with the ignition torn out.

Aunt Elizabeth, as was her custom, retired at nine. Suzan and David crept down the back stairs to confer in the basement. "Now," Suzan said in a hoarse whisper, "we must be methodical about this. Before we act we must think."

"You think," said David. "I'll just sit here and recover from the thinking I was doing at dinner."

"What would be the most logical thing to take on a panther hunt?"

"A bigger panther," David said.

"If you were a panther," said Suzan, "where would you go?"

"I'd come home to Aunt Elizabeth."

They set out finally with a length of rope and a landing net which Suzan insisted upon taking despite the fact that it was for fish. She said that it might come in handy and that it would be no trouble to carry it. It was no trouble for anyone but David, who carried it.

They saw the panther only once, and briefly. He was with George, and seemed willing enough to come home, but when Suzan bent down and temptingly held out a bit of Baby's dinner meat, George growled insinuatingly and walked away. Baby, stretching luxuriously, hesitated only a moment between love and duty. He followed the dog, disappearing into the woods in three leaps. They started after him. It kept growing darker.

The quarrel started at twelve o'clock. It was born when Suzan tripped and fell over a log. She lay there, flat on her face, until David picked her up. He made the mistake of saying, "Watch where you're going."

They'd been walking since nine-thirty. Suzan had torn her frock. Privately, she had despaired of finding Baby and that made matters worse. Her voice trembled. She said, "Watch where I'm going yourself, smart aleck—I mean watch where—" and then she began crying.

"Now, look," David said. "I'd suggest that we go home."

Suzan stamped her wrath out on innocent shrubs. "Go home and tuck yourself into bed, quitter! Go *on* home. I'm going to find that beast if it—t-takes me the rest of my natural life! The idea, turning a wild animal loose on an innocent countryside and then g-going home and sleeping—with lives in danger—all over—"

David said, "Oh, Suzan, do stop making an ass of yourself."

"So," said Suzan. She jumped back hastily onto her dignity. "So," she said, and stalked off. David followed. Suzan stopped. "Please, David," she said, "I'd rather you didn't."

"Didn't what?"

"Didn't come with me," said Suzan frigidly. "This time, David, I am through. The other times have been silly quarrels, but this time I am thoroughly, quite thoroughly, through."

"Oh, very well," David said. He sat down on a log.

He could hear Suzan crashing away from him. Then she crashed back toward him after a bit. Presently, in a quavering voice quite near him she said, "David?"

David kept quiet.

"Oooh!" said Suzan, and headed straight for the main road. Establishing your independence is one thing and mucking about in the woods alone at twelve o'clock at night is another.

David followed at a reasonable distance. He threw away the landing net but retained the rope, mindful of the fact that it was a clothesline and useful in its way.

The moon was up. Ahead, he could see Suzan looking from side to side but she wasn't looking for Baby. She was looking for something to jump out at her from behind a tree. David was resigned to the fact that the most baleful and horrible revenge that has ever been perpetrated on a man by a woman was being cooked up but it didn't seem to matter. The only thing of importance in the whole world was a bed. A wide, comfortable bed with big, soft pillows. A bed that was sturdy. A bed where a man could sink back, close his eyes and just ache in peace until he fell asleep.

As Suzan came abreast of a large, white house, she stopped suddenly. She dropped to her hands and knees and started crawling. David thought, "The little beast has sprained her ankle," but after a moment he realized that she was crawling toward an objective. The objective was a monotonous, low growling sound. George. Suzan disappeared behind a largish clump of hydrangeas. David advanced. After looking a moment he could distinguish a big, cat-like form outlined against the sky, comfortably ensconced on the veranda roof of the white house.

Suzan was saying, "Good Baby. Nice Baby, come down."

David gave up and sat down in a clump of sumac.

Suzan was waxing indignant. Knowing Suzan, David knew that she was stamping her foot. "Come down at *once!*" George growled louder.

There was a short silence. Suzan was thinking. David hoped she wouldn't decide to climb the trellis and come to grips with her problem.

The fruit of her thought came, after a moment. She lifted her voice in song.

"I can't give you anything but love, ba-by,
That's the only thing I've plenty o-of, ba-by,
Dream a while, scheme a while, you're sure to—"

A window was flung up and a pajama-clad man appeared in the aperture. Obviously, he was at a loss to know where to start. He said finally, "What are you doing, may I ask?"

"Singing," Suzan said.

"If you're paying a bet there must be someplace else you can pay it," the man said. By this time his wife had joined him at the window. Clearly, she didn't like Suzan's looks.

"I'm not paying a bet," Suzan said distinctly. "There's a panther on your roof."

"I'm not going to bandy words with you at this time of night." He, too, was beginning not to like Suzan.

"There's a panther on your roof and it's my panther," Suzan said stubbornly, "and I'm going to get him. To get him, I have to sing."

"There is nothing on my roof," he said.

"There is! Come out and look!"

The woman's face softened. She said something to her husband. He drew back from the opening like a turtle whose shell has been tapped. The woman leaned farther out and said, "Sing if you like, dear."

Suzan started. "I can't give you anything but love, baby . . ."

The woman regarded her pityingly, shaking her head a little.

A door banged. The man had put on his pants hurriedly. Baby, alarmed, disappeared over the edge of the roof.

Suzan was yelling. "He went that way!"

She struggled in the gentle but firm grip of a man who knew his duty. He kept saying, "Hush, hush. It's all right."

"You've frightened him away," Suzan wailed furiously, "and now I'll never find him again."

"See, he's still there," her captor said soothingly. "See him?"

"He's not!" Suzan yelled. "Let go of my arm! Let go!"

"He'll come back, don't worry. Now you tell me where you live. Do you know?"

"Of course, I know," Suzan said indignantly, "but that's not the point. I have to get my panther." She appealed desperately to him. "Won't you help me?"

"I certainly will," he said.

With a sigh of relief, David pushed his way through the sumac thicket. Suzan was safe. Of course, when she discovered that the man thought her batty, the man wasn't safe, but that was his responsibility, not David's.

It was dark among the trees. David stumbled around looking up into them for Baby and under them for George. Now and then he called, hoping that George would growl in reply.

He came upon them in a small clearing. Baby was lying in a wagon track and George was standing beside him. David had an unpleasant feeling that they'd been watching him all the time. He tried to remember all the things he'd ever heard about dealing with animals. Looking Baby straight in the eye was a bit difficult in the dark and from a distance. He tried cooing at them and making wild promises about steak at home, but George only growled.

Only the picture of sitting all night in that clearing, watching Baby, drove him to unwind the rope and walk toward them. Baby rolled over on his back to have his stomach scratched. David scratched it and put the rope around his neck. From there on it was simple. He merely walked home. Baby padded along at his side and George followed at his heels, growling.

Every light in the house was on and Aunt Elizabeth, in a fury, was on the telephone. David went in, towing Baby.

Aunt Elizabeth was shouting, "Of course I have a niece but she's decently in bed, not singing around under windows! Why should I come to the police station and identify her? It's no responsibility of mine or my niece's if you've picked up a feeble-minded female! There's no insanity in our family! Don't take any checks from her, mind."

David grinned, feeling a twinge of sympathy for the local police force.

"I tell you," Aunt Elizabeth shouted, "that the girl's an impostor! My niece is a sober, self-respecting citizen!" Then she looked up and saw David. She stared at Baby. She looked back at David. She turned to the telephone. "Wait a minute, my good man," she said. "I might be wrong."

David handed Aunt Elizabeth the end of the clothesline. He took the telephone from her unresisting hand. "Put your prisoner on the wire, Sergeant," he said. "If it's Miss Vance we'll be able to identify her by her voice."

A furious squeaking sailed into the room from the receiver.

"Don't take that tone," David said warningly.

"Da-*vid!*" said Suzan.

"Am I marvelous?"

"You're anything you say," wailed Suzan.

"Are we engaged or aren't we?"

"All right," Suzan said sulkily.

"I'll be right over," David said. He hung up.

After he'd gone Aunt Elizabeth stood staring at Baby, who was rolling over to have his stomach scratched. "Imagine," she said into space, "Mark can't send me a panther from the wilds of Brazil but these two can scare one up in the Connecticut woods. That's rather sweet. I've misjudged Suzan. I think—yes, I think I'll cut Mark off and give Suzan all the money."

Interviews, Reviews, and Commentaries

Interviews

In the final fifteen years of his life, Hawks gave at least a dozen public interviews. He had become a central figure to the arguments of *auteurists*. The interviews were rather consistent in both tone and content. Hawks adopted a folksy midwestern modesty in which he claimed merely to have accomplished very simple things in very simple ways. The following selection is adapted from Joseph McBride's collection of interviews with Hawks, *Hawks on Hawks*, published by the University of California Press, 1982. A complete bibliography of Hawks's published interviews is as follows: *Cahiers du cinéma* 10, no. 56 (February 1956); *Movie* 5 (December 1962); *Cinema* 1 (November-December 1963); *Films and Filming* 1 (October 1968); *Focus on Howard Hawks,* ed. Joseph McBride (Englewood Cliffs, N.J.: Prentice-Hall, 1972); *Sight and Sound* 40, no. 2 (Spring 1971); *Take One* 3, no. 8 (July-August 1971); Donald C. Willis, *The Films of Howard Hawks* (Metuchen, N.J.: Scarecrow Press, 1976); *Wide Angle* 1, no. 2 (Summer 1976); *Hawks on Hawks,* ed. Joseph McBride (Berkeley and Los Angeles: University of California Press, 1982). This McBride excerpt serves as both a distillation and a culmination of all these Hawks interviews.

Interview with Joseph McBride

All I'm doing is telling a story. I don't analyze or do a lot of thinking about it. I work on the fact that if I like somebody and think they're attractive, I can make them attractive. If I think a thing's funny, then people laugh at it. If I think a thing's dramatic, the audience does. I'm very lucky that way. I don't stop to analyze it. We just made scenes that were fun to do. I think our job is to make entertainment.

You say that you are an entertainer, but critics in the last few years have been treating you as something more than that. Do you think they're right?

Oh, I listen to them, and I get open-mouthed and wonder where they find some of the stuff that they say about me. I'm very glad that they like it, and I'm very glad that a lot of them are copying what I do, but they find things. They give me credit for an awful lot of things that I don't pay any attention to.

Do all good directors have a personal style?

The men that I think are good directors certainly have a style. I can go and tell who directed it. If you were listening to a comedian tell a joke, you'd certainly know the way Bob Hope tells it, and you can just go right down the line—everybody has his own particular way of telling his story, and I think if a director's any good he's got his own way of telling it. . . .

You have a reputation as one of the most astute businessmen of all directors. You've never been tied for a long time to any studio, and you've always maintained a high degree of control over your work. The producing aspect of your career is very important because you only exercise creative control by controlling the money.

I've been independent except for two or three pictures in the first couple years. It's very easy to figure out that I didn't have much to do with 'em. I've been independent ever since that time. And I started a lot of trouble by saying "Directed by Howard Hawks" and "Produced" afterward, making the direction more important. A lot of producers didn't like that.

How much correlation is there between how much you like a film personally and how well it does commercially?

I hate to say this, but I don't think any of them that I didn't like did any good. I

From *Hawks on Hawks*, ed. Joseph McBride (Berkeley and Los Angeles: University of California Press, 1982).

made those films trying to do favors for people who I liked very much. I'd say, "I don't know how to make that kind of a goddam film." They'd say, "Oh, yes, you do," and I'd make it, and it wasn't any good. I won't say what pictures they were.

How much control do you have over the editing of your films?

Oh, practically complete control. I've had a little trouble on a couple of pictures that they thought were too long. I made the mistake of making them too long, and they made the mistake of trying to shorten them.

Since you also produce your own pictures, do you find that you have to worry much about money matters during production?

It all depends. For fifteen or twenty years, I've worked on the profits of my pictures, not working for a company, so I'm damned interested in how much they cost and how much they gross. But I don't think it has any effect at all. I think you're out to do as well as you can, but you're not about to throw money away. If you do, you find yourself pretty soon without a picture.

What are the differences you find in the economics of filmmaking and distribution between today and the past?

There isn't any comparison. In the 1920s I made *Fig Leaves,* and it got its cost back in one theater. And that was at about ten cents admission or twenty cents admission. Nowadays—oh, we made a picture up in Idaho, every Indian pony cost us $86 a day to work with. You could have gone up there and rented the pony for fifty cents. And they'd have been happy to have rented it to you. It's almost impossible to make a picture around here. The shooting schedule of *El Dorado* [1967] was at least twice as long as on *Rio Bravo* [1959], which was made in the same location, practically the same cast. The prices in making a picture went up so that it cost us three times as much to make *El Dorado* as it did to make *Rio Bravo.* The last movie, the last western [*Rio Lobo,* 1970], cost $1,000,000 less by going down to Mexico than it would cost here. Used the same people, the same sets, same film, same everything. Just didn't have the unions to combat. If anything's the matter, it's the unions. We had a little two-sided shack to put up for *El Dorado.* Cost $14,000 to build it. In the 1920s they'd have put it up for $250. As a matter of fact, you wouldn't have gotten a gang, you'd just ask the one grip to put it up, and he had it up in two hours.

Today a filmmaker has to spend two years making the deal and then, after he makes a film, another year supervising the contracts and the foreign versions. Do you feel that has hurt the industry?

I don't think they're doing anything right in the whole industry at the present time. Some agents are trying to make more money than the director or the writers and everything. There's nothing you can do about it unless you get in there and go through it, right from top to bottom. And that's an awful job.

Do you believe in previewing, especially in the case of comedies? Do you get audience response and then cut the film accordingly?

Not too much. I'm not too great a believer in previews, but sometimes they're good. Sometimes they tell you a lot. When we previewed *To Have and Have Not*, we had a new girl [Lauren Bacall], and she was different. I was a little worried about her, about whether the audience would like her, if they would laugh. She had one line in the beginning of the thing, so I waited until they laughed like hell, and then I went out and got a couple of drinks. I came back in and Jack Warner said, "Where the hell have you been?" I said, "Out having some drinks. How's it going?" He said, "Just great. Why did you leave?" I said, "I knew when they laughed at that thing, they were going to laugh at her all the way through." You can find out whether you've got a funny character. The first time I used Walter Brennan [in *Barbary Coast*] I was quite worried about him, whether he was going to be funny. I never worried after the first time. We took the picture out one night to preview it. Nobody laughed at all. The audience just sat there. I came out rather stunned and looked up to see what picture was playing, and it was Will Rogers; he was killed that afternoon [August 15, 1935]. But for about half an hour, I didn't know what had happened. We took the picture out the next night, and people laughed and roared. That was the most frustrating thing that ever happened to me. If you make a comedy, you take it out and the people laugh, you're *immediately* pleased, you get an immediate reaction and the pleasure that you've done a good job. If you make a drama, it takes a little bit longer. You have to have people come up to you and say, "I enjoyed that," because they can give you no visible expression in a theater. Oh, if they don't walk out, that's pretty good. I think probably the last picture that worked out well is your favorite for a while, and then you start thinking about it, and you go back a little further. Not that you're trying to make every scene a great scene, but you try not to annoy the audience. I told John Wayne when we started to work together, "Duke, if you can make three good scenes in this picture and don't annoy the audience the rest of the time, you'll be good." He said, "Do you believe that?" I said, "Yeah. If I make five good scenes in this picture, and don't annoy the audience, I think I'll be good." So he started to work on that. And he always comes up to me and says, "Hey, is this one of those scenes?" I'd say, "This is the one where you get it over just as quickly as you can and don't annoy the audience." "OK." We work that way, and now he preaches that as though it's gospel, and he does a great job of not annoying the audience. As we got to be better friends working together, I could hear him telling some actor who was trying to ham it up, "Look, the boss says this. You see that you do it. Get it over in a hurry. This is one of those scenes." I never realized that he was playing policeman for me on the last two or three pictures.

Some people feel that a comedy should run only about ninety minutes. Do you think there's a particular rule about running time when it comes to comedy?

I think it would be a good idea to keep those people from expressing their ideas. They don't know what the hell it's all about. . . .

How do you rehearse actors?

Part of it is if I'd think of something, I'd go to the actor and say, "Don't tell this other guy about it, but read such-and-such a line." He throws the line to the other actor, and the other actor at first doesn't know what to say, and then he responds in his own way, and it always works out well. You don't have to do a lot of rehearsing with any good actor. You merely tell them what you're trying to get out of a scene, then you just turn them loose and let them go.

In Rio Bravo, *when Walter Brennan mimics John Wayne at one point, did Dean Martin know it was coming? There's something about the way Martin looks that makes me think it was a complete surprise to him.*

If I answer yes, I'll have at least a fifty percent chance of being right, because I don't do scenes twice if I can help it. Did you see the George Plimpton show [*Shootout at Rio Lobo*, a 1970 TV documentary about Hawks at work]? It typifies the way we work more than anything else that's ever been made. I told John Wayne to show Plimpton how to walk the way he does. But I didn't tell him to go through that marvelous routine that he went through. That was almost all ad-lib, as it were. I told him what to do, but he did it much better than I told him. And I told the rest of the actors the dumbest thing in the world is an actor getting serious about himself. For God's sake, don't get so serious about it.

That reminds me of something funny that happened on the Academy Awards show when you received your Oscar. Wayne presented it to you after making a crack about how he "directed" you onto the stage for the award, but then when the two of you walked off, Wayne started to leave the stage in the wrong direction, and you had to motion him which way to go. Was that an accident?

No. I said, "Duke, go off the wrong way and I'll stop you."

How do you keep the atmosphere from getting too serious on the set when the cameras start to roll?

Instead of saying "Action!" which I think is a silly way to start a scene, I say "Camera." Because if you're gonna do a quiet scene and you say "Action!"— oh, God, you should have seen some of the early directors, some of the silent directors over at Fox. There was one fellow who used to stand right under the camera, and he'd crouch as though he was going to spring at 'em. And he'd say, "Now is everybody ready? Are you ready? All right! *Number One!*" And then in the middle of the scene he'd say. *"Number Two! Three and Four!"*

When you're doing comedy, take after take after take, how do you keep it fresh?

I don't *let* them do take after take after take. If a person isn't good enough to do it, I just have somebody else walk in, or else I forget that scene and start on something else. I don't go back to it. I don't believe in getting myself tired out along with the actors. You just try and make a funny picture. If it isn't funny, you drop the thing. I think that when actors get to mumbling over lines so long, they get very bad, but if they just come out with it, they usually say the right thing. Brando started out as a great actor. I had a talk with him when he made a picture called *One-Eyed Jacks*. Paramount asked me if I could do anything to make it better, because they lost their shirt on it. He said, "Did you like it?" And I said, "No." He said, "Don't you think I'm a good actor?" I said, "You take much too long to do a scene." He slowed up until he got so dull that it drove me nuts, I couldn't stand watching him. But if you've got a good scene, you can let an actor stall and play with it. If it isn't a good scene, the quicker you get it over with the better you are. I work at about twenty percent faster speed than the average picture. When an actor does a scene, I say, "Do it in twenty seconds less and it'll be pretty good." And if they *don't* do it in twenty seconds less, then I cut it down to practically nothing and tell them to go ahead with it. Because it's just as good a scene, and it gets it over in a hurry. Actors get all confused. They stall in making scenes. It takes you a couple of days to get with them. They don't like to hop on somebody's lines. I would say, "If you *don't* hop on the line, I'll throw you out of here." So they hop on the line. The old school as far as theater goes is, "Don't speak over somebody's lines." I *want* them to speak over the lines. I want the sound man to tell me whether or not he can understand. If he can understand, that's fine.

It occurs to me that you are so much like some of the characters in your films. You have that same laconic wit.

I think I'm probably the worst actor that's ever been in a film. The first time I tried to do it, I stumbled and fell down. I can't remember a line.

It's sometimes said that a director can bludgeon an actor into giving a good performance.

I don't think that's true. . . .

Your attitude is basically comic, even in a tragic situation. For instance, Al

Capone [Scarface] *is not really a funny story, but you made a comedy out of it.*
Well, would you rather see something dead serious or laugh at something? In the first place, true drama is awfully close to being comedy. The greatest drama in the world is really funny. A man who loses his pants out in front of a thousand people—he's suffering the tortures of the damned, but he's awfully funny doing it. I had a damn good teacher, Chaplin. Probably our greatest comic. And everything he did was tragedy. He made things funny out of tragedy. I work a lot on that. I wanted to do *Don Quixote* with Cary Grant and Cantinflas, and people said, "But that isn't a comedy—that's a tragedy." I'd have to go into a long explanation. I think we could have a lot of fun with it. I think that Don Quixote's the basis really for the Chaplin character. Maybe we'll do it; I don't know. Before Cary gets too old or I get too old, we hope to do it.
Your movies have been compared to Buster Keaton's in some ways, for the visual sparsity, the lack of frills. Do you like Keaton's movies?
I like Keaton's. But Chaplin is the best of 'em all.
I would have thought you'd prefer Keaton, because Chaplin is very sentimental, and Keaton is sort of tough, like your characters.
Well, I couldn't do the sentimental type, and so I happen to like 'em better.
You're famous for taking a scene that has elements of pain and humiliation, such as the finger amputation in The Big Sky *or the "Who's Joe?" scene in* Only Angels Have Wings, *and either playing it lightly or for outright slapstick. Can you explain why you like to do something like that?*
You're looking for something new to be funny. The only time John Wayne ever objected to a scene was on our first picture, *Red River.* I said, "Duke, I've got a good idea. You get your finger caught between the rope and the saddle horn, and it's all smashed. You show it to Walter Brennan, and he says, 'That finger ain't gonna be much good to you.' And you say, 'No, I guess it isn't.' So Brennan calls for somebody and says, 'Stick an iron in the fire. Get a block of wood, and get a nice big jug of whiskey.' And they get you drunk, and they heat up the iron to cauterize the thing. Brennan starts sharpening his knife. Then we'll fuss around in there until somebody says, 'I think he's about ready for it.' And then they'll hold your finger over a chopping block, and cut if off. They say, 'He never even felt it.' And just when everything is very happy, why, you say, 'Where's my finger? A man oughta have his finger. He should be buried with it, whole.' And you all end up on your behinds looking in the ashes." He said, "You think that's *funny?*" "Oh," I said, "if you're not good enough then we won't do it. I'll do it sometime with somebody who's a better actor." So I did it with Kirk Douglas,

who is not as good an actor, but Kirk did it, and it was very funny. Duke saw it, and he told me, "If you tell me a funeral is funny I'll do a funeral." One of the best scenes that I ever made was in *Rio Bravo*. Wayne hit a fellow across the face the most horrible way. Dean Martin said, "Hey, take it easy." And Wayne said, "I'm not gonna hurt him." The audience thought it was funny. In *Rio Lobo*, we set a man on fire. He tries to hit Wayne with an oil lamp, and Wayne knocks him against a wall, and the lamp breaks, and the oil spills over him. He's burning, and somebody goes to pick up a blanket to put the thing out. Wayne says, "Let him burn." And the other fellow [Jack Elam] says, "Don't let him burn so much he can't sign the papers we want him to sign." And, I don't know, to me it was funny.

Why do you think it is?

I've seen so many people laugh at violence when it happens. Kind of hysterical laughter. It's the easiest time for you to get a laugh. I'm getting goddam sick of these pictures, you know, nothing but violence. Peckinpah and I believe in exactly the opposite thing. I like it when it's so quick that you say, "My God, did it really happen?" And it's much easier to get comedy if you don't start out trying to be funny. That's a particular theory of mine, that if people start a picture and they have a funny main title, a lot of funny things, it's as much as to say, "We expect you to laugh." I think that's committing suicide. They're going to go against it. So I start out and try to get their attention with a good dramatic sequence, and then find a place to start getting some laughs. We did that with *Rio Bravo*, we did that with *El Dorado*, and we did it very much with *Rio Lobo*. It starts off being *very* serious, and then before the audience realizes it, you're starting in having some fun. Look at *His Girl Friday*. It's the story of a poor little guy, an escaped murderer, and his girl commits suicide. Now, you can't tell anybody that you're gonna make a comedy about an escaped murderer. It has no relation to a comedy except for the way that Hecht and MacArthur treated the thing.

It's funny because it's done from the viewpoint of the reporters, who are not involved in the main action, at least initially. But if you were doing the story from the viewpoint of the escaped murderer, wouldn't it tend to be a tragedy then?

Oh, yes, it certainly would. It's all in the point of view.

Some of your comedies actually get pretty grim at times. Such as Bringing Up Baby *or* I Was a Male War Bride. *The predicaments the people get into become rather harrowing.* Bringing Up Baby, *particularly in the later scenes, is so dark photographically, it's lit almost like a tragedy.*

Well, it was pretty sad for Cary Grant going around on his hands and knees looking for a bone.

How do you write comic dialogue?

I don't use funny lines. They're not funny unless you see them. Some friends once came up to me and said they saw two of the greatest comics you've ever seen in your life—Rowan and Martin. So I went to see them expecting somebody funny. I didn't see anybody funny at all. All they had was a few funny lines. They'd been rehearsing those lines for two years. You can split an audience right down the middle, and half of them will laugh at one line and half at another; that isn't good enough. I can't remember ever using a funny line in a picture.

In your comedies, you always have the woman pursuing a very shy man. It's unusual on the screen to have men be so shy and women be so aggressive. Yet you were doing it in the 1920s and 1930s before that kind of thing was seen much in comedies.

You take a professor, and you use the girl's part to knock his dignity down— Katie Hepburn and Cary were a great combination [in *Bringing Up Baby*]. It's pretty hard to think of anybody but Cary Grant in that type of stuff. He was so far the best that there isn't anybody to be compared to him. But I can almost make you eat those words. In *His Girl Friday,* that was a battle from beginning to end; Rosalind Russell didn't have an easy job at all. He was giving her a really rough time. Even in the end of the picture, where they were going off very happily, she was having trouble carrying their luggage. He said, "Can't you do a better job of carrying that?" But I will admit that in most of the comedies, the woman had the dominant part. Because Cary is such a great receiver. He was so marvelous. We finally got so that I'd say, "Cary, this is a good chance to do Number Seven." Number Seven was trying to talk to a woman who was doing a lot of talking. We'd just do Number Seven. And he'd have to find variations on that. He and Hepburn were just great together. It was such a funny story, it was easy to be funny in it. I bought a short story written by a girl [Hagar Wilde]. I got the girl to come over, and she didn't know anything about pictures. But I wanted to keep exactly the same thought, that method of treating it. She had the characters for both Hepburn and Grant so well. So Dudley Nichols worked with her on the script. They worked right together. And he was awful good.

The scene you use in some of the comedies with Grant dressing up in women's clothing, such as when he wears the negligee in Bringing Up Baby, *was that done to humiliate the character to the utmost possible degree?*

The girl was playing a part of someone without a care in the world, and everything that she did got him farther and farther and farther into trouble. He stepped on her dress, he bitched up a golf game, she had a leopard—she just put him on a hook. It's logical that one of the craziest things was to put him in a woman's negligee. Anything we could do to humiliate him, to put him down and let her sail blithely along, made it what I thought was funny. I think it's fun to have a woman dominant and let the man be funniest. Katie and Rosalind Russell and Ann Sheridan in *I Was a Male War Bride* did their share in being funny, but they played much straighter and left the other stuff to Cary. . . .

How was Hepburn to work with on Bringing Up Baby?

We had trouble with Kate at first. The great trouble is people trying to be funny. If they don't try to be funny, then they are funny. I couldn't do any good with her, so I went over to an actor who was a comic for the Ziegfeld Follies and everything, Walter Catlett, and I said, "Walter, have you been watching Miss Hepburn?" He said, "Yeah." "Do you know what she's doing?" "Yeah." And I said, "Will you tell her?" He said, "No." "Well," I said, "supposing she asks you to tell her?" "Well, then I'll have to tell her." So I went over to Kate, and I said, "We're not getting along too well on this thing. I'm not getting through to you, but there's a man here who I think could. Do you want to talk to him?" She came back from talking with him and said, "Howard, hire that guy and keep him around here for several weeks, because I need him." And from that time on, she knew how to play comedy better, which is just to read lines. I can tell you another little story about Katie. Katie was making a lot of noise on the set one day, and we couldn't quiet her down. The assistant director called "Quiet!" a couple of times, and finally I motioned him, "Sit down here and watch." So Katie all of a sudden turned around and said, "What's the matter?" I said, "You're acting a good part of a parrot, and if you're going to keep on doing it, we'll just sit here and watch you." She said, "I want to talk to you." So we went behind the set and she said, "Howard, you can't talk that way to me. I've got a lot of friends here." I looked up on the scaffold at the electrician, and I said to him, "If you had the choice of dropping a lamp on Miss Hepburn or me, who would you drop it on?" And he said, "Get out of the way, Hepburn!" Katie was just marvelous. She said, "I guess I'm wrong." From that time on we got along beautifully, no trouble at all. They're great people.

Reviews

These three reviews—originally published in the *New York Times, Variety,* and *The New Republic*—indicate the range of original reponses to the film. Nugent's is an intellectual sneer, a contemptuous dismissal of a piece of mass entertainment to which he felt superior. Ironically, Nugent would move from journalism to Hollywood, where he would both write and direct films. Not one of his own projects ever achieved the distinction of *Bringing Up Baby.* The *Variety* review is a solid estimation of the film's commercial potential. Trade reviews in *Variety* frequently proved more accurate and more perceptive than reviews in journals and newspapers. The final review, by Otis Ferguson, appeared in the literate *New Republic,* where Ferguson worked as film critic before he was killed in World War II. Ferguson's review reveals his usual mix of intellectual sensitivity and movie sense.

New York Times
Frank S. Nugent

To the Music Hall yesterday came a farce which you can barely hear above the precisely enunciated patter of Miss Katharine Hepburn and the ominous tread of deliberative gags. In "Bringing Up Baby" Miss Hepburn has a role which calls for her to be breathless, senseless and terribly, terribly fatiguing. She succeeds, and we can be callous enough to hint it is not entirely a matter of performance.

And the gags! Have you heard the one about the trained leopard and the wild leopard who get loose at the same time? Or the one about the shallow brook with the deep hole? Or the one about the man wearing a woman's negligee? Or the one about the Irishman who drains his flask and sees a wild animal which really is a wild animal?

You have? Surprising. Indeed. But perhaps you haven't heard the one about the annoying little wirehaired terrier who makes off with a valuable object and buries it somewhere and has the whole cast on his heels. That one, too? Well then, how about the one where the man slips and sits on his top hat? Or the one where the heroine is trying to arouse a sleeper by tossing pebbles at his window and, just as he pokes his head out, hits him neatly with a bit of cobblestone? Or, getting back to the leopard who is the "baby" of the title, would you laugh madly if Charles Ruggles did a leopard-cry imitation as an after-dinner stunt and commented two minutes later upon the unusual echo?

Well, neither did we. In fact, after the first five minutes of the Music Hall's new show—we needed those five to orient ourselves—we were content to play the game called "the cliché expert goes to the movies" and we are not at all proud to report that we scored 100 per cent against Dudley Nichols, Hagar Wilde and Howard Hawks, who wrote and produced the quiz. Of course, if you've never been to the movies, "Bringing Up Baby" will be all new to you—a zany-ridden product of the goofy farce school. But who hasn't been to the movies?

From the *New York Times*, March 4, 1938.

Variety

"Wear"

This harum-scarum farce comedy is Katharine Hepburn's first of this type. Opposite her is Cary Grant, who is perfectly at home as a farceur after his work in "The Awful Truth." Picture is moulded along same lines and is definite box office.

"Bringing Up Baby" is constructed for maximum of laughs with Ruggles and Catlett adding to the starring team's zany antics. There is little rhyme or reason to most of the action, but it's all highly palatable.

Wacky developments include pursuit of an heiress after a zoology professor who expects to wed his femme assistant in the museum on the same day he plans to complete a giant brontosaurus; a pet leopard "Nissa" who makes a playmate of "Asta" the redoubtable Scotch terrier; a wealthy woman who may endow the prof's museum with $1,000,000; an escaped wild leopard from the circus; a stupid town constable; a forgettable ex-big game hunter; a scientifically-minded brain specialist; and a tippling gardener. Under Howard Hawks' skillful pacing it is an hilarious farce.

Katharine Hepburn, as the heiress who goes after her man once she spots him, contributes one of her most invigorating screen characterizations, as a madcap deb. Cary Grant, the zoology prof who thinks more of recovering the priceless missing bone for his uncompleted brontosaurus than his impending wedding and the companionship of the playful heiress performs his role to the hilt.

Ruggles, as the former African game hunter, does wonders with a minor characterization brought in late in picture. May Robson, obviously out of her element here, provides a few sober moments to the mad proceedings, being as effectual as ever. Catlett gives an expertly comic portrayal of the constable, Fritz Feld is the brain specialist and excellent support is furnished by Barry Fitzgerald, Tala Birell, John Kelly and the animal actors.

Hagar Wilde's story has been neatly scripted by himself [sic] and Dudley Nichols. Developments are paced by sizzling dialog. Chief shortcoming is that

From *Variety*, February 16, 1938.

too much time is consumed with the jail sequence. It diverts interest from the attempt to locate the missing pet leopard and dog. Prime reason for it, of course, is that it gives Miss Hepburn a chance to imitate a gunmoll.

Both Vernon Walter, with his special effects, and Russell Metty's photography are well up to the elaborate productions given the film.

The New Republic

Otis Ferguson

I n view of the heavy thought that has recently gone into the question Is Humor Best for Us? I am happy to report that *Bringing Up Baby* is funny from the word go, that it has no other meaning to recommend it, nor therapeutic quali- ties, and that I wouldn't swap it for practically any three things of the current season. For comedy to be really good, of course, there is required something more in the way of total design than any random collection of hilarities. There must be point—not *a* point to be *made,* which is the easy goal of any literary tortoise, but a point from which to start, as implicit throughout as the center of a circle. *Bringing Up Baby* has something of the sort. The actual story goes into the troubles of a paleontologist who first offends a prospective angel for his museum, then his fiancée, and then gets into the wild-goose affairs of a girl and her leopard and terrier and other family members, ending up in jail and of course in love. That could be done in two reels. What puts the dramatic spirit into it is the character of the harebrained young thing who gets him mixed up in all this.

Katharine Hepburn builds the part from the ground, breathless, sensitive, headstrong, triumphant in illogic, and serene in that bounding brassy nerve pos- sible only to the very very well bred. Without the intelligence and mercury of such a study, the callous scheming of this bit of fluff would have left all in confusion and the audience howling for her blood. As it is, we merely accept and humor her, as one would a wife. Cary Grant does a nice job of underlining the situation; there is good support from Barry Fitzgerald, Walter Catlett, May Rob- son (the leopard was better than any of them, but is it art?). The film holds together by virtue of constant invention and surprise in the situations; and Howard Hawks' direction, though it could have been less heavy and more supple, is essentially that of film comedy. All of which could be elaborated, techniques analyzed, points cited, etc. But why? *Bringing Up Baby* is hardly a departure; it settles nothing; it is full of an easy inviting humor. So do you want to go or don't you?

From *The New Republic*, March 2, 1938.

Commentaries

In the two decades following Hawks's retirement from filmmaking, intellectual and academic film critics addressed the very questions which his popular reviewers avoided when the films were released. Unlike Otis Ferguson, this later generation of critics wonders if *Bringing Up Baby* has some other "meaning to recommend it." These meanings tended to fit Hawks's films into respected and long-standing traditions of either filmmaking or storytelling in general. Hawks could be taken as representative of the *auteur,* the often invisible author who smuggled his own personal views, tastes, and ideas into the conventional assumptions of reigning Hollywood genres. Or Hawks could be shown to be borrowing and expanding upon the familiar devices of romantic comedy, descending from comedies that preceded the movies by centuries. Or Hawks could be shown to be a meticulous craftsman, like every master of playwriting and storytelling before him, disguising his craft beneath conventions that seemed either overly familiar or overly idiotic. Each of the essays that follows takes one of these paths.

The *Auteur* Theory

Peter Wollen

. . . The test case for the *auteur* theory is provided by the work of Howard Hawks. Why Hawks, rather than, say, Frank Borzage or King Vidor? Firstly, Hawks is a director who has worked for years within the Hollywood system. His first film, *Road to Glory,* was made in 1926. Yet throughout his long career he has only once received general critical acclaim, for his wartime film, *Sergeant York,* which closer inspection reveals to be eccentric and atypical of the main *corpus* of Hawks's films. Secondly, Hawks has worked in almost every genre. He has made westerns (*Rio Bravo*), gangsters (*Scarface*), war films (*Air Force*), thrillers (*The Big Sleep*), science fiction (*The Thing from Another World*), musicals (*Gentlemen Prefer Blondes*), comedies (*Bringing Up Baby*), even a Biblical epic (*Land of the Pharaohs*). Yet all of these films (except perhaps *Land of the Pharaohs,* which he himself was not happy about) exhibit the same thematic preoccupations, the same recurring motifs and incidents, the same visual style and tempo. In the same way that Roland Barthes constructed a species of *homo racinianus,* the critic can construct a *homo hawksianus,* the protagonist of Hawksian values in the problematic Hawksian world.

Hawks achieved this by reducing the genres to two basic types: the adventure drama and the crazy comedy. These two types express inverse views of the world, the positive and negative poles of the Hawksian vision. Hawks stands opposed, on the one hand, to John Ford and, on the other hand, to Budd Boetticher. All these directors are concerned with the problem of heroism. For the hero, as an individual, death is an absolute limit which cannot be transcended: it renders the life which preceded it meaningless, absurd. How then can there be any meaningful individual action during life? How can individual action have any value—be heroic—if it cannot have transcendent value, because of the absolutely devaluing limit of death? John Ford finds the answer to this question by placing and situating the individual within society and within history, specifically within American history. Ford finds transcendent values in the historic vocation of America as a nation, to bring civilisation to a savage land, the garden to the wilderness. At the same time, Ford also sees these values themselves as problematic; he begins to question the movement of American history itself. Boetticher, on the contrary, insists on a radical individualism. "I am not interested in making

From *Signs and Meaning in the Cinema* (Bloomington: Indiana University Press, 1969).

films about mass feelings. I am for the individual." He looks for values in the encounter with death itself: the underlying metaphor is always that of the bull-fighter in the arena. The hero enters a group of companions, but there is no possibility of group solidarity. Boetticher's hero acts by dissolving groups and collectives of any kind into their constituent individuals, so that he confronts each person face-to-face; the films develop, in Andrew Sarris's words, into "floating poker games, where every character takes turns at bluffing about his hand until the final showdown." Hawks, unlike Boetticher, seeks transcendent values beyond the individual, in solidarity with others. But, unlike Ford, he does not give his heroes any historical dimension, any destiny in time.

For Hawks the highest human emotion is the camaraderie of the exclusive, self-sufficient, all-male group. Hawks's heroes are cattlemen, marlin-fishermen, racing-drivers, pilots, big-game hunters, habituated to danger and living apart from society, actually cut off from it physically by dense forest, sea, snow or desert. Their aerodromes are fog-bound; the radio has cracked up; the next mail-coach or packet-boat does not leave for a week. The *élite* group strictly preserves its exclusivity. It is necessary to pass a test of ability and courage to win admittance. The group's only internal tensions come when one member lets the others down (the drunk deputy in *Rio Bravo,* the panicky pilot in *Only Angels Have Wings*) and must redeem himself by some act of exceptional bravery, or occasionally when too much 'individualism' threatens to disrupt the close-knit circle (the rivalry between drivers in *Red Line 7000,* the fighter pilot among the bomber crew in *Air Force*). The group's security is the first commandment: "You get a stunt team in acrobatics in the air—if one of them is no good, then they're all in trouble. If someone loses his nerve catching animals, then the whole bunch can be in trouble." The group members are bound together by rituals (in *Hatari!* blood is exchanged by transfusion) and express themselves univocally in communal sing-songs. There is a famous example of this in *Rio Bravo.* In *Dawn Patrol* the camaraderie of the pilots stretches even across the enemy lines: a captured German ace is immediately drafted into the group and joins in the sing-song; in *Hatari!* hunters of different nationality and in different places join together in a song over an intercom radio system.

Hawks's heroes pride themselves on their professionalism. They ask: "How good is he? He'd better be good." They expect no praise for doing their job well. Indeed, none is given except: 'The boys did all right.' When they die, they leave behind them only the most meagre personal belongings, perhaps a handful of medals. Hawks himself has summed up this desolate and barren view of life:

It's just a calm acceptance of a fact. In *Only Angels Have Wings,* after Joe
dies, Cary Grant says: "He just wasn't good enough." Well, that's the only
thing that keeps people going. They just have to say: "Joe wasn't good
enough, and I'm better than Joe, so I go ahead and do it." And they find
out they're not any better than Joe, but then it's too late, you see.

In Ford films, death is celebrated by funeral services, an impromptu prayer, a few
staves of "Shall we gather at the river?"—it is inserted into an ongoing system of
ritual institutions, along with the wedding, the dance, the parade. But for Hawks
it is enough that the routine of the group's life goes on, a routine whose only
relieving features are "danger" (*Hatari!*) and "fun." Danger gives existence
pungency: "Every time you get real action, then you have danger. And the question, 'Are you living or not living?' is probably the biggest drama we have." This
nihilism, in which 'living' means no more than being in danger of losing your
life—a danger entered into quite gratuitously—is augmented by the Hawksian
concept of having "fun." The word "fun" crops up constantly in Hawks's interviews and scripts. It masks his despair.

When one of Hawks's *élite* is asked, usually by a woman, why he risks his
life, he replies: "No reason I can think of makes any sense. I guess we're just
crazy." Or Feathers, sardonically, to Colorado in *Rio Bravo:* "You haven't even
the excuse I have. We're all fools." By "crazy" Hawks does not mean psycho-
pathic: none of his characters are like Turkey in Peckinpah's *The Deadly Companions* or Billy the Kid in Penn's *The Left-Handed Gun.* Nor is there the sense
of the absurdity of life which we sometimes find in Boetticher's films: death, as
we have seen, is for Hawks simply a routine occurrence, not a *grotesquerie,* as in
The Tall T ('Pretty soon that well's going to be chock-a-block') or *The Rise and
Fall of Legs Diamond.* For Hawks "craziness" implies difference, a sense of
apartness from the ordinary, everyday, social world. At the same time, Hawks
sees the ordinary world as being "crazy" in a much more fundamental sense,
because devoid of any meaning or values. "I mean crazy reactions—I don't think
they're crazy, I think they're normal—but according to bad habits we've fallen
into they seemed crazy." Which is the normal, which the abnormal? Hawks
recognises, inchoately, that to most people his heroes, far from embodying ra-
tional values, are only a dwindling band of eccentrics. Hawks's 'kind of men'
have no place in the world.

The Hawksian heroes, who exclude others from their own *élite* group, are
themselves excluded from society, exiled to the African bush or to the Arctic.

Outsiders, other people in general, are perceived by the group as an undifferentiated crowd. Their role is to gape at the deeds of the heroes whom, at the same time, they hate. The crowd assembles to watch the showdown in *Rio Bravo*, to see the cars spin off the track in *The Crowd Roars*. The gulf between the outsider and the heroes transcends enmities among the *élite*: witness *Dawn Patrol* or Nelse in *El Dorado*. Most dehumanised of all is the crowd in *Land of the Pharaohs*, employed in building the Pyramids. Originally the film was to have been about Chinese labourers building a "magnificent airfield" for the American army, but the victory of the Chinese Revolution forced Hawks to change his plans. ("Then I thought of the building of the Pyramids; I thought it was the same kind of story.") But the presence of the crowd, of external society, is a constant covert threat to the Hawksian *élite*, who retaliate by having "fun." In the crazy comedies ordinary citizens are turned into comic butts, lampooned and tormented: the most obvious target is the insurance salesman in *His Girl Friday*. Often Hawks's revenge becomes grim and macabre. In *Sergeant York* it is "fun" to shoot Germans "like turkeys"; in *Air Force* it is "fun" to blow up the Japanese fleet. In *Rio Bravo* the geligniting of the badmen "was very funny." It is at these moments that the *élite* turns against the world outside and takes the opportunity to be brutal and destructive.

Besides the covert pressure of the crowd outside, there is also an overt force which threatens: woman. Man is woman's "prey." Women are admitted to the male group only after much disquiet and a long ritual courtship, phased round the offering, lighting and exchange of cigarettes, during which they prove themselves worthy of entry. Often they perform minor feats of valour. Even then though they are never really full members. A typical dialogue sums up their position:

> *Woman*: You love him, don't you?
> *Man* (embarrassed): Yes . . . I guess so. . . .
> *Woman*: How can I love him like you?
> *Man*: Just stick around.

The undercurrent of homosexuality in Hawks's films is never crystallised, though in *The Big Sky*, for example, it runs very close to the surface. And he himself described *A Girl in Every Port* as "really a love story between two men." For Hawks men are equals, within the group at least, whereas there is a clear identification between women and the animal world, most explicit in *Bringing Up Baby*, *Gentlemen Prefer Blondes* and *Hatari!* Man must strive to maintain his mastery.

It is also worth noting that, in Hawks's adventure dramas and even in many of his comedies, there is no married life. Often the heroes were married or at least intimately committed, to a woman at some time in the distant past but have suffered an unspecified trauma, with the result that they have been suspicious of women ever since. Their attitude is "Once bitten, twice shy." This is in contrast to the films of Ford, which almost always include domestic scenes. Woman is not a threat to Ford's heroes; she falls into her allotted social place as wife and mother, bringing up the children, cooking, sewing, a life of service, drudgery and subordination. She is repaid for this by being sentimentalised. Boetticher, on the other hand, has no obvious place for women at all; they are phantoms, who provoke action, are pretexts for male modes of conduct, but have no authentic significance in themselves. "In herself, the woman has not the slightest importance."

Hawks sees the all-male community as an ultimate; obviously it is very retrograde. His Spartan heroes are, in fact, cruelly stunted. Hawks would be a lesser director if he was unaffected by this, if his adventure dramas were the sum total of his work. His real claim as an author lies in the presence, together with the dramas, of their inverse, the crazy comedies. They are the agonised exposure of the underlying tensions of the heroic dramas. There are two principal themes, zones of tension. The first is the theme of regression: of regression to childhood, infantilism, as in *Monkey Business*, or regression to savagery: witness the repeated scene of the adult about to be scalped by painted children, in *Monkey Business* and in *The Ransom of Red Chief*. With brilliant insight, Robin Wood has shown how *Scarface* should be categorised among the comedies rather than the dramas: Camonte is perceived as savage, child-like, subhuman. The second principal comedy theme is that of sex-reversal and role-reversal. *I Was A Male War Bride* is the most extreme example. Many of Hawks's comedies are centred round domineering women and timid, pliable men: *Bringing Up Baby* and *Man's Favorite Sport*, for example. There are often scenes of male sexual humiliation, such as the trousers being pulled off the hapless private eye in *Gentlemen Prefer Blondes*. In the same film, the Olympic Team of athletes are reduced to passive objects in an extraordinary Jane Russell song number; big-game hunting is lampooned, like fishing in *Man's Favorite Sport;* the theme of infantilism crops up again: "The child was the most mature one on board the ship, and I think he was a lot of fun."

Whereas the dramas show the mastery of man over nature, over woman, over the animal and childish; the comedies show his humiliation, his regression. The heroes become victims; society, instead of being excluded and despised, breaks in with irruptions of monstrous farce. It could well be argued that Hawks's outlook, the alternative world which he constructs in the cinema, the Hawksian heterocosm, is not one imbued with particular intellectual subtlety or sophistication. This does not detract from its force. Hawks first attracted attention because he was regarded naïvely as an action director. Later, the thematic content which I have outlined was detected and revealed. Beyond the stylemes, semantemes were found to exist; the films were anchored in an objective stratum of meaning, a plerematic stratum, as the Danish linguist Hjelmslev would put it. Thus the stylistic expressiveness of Hawks's films was shown to be not purely contingent, but grounded in significance.

Something further needs to be said about the theoretical basis of the kind of schematic exposition of Hawks's work which I have outlined. The 'structural approach' which underlies it, the definition of a core of repeated motifs, has evident affinities with methods which have been developed for the study of folklore and mythology. In the work of Olrik and others, it was noted that in different folk-tales the same motifs reappeared time and time again. It became possible to build up a lexicon of these motifs. Eventually Propp showed how a whole cycle of Russian fairy-tales could be analysed into variations of a very limited set of basic motifs (or moves, as he called them). Underlying the different, individual tales was an archi-tale, of which they were all variants. One important point needs to be made about this type of structural analysis. There is a danger, as Lévi-Strauss has pointed out, that by simply noting and mapping resemblances, all the texts which are studied (whether Russian fairy-tales or American movies) will be reduced to one, abstract and impoverished. There must be a moment of synthesis as well as a moment of analysis: otherwise, the method is formalist, rather than truly structuralist. Structuralist criticism cannot rest at the perception of resemblances or repetitions (redundancies, in fact), but must also comprehend a system of differences and oppositions. In this way, texts can be studied not only in their universality (what they all have in common) but also in their singularity (what differentiates them from each other). This means of course that the test of a structural analysis lies not in the orthodox canon of a director's work, where resemblances are clustered, but in films which at first sight may seem eccentricities.

In the films of Howard Hawks a systematic series of oppositions can be seen very near the surface, in the contrast between the adventure dramas and the crazy comedies. If we take the adventure dramas alone it would seem that Hawks's work is flaccid, lacking in dynamism; it is only when we consider the crazy comedies that it becomes rich, begins to ferment: alongside every dramatic hero we are aware of a phantom, stripped of mastery, humiliated, inverted. With other directors, the system of oppositions is much more complex: instead of there being two broad strata of films there are a whole series of shifting variations. In these cases, we need to analyse the roles of the protagonists themselves, rather than simply the worlds in which they operate. The protagonists of fairy-tales or myths, as Lévi-Strauss has pointed out, can be dissolved into bundles of differential elements, pairs of opposites. Thus the difference between the prince and the goose-girl can be reduced to two antinomic pairs: one natural, male versus female, and the other cultural, high versus low. We can proceed with the same kind of operation in the study of films, though, as we shall see, we shall find them more complex than fairy-tales. . . .

Leopards in Connecticut

Stanley Cavell

[It] opens in a museum of natural history where an absent-minded professor (Cary Grant) is trying to finish his reconstruction of the skeleton of a brontosaurus. Standing as it were before the curtain, he finds out, or is reminded of, five or six things: that the expedition has just found the crucial bone, the intercostal clavicle, to complete the skeleton; that he is getting married tomorrow to his assistant, Miss Swallow; that after their wedding there will be no honeymoon; that the reconstructed skeleton will be their child; that he has an appointment to play golf with a Mr. Peabody and discuss a donation of a million dollars to the museum; and that he is to remember who and what he is. Call this Prologue the first sequence. There is a natural breakdown into ten further sequences. (2) On a golf course, the professor is drawn from his game and conversation with Mr. Peabody by a young woman (Katharine Hepburn) who first plays his golf ball and then dents and rends his car unparking it, amused at his claim that she has made a mistake and that the car, too, belongs to him, and then drives off with it while he is hanging onto its side as perhaps the bull did with Europa. The sequence ends with his yelling back for the third or fourth time: "I'll be with you in a minute, Mr. Peabody." (3) At night, in the restaurant of some Ritz Hotel; Grant slips on an olive dropped by Hepburn and sits on his hat on the floor. Their argument is resumed concerning who is following whom. After further parapraxes, each rips open part of the other's clothing: she splits the tails of his swallow-tail coat up the back and he rips off the back of the skirt of her evening dress. He walks out behind her, guiding her, to cover what he's done (not, however, what he's doing). As he does so, Mr. Peabody appears again, with whom he again had an appointment, and again he says, "I'll be with you in a minute, Mr. Peabody." (4) In her apartment Hepburn sews Grant's tails, after which they set out to find Mr. Peabody, whom she knows and whom she throws stones at after giving Grant his second drive around. They are on a first-name basis by now. David tells Susan that he's getting married tomorrow. (5) The prehistoric bone is delivered to Grant's apartment and he rushes to hers, the bone in a box under his arm, to save

From *Pursuits of Happiness: The Hollywood Comedy of Remarriage* (Cambridge, Mass.: Harvard University Press, 1981).

her from a leopard, who turns out to be Baby, a tame present from her brother. Susan and Baby arrange that the leopard is not to be Susan's problem alone. (6) Driving Baby to Susan's house in Connecticut, they hit a truck of fowls, buy thirty pounds of raw meat, and Susan steals, this time quite consciously, another car. (7) At the house, Susan does not rip David's clothes off but steals them while he is showering. So David puts on Susan's negligee, and later is discovered in bits of her brother's riding habit, which is appropriate since they soon have to hunt for something rare and precious, the bone which the dog George has taken from the box on the bed. David says to Susan's aunt (May Robson) that he went gay all of a sudden. He learns that the aunt is the potential donor of the million and that Susan expects to inherit it. He asks Susan most earnestly not to tell her aunt who he is. Susan tells her that he's had a nervous breakdown and that his name is Bone, and that is what the aunt tells her friend the major (Charles Ruggles) who appears for dinner. (8) The four are at dinner during which David stalks George. The major gives the mating cry of the leopard, which is answered. He asks, "Are there leopards in Connecticut?" (9) Baby escapes, George disappears, and David and Susan spend most of the night exploring the woods. Susan enjoys it. They are captured, she by a recurring psychiatrist, he by a recurring sheriff. (10) They are behind bars; eventually most of the household is, from trying to identify them. Susan talks her way out of her cell, then out a window, to get the proof that there really is a leopard in Connecticut. She returns dragging a circus leopard behind her, whom we know to be a killer. David does what he once ran to her apartment to do—saves her from a wild beast. (11) In the Epilogue, back in daylight at the museum, Susan shows up, having recovered the bone and inherited the money. Running up high ladders, they talk across the back of the brontosaurus; he says he thinks he loves her. He rescues her again as she has jumped from her swaying ladder onto the brontosaurus pulling her by one arm up to his ledge as the skeleton collapses under her weight. They embrace.

At some point it becomes obvious that the surface of the dialogue and action of *Bringing Up Baby*, their mode of construction, is a species of more or less blatant and continuous double entendre. The formal signal of its presence in the dialogue is the habitual *repetition* of lines or words, sometimes upon the puzzlement of the character to whom the line is addressed, as though he or she cannot have heard it correctly, sometimes as a kind of verbal tic, as though a character has not heard, or meant, his own words properly. I qualify this presence of doubleness thus heavily (calling it a "species" and claiming that it is "more or less blatant") for two reasons.

(1) While an explicit discussion, anyway an open recognition, of the film's obsessive sexual references is indispensable to saying what I find the film to be about, I am persistently reluctant to make it very explicit. Apart from more or less interesting risks of embarrassment (for example, of seeming too perverse or being too obvious), there are causes for this reluctance having to do with what I understand the point of this sexual glaze to be. It is part of the force of this work that we shall not know how far to press its references.

At some juncture the concept and the fact of the contended bone will of course threaten to take over. (Its mythical name, the intercostal clavicle, suggests that it belongs to creatures whose heads are beneath their shoulders, or anyway whose shoulders are beneath at least some of their ribs.) This threat will occur well before the long recitative and duet on the subject (beginning with Grant's thunderous discovery of the empty box and the lines "Where's my intercostal clavicle?" "Your *what?*" "My intercostal clavicle. My bone. It's rare; it's precious," and continuing with Hepburn's appeal to the dog: "George. George. David and Susan need that bone. It's David's bone"; hence well before the quartet on the words "Mr. Bone," a title that both claims Grant as the very personification of the subject at issue (as someone may be called Mr. Boston or Mr. Structuralism) and suggests, pertinently, that he is an end man in a minstrel show.

By the close of the sequence in the restaurant, the concept and the fact of the behind will be unignorable. Neither the bone nor the behind will give us pause, on a first viewing, in Grant's opening line, the second line of the film: gazing fixedly down at a bone in his hand he says: "I think this one must belong in the tail." His assistant, Miss Swallow, corrects or reminds him: "You tried it in the tail yesterday." That we are not given pause on a first viewing means both that this film is not made for just one viewing and also that this early line works well enough if it underscores the plain fact that this man is quite lost in thought, and prepares us for amazement when we discover what it is he is lost in thinking about, and for discovering that his preoccupation is the basis of the events to come. This is not asking too much. The broad attitude of this comedy is struck at once, at Miss Swallow's opening line, "Sh-h-h. Dr. Huxley is thinking," as the camera rises to discover Cary Grant in the pose of Rodin's *The Thinker*, a statue already the subject of burlesque and caricature. (The rightness in its being Cary Grant who takes this pose is a special discovery of Howard Hawks's about Grant's filmic presence, his photogenesis, what it is the camera makes of him. What Grant is thinking, and that what he is doing is thinking, is as much the subject of *His Girl Friday* as it is of the time he reverts to playing professor, in *Monkey Business*.)

Then are we to pause over the lines stated by Grant to Hepburn when they discover that Baby has escaped?: "Don't lose your head." "My *what?*" "Your head." "I've got my head; I've lost my leopard." And how much are we to do with Hepburn's line, genuinely alarmed, to Grant as he is trying to cover her from behind in the restaurant? "Hey. Fixation or no fixation . . . Will you stop doing that with your hat?" (What does she think he is doing and what does she think he should be doing it with?) And we are to gasp as Hepburn, in the last scene before the Epilogue, in jail, drops what she calls her "society moniker" and puts on a society woman's version—or a thirties movie version—of a gun moll, drawling out, in close-up: "Lemme outta here and I'll unbutton my puss and shoot the works." I say we do not know how far to press such references, and this is meant to characterize a certain anxiety in our comprehension throughout, an anxiety that our frequent if discontinuous titters may at any moment be found inappropriate. If it is undeniable that we are invited by these events to read them as sexual allegory, it is equally undeniable that what Hepburn says, as she opens the box and looks inside, is true: "It's just an old bone." Clearly George agrees with her. The play between the literal and the allegorical determines the course of this narrative, and provides us with contradicting directions in our experience of it.

(2) The threat of inappropriateness goes with a slightly different cause of my reluctance to be explicit, namely that the characters are themselves wholly unconscious of the doubleness in their meaning. This is a familiar source of comic effect. But so is its opposite. In particular, the effect here contrasts specifically with Shakespearean exchanges in double entendre, where the characters are fully conscious of the other side of their words. The similarity between our characters and comparable ones in Shakespeare is that the women in his plays are typically virgins and the men typically clowns. They are, that is to say, figures who are not yet (or by nature not) incorporated into the normal social world of law and appropriateness and marriage and of consonant limitations in what we call maturity and adulthood.

The critical problem in approaching these characters, or the problem in describing them, can then be put this way: If we do not note the other side of their words and actions, then we shall never understand them, we shall not know why the one is in a trance and the other in madcap. But if we do note the other side of their words and actions, we shall lose our experience of them as individuals, we shall not see their exercises of consciousness. We have neither to know them nor to fail to know them, neither to objectivize nor to subjectivize them. It is a way of defining the epistemological problem of other minds.

Let us note some further features of the world of this film that there should be no reluctance or difficulty in making explicit. Not surprisingly, given that the film is some kind of comedy, it ends with a marriage, anyway with a promise of marriage, a young pair having overcome certain obstacles to this conclusion. Apart from these central characters, we have a cast of humors—an exasperated aunt; a pedant (in the guise, not uncommon in Hollywood films, of a psychiatrist); a sexless zany who talks big-game hunting; an omni-incompetent sheriff; a drunken retainer—none of whom can act beyond their humorous repetitions. The exposition of the drama takes place, roughly, in the town, and is both complicated and settled in a shift to the countryside. It carefully alternates between day and night and climaxes around about midnight.

Are we beginning to assemble features whose combination, could we find their laws, would constitute a dramatic genre? And should such a genre be called "a Hollywood comedy"? This seems unpromising. Not all the considerable comedies made in Hollywood will contain even the features so far mentioned; and the label hardly captures our intuition that the mood, to go no further, of this film is quite special. Yet Northrop Frye, in an early statement of his work on comedy, allows himself to say: "The average movie of today [he is writing in 1948] is a rigidly conventionalized New Comedy proceeding toward an act which, like death in Greek tragedy, takes place offstage, and is symbolized by the final embrace." This is a nice example of academic humor, and strikes a conventional note of complacency toward movies in general. But is it true?

I cannot speak of the "average movie" of 1948 or of any other time, but of the Hollywood comedies I remember and at the moment care most about, it is true of almost none of them that they conclude with an embrace, if that means they conclude with a shot of the principal characters kissing. It is, in particular, not the way the other members of our genre conclude.

So let us not speak hastily and loosely of final embraces and happy endings. There are few festivals here. The concluding moments I have cited are as carefully prepared and dramatically conclusive (if, or because, fictionally inconclusive) as the closing of an aphorism, and it may be essential to a certain genre of film comedy that this should be so.

Bringing Up Baby, it happens, does conclude with an embrace, anyway with some kind of clinch. It is notably awkward; one cannot determine whether the pair's lips are touching. And it takes place on the platform of a work scaffold, where the film began, and in the aftermath of a collapsing reconstructed skeleton of a brontosaurus. What act does *all* of this symbolize? The collapsing of the skeleton poses the obvious discomfort in this conclusion, or shadow on its happiness. One is likely to ask whether it is necessary, or positively to assert that it is not. Is it meant to register the perimeter of human happiness, or the happenstance of it—like the breaking of the glass at the end of a Jewish wedding? Both surely comment upon the demise of virginity, but in this film it is the woman who directly causes it. Perhaps, then, our question should be, not whether it is necessary, but how it is that this man, afterwards, can still want to embrace. Are we to imagine that his admission of love requires that he no longer care about his work? Or can we see that he finally feels equal to its disruption and capable of picking up the pieces?

It should help us to recognize that the pose of the final clinch—something that to me accounts for its specific awkwardness—is a reenactment of a second popular statue of Rodin's, *The Kiss;* a concluding *tableau vivant* to match the opening one.—So what? Are we accordingly to conclude that the opening man of stone after all retreats into stone? But surely the intervening events have produced some human progress, or some progress toward the human? At least he now has company. The isolation of the scaffold has emphatically become the isolation of a pedestal. It looms so large and shadowy in the final shot as to mock the tiny figures mounted on it. Surely they will make it down to earth?—How did they get up there? It started as Hepburn entered the museum holding the recovered bone, upon which Grant instinctively ran up the scaffold—perhaps *in order* to be followed up. In any case he does at least acknowledge, over the skeleton, that he ran because he is afraid of her, which prepares his declaration of love. So he, or his prehistoric instinct, was as much the cause of the collapse of science as she was; as much the cause of its collapse as of its construction.

The issue of who is following whom presides over their relationship from its inception. At the end of the first scene, on the golf course, he responds to her accusation by denying that he is following her, and in the conventional sense he is not; but it cannot be denied that literally he is. Whereupon she gallops off with him. (She does this again later, and again in a stolen chariot, after their stop in Connecticut to buy food for Baby.) At the close of the restaurant sequence, their walk-off—the man leading the woman yet following her pace, as in some dream tango, dog fashion—identifies the issue of who is following whom with the matter of who is behind whom, which remains thematic in subsequent scenes. Notably, as the two are hunting through the night woods for Baby, Grant with a rope and a croquet mallet, Hepburn with a butterfly net, he turns around to discover her on all fours (she is trying to avoid his wake of branches swinging in her face) and he says, "This is no time to be playing squat-tag"; she replies that she is not playing and, upon asking whether she shouldn't go first, is told, "Oh no. You might get hurt." The question of who belongs where reaches its climax inside the jailhouse in the last scene before the Epilogue. We will get to that.

I have suggested that the work of the romance of remarriage is designed to avoid the distinction between Old and New Comedy and that this means to me that it poses a structure in which we are permanently in doubt who the hero is, that is, whether it is the male or the female, who is the active partner, which of them is in quest, who is following whom. A working title for this structure might be "the comedy of equality," evoking laughter equally at the idea that men and women are different *and* at the idea that they are not. The most explicit conclusion of this theme among the films I can recognize as of this genre is arrived at in *Adam's Rib*. Once more we are in the expensive Connecticut countryside; once more the pair is alone. And we are given what sounds like a twice-told, worn-out joke. Tracy says: Vive la différence. Hepburn asks: What does that mean? Tracy replies: It means, Hooray for that little difference. Then they climb behind the curtains of a fourposter bed and the film concludes. If what I have claimed about the conclusions of such films is correct, then a film so resourceful and convincing as *Adam's Rib* cannot vanish on the sounding of a stale joke. And it does not. It vanishes with a joke on this joke. It is not conceivable that this woman—to whom Tracy had cracked earlier, when she was turning on a superior note, "Oh. Giving me the old Bryn Mawr business, eh?"—it is not conceivable that this woman does not know what the French words mean. She is asking solemnly, what difference is meant by that little difference. So it is upon the repetition of a question, not upon the provision of an answer, that they climb together out of sight into bed, with, surrealistically, their hats on. (How their hats get put on makes a nice story. Her putting hers on is a reacceptance of an important and intimate present from him. His putting his on acknowledges that hers is on. He puts his on without thinking, as another man would take his off in the presence of a lady. This pair is inventing gallantry between one another.)

The equality of laughter at the idea of difference is enough to ensure that, unlike the case of classical comedies, there can in general be no new social reconciliation at these conclusions, for society does not regard the difference between men and women as the topic of a metaphysical argument; it takes itself to know what the difference means. So the principal pair in this structure will normally draw the conclusion on their own, isolated within society, not backed by it. The comedy of equality is a comedy of privacy, evoking equal laughter at the fact that they are, and are not, alone. In particular, the older generation will not be present. Where this rule seems to be infringed, say in *The Philadelphia Story*, the moment is radically undercut; we are ripped from our supposed presence at this wedding festival by being shown that we are looking at a gossip shot—one way of looking at a movie—giving us the sort of inside knowledge that merely underlines our position as members of an outside public. Contrariwise, the pull of the private conclusion can mislead a director into supposing that his picture has earned it. I am thinking of Cukor's *Holiday*, which he concludes with a kiss. This conclusion feels wrong, feels like violation, every way you look at it—from Grant's point of view, from Hepburn's, but especially from the point of view of their older friends, a couple who in this case, themselves being shown out of sympathy with the conventional world, have provided an alternative social world for this young pair and who therefore deserve to be present, whose presence therefore feels required. I mention this in passing partly to enlist another item of evidence for investigating the idea of the final embrace, but also to suggest that the wrongness of this conclusion cannot be accounted for by appealing to a lack in the psychological development of the characters (their development is complete), nor excused by appealing to a general movie convention of the final embrace, first of all because there is no such general convention, and second, and more important, because the wrongness in question consists in breaking the structure of this narrative.

Is there present a definite structure of the kind I have named the comedy of equality? And if there is, what has it to do with the thematic or systematic allegory in *Bringing Up Baby?* How does it help us to understand who or what Baby is, and where a Baby belongs, and where a Baby comes from?

I might bypass my intuition of a definite structure in force here and directly seek an interpretation of the mode of sexuality in play, in particular, of the ambivalence or instability in it: the situation between this pair cannot remain as it is. Here I would wish to put together the following facts: first, the texture of certain speeches and actions that I have noted as a play between their literal and their allegorical potentialities; second, the sense that the principals' actions consist of, or have the quality of, a series of games (from actual golfing, to rock-throwing at the windows of the rich, to various species of follow-the-leader and hide-and-seek, to playing dress-up and playing house, to finding the hidden object, all framed by pinning the tail on the brontosaurus); third, the fact that the female of the pair likes the games whereas the male plays unwillingly and is continuously humiliated by their progress; fourth, the mystery of their behavior to everyone around them (to Mr. Peabody, from before whose eyes Grant is continually disappearing; to the man's fiancée and to the woman's aunt and to the aunt's major and her cook's husband; to the psychiatrist and the sheriff; and even to the butcher from whom Grant orders thirty pounds of meat for Baby to eat raw).

Such facts add up to a representation of a particular childhood world, to that stage of childhood preceding puberty, the period Freud calls latency, in which childish sexual curiosity has been repressed until the onset of new physiological demands, or instincts, reawakens it. In this film we are attempting to cross the limit of this stage, one whose successful and healthy negotiation demands a satisfaction of this reawakened curiosity, a stage at which the fate of one's intelligence, or ability and freedom to think, will be settled. This stage is confirmed by the air of innocence and secrecy between the two; by the obviousness of the sexuality implied, or rather by the puzzles of sexuality seeming to concern merely its most basic mechanics; and by the perception we are given of the humorous collection of figures surrounding them, a perception of these figures as, one might simply say, grown-ups—not exactly mysterious, yet foreign, asexual, grotesque in their unvarying routines, the source primarily of unearned money and of unmerited prohibitions.

This representation of this period implies two obstacles in the way of this pair's achieving some satisfactory conclusion in relation to one another and to the world, a conclusion both refer to as "marriage." Or, two questions stand in the way of the man's awakening from his entrancement ("I can't seem to move") and of the woman's doffing her madcap ("I just did whatever came into my head"). One question is: If adulthood is the price of sexual happiness, is the price fair? If the grown-ups we see around us represent the future in store for us, why should we ever leave childhood? A second question is: If virginity at some point becomes humiliating and laughable, then why must departing from it be humiliating and laughable? Why are the vaunted pleasures of sexuality so ludicrous and threatening? In the middle of their chase through the woods, they come upon Baby and George growling and rolling in one another's arms on a clear, moonlit patch of ground. Thus seeing themselves, the female is relieved ("Oh look. They like one another"—but she had earlier said that she doesn't know whether, having been told that Baby likes dogs, that means that he is fond of them or eats them); the male is not happy ("In another minute my intercostal clavicle will be gone forever"). I think it would be reasonable, along such lines, to regard the cause of this comedy as the need, and the achievement, of laughter at the physical requirements of wedded love, or, at the romance of marriage; laughter at the realization that after more than two millennia of masterpieces on the subject, we still are not clear why, or to what extent, marriage is thought to justify sexual satisfaction. (That such comedies are no longer made perhaps means that we have given up on this problem, or publicized it to death.) Accordingly, we should regard the midsummer's eve in the Connecticut forest not as the preparation for a wedding ceremony but as an allegory of the wedding night, or a dream of that night. Grant, sensing his entrancement, at one point almost declares himself asleep: "What I've been doing today I could have done with my eyes shut." (At the beginning of the end of the Ritz sequence, he had said: "Let's play a game. I'll close my eyes and count to ten and you go away.") And just before they discover Baby's escape and leave for the woods, he behaves as if he is walking in his sleep, rising stiffly from the dinner table and following George out of the house, his soupspoon still in his hand, stopped in midair on the way to his mouth.

But while I find such considerations pertinent, they seem to me to leave out too much, in particular they do not account for the beginning and the ending of this narrative, for why just this couple finds just these obstacles on their road to marriage. More particularly, they do not account for the overall drive of the plot, which appears to be a story not of a man seeking marriage but of a man seeking extrication, divorce. One might say that according to this plot he is seeking extrication from Hepburn in order to meet his engagement with Miss Swallow. But that hardly matches our experience of these events, which could just as well be described, attending to the introductory sequence, as his attempt to extricate himself from Miss Swallow, who promises him, or threatens him with, a marriage that, as she puts it, must "entail [that word again] no domestic entanglements *of any kind*." Upon which promise, or threat, he leaves to seek his fortune.

The film, in short, poses a question concerning the validation of marriage, the reality of its bonding, as that question is posed in the genre of remarriage comedy. Its answer participates in, or contributes its particular temperament to, the answer of that structure—that the validity of marriage takes a willingness for repetition, the willingness for remarriage. The task of the conclusion is to get the pair back into a particular moment of their past lives together. No new vow is required, merely the picking up of an action which has been, as it were, interrupted; not starting over, but starting again, finding and picking up the thread. Put a bit more metaphysically: only those can genuinely marry who are already

married. It is as though you know you are married when you come to see that you
cannot divorce, that is, when you find that your lives simply will not disentangle.
If your love is lucky, this knowledge will be greeted with laughter.

   Bringing Up Baby shares, or exaggerates, two of the features of this structure.
First, it plots love-making in the form of aborted leavetaking. It adds to this,
more particularly, the comic convention according to which the awakening of
love causes the male to lapse into trances and to lose control of his body, in
particular to be everywhere in danger of falling down or of breaking things. *The
Lady Eve* contains, as we saw, another virtuoso treatment of this convention.
And even Spencer Tracy, whom it is hard to humiliate, is asked by the genre to
suffer these indignities. Second, it harps upon repetition. Beyond the texture of
verbal repetitions and the beginning and ending *tableaux vivants,* and beyond the
two "I'll be with you in a minute, Mr. Peabody" exits, and the two kidnappings
in stolen cars, and the two scenes of serenade under the second-story windows of
respectable houses, and two golf balls and two convertible coupés and two purses
and two bones and two bent hats, there is the capping discovery that there are two
leopards in Connecticut. My idea, then, is that this structure is to be understood
as an interpretation of the genre of remarriage in the following way: the principals accept the underlying perception that marriage requires its own proof, that
nothing can show its validity from outside; and its comedy consists in their attempts to understand, perhaps to subvert, to extricate themselves from, the necessity of the initial leap, to move directly into a state of reaffirmation. It is as
though their summer night were spent not in falling in love at first or second
sight, but in becoming childhood sweethearts, inventing for themselves a shared,
lost past, to which they can wish to remain faithful. (Among the other, nonex-
clusive, perceptions of their final setting, it can be read as a tree house or a crib.)
It is a kind of prehistoric reconstruction. That this must fail is not exactly funny.
Grant, in particular, never smiles.

   The concluding tableau is a repetition, or interpretation, not alone of the opening shot of Grant, but of the image upon which the final scene (preceding the
Epilogue) had closed. There Grant faces the second leopard, the wild one, the
killer, using correctly this time an appropriate implement, a tamer's tool before
him, and coaxes the beast into a cage, or rather a cell; it is, as it happens, the
particular cell in which Hepburn had been locked. In this final game (playing
tamer and rescuer), the woman is now standing behind the man, and, after their
victory, he turns to face her, tries to say something, and then loses conscious-

ness, collapsing full-length into her arms for their initial embrace. Somewhat to our surprise, she easily bears his whole weight. Nature, as in comedies it must, has taken its course.

This sub-conclusion is built upon a kind of cinematic, or grammatical, joke. The cutting in this passage back and forth between the leopards emphasizes that we are never shown the leopards within the same frame. It thus acknowledges that while in this narrative fiction there are two leopards, in cinematic fact there is only one; one Baby with two natures; call them tame and wild, or call them latent and aroused. It is this knowledge, and acknowledgment, that brings a man in a trance of innocence to show his acquisition of consciousness by summoning the courage to let it collapse.

Common to some who like and some who dislike *Bringing Up Baby* is an idea that the film is some kind of farce. (It would be hard to deny that some concept of the farcical will be called upon in dealing with the humor in marriage.) But if the home of this concept of farce lies, say, in certain achievements of nineteenth-century French theater, then, as in other cases, this concept is undefined for film. I do not deny that such achievements are a source of such films, but this merely asks us to think what a source is and why and how and by what it is tapped. Nor would I put it past Howard Hawks, or those whose work he directed, to be alluding in their title to, even providing a Feydeauian translation of, Feydeau's *On purge Bebé*. This would solve nothing, but it might suggest the following line of questioning: Why, and how, and by what, is such a source tapped in this film since neither the treatment of dialogue nor of character nor of space nor of the themes of sexuality and marriage in *Bringing Up Baby* are what they are in Feydeau?

One line of response might undertake to show that this question encodes its own answer, that *Bringing Up Baby* is what it is precisely in negating Feydeauian treatments. This would presumably imply a negation or redemption of (this species of) farce itself, that is, an incorporation, or sublimation, of the bondage in marriage into a new romanticizing of marriage.—Would an implied criticism of society be smaller in the latter than in the former case? Not if one lodges one's criticisms of society irreducibly, if not exclusively, from within a demand for open happiness. Feydeauian comedy cedes this demand on behalf of its characters; Hawksian comedy, through its characters' struggles for consciousness, remembers that a society is crazy which cedes it, that the open pursuit of happiness is a standing test, or threat, to every social order. (Feydeau and Hawks are as distant conceptually as the Catholic and the Protestant interpretations of the institution of marriage, hence of the function of adultery.)

What is it about film that could allow the "negation" of theatrical "treatments"? Take the treatment of character, and film's natural tendency to give precedence to the actor over his or her character. This precedence is acknowledged in the capping repetition of the line—the curtain-line for each of the first two scenes—"I'll be with you in a minute, Mr Peabody." It scans and repeats like the refrain of a risqué London music hall ballad, of course to be sung by a woman. This contributes to an environment for our response to the *expertness* of the pair's walk-off through the revolving door of the restaurant. (That they are as on a stage is confirmed by the inset cut, in mid-walk, to a tracking shot past the astonished Mr. Peabody, who takes the place of an audience.) The authority of this exit, which calls for a bent hat held high in salute in the hand upstage, is manageable only by a human being with Cary Grant's experience and expertise in vaudeville.

As well as in its allusions to, and sources in, farce and vaudeville, this film insists upon the autonomy of its existence as film in its allusions to movies. When I took in Grant's line, in the jailhouse scene, "She's making all this up out of old motion pictures," I asked myself, Which ones? (There is a similar jail-house scene in John Ford's earlier *The Whole Town's Talking*.)* But of course one is invited further to ask oneself why, in so self-conscious a film, Hawks places this allusion as he does. It is a line that immediately confesses the nature of movies, or of a certain kind of movie making: the director of the movie is the one who is making all this up out of old motion pictures. (As Hitchcock will incorporate the conclusion of *Bringing Up Baby* into the conclusion of *North by Northwest*, where Grant's powerful hand and wrist save another woman from falling, and we see that the ledge he hauls her onto is his cavebed.) Or: a director makes a certain *kind* of movie; or: a director works within, or works to discover, a maze of kinships. Anyway *this* director does, demanding his inheritance. So Hepburn is characterized by Grant as having or standing for some directorial function. The implication is that the spectator is to work out his or her relation to (the director of) this film in terms of Grant's relation to Hepburn.—So, after all, criticism comes down to a matter of personal attachment! This is why we must

---

* Andrew Sarris provided this answer at the New York conference at which a version of this reading was presented. I have not seen the Ford film.

adopt some theoretical position toward film!—But I rather imagined that Grant's relation to Hepburn itself might provide a study in personal attachment. At any rate, a theory of criticism will be part of a theory of personal attachment (including a theory of one's attachment to theory, a certain trance in thinking).

I have thus, encouraged by this film, declared my willingness, or commitment, to go back over my reading of it, construed as my expressions of attachment to it. Reconsideration of attachments, and of disaffections, ought to be something meant by education, anyway by adult education, by bringing oneself up. Since for this film I am to proceed in terms proposed by Grant/David's relation to Hepburn/Susan, then before or beyond testing any given form in which I have so far expressed myself about the film, for its accuracy at once to what is there and to what I feel in what is there, I am to ask what I know and do not know about this relation, and what Grant knows and does not know about it. The principal form this question takes for him is, in essence: What am I doing here, that is, how have I got into this relation and why do I stay in it? It is a question all but continually on his mind. So I, as his spectator, am to learn to ask this question about my relation to this film. It will not be enough to say, for example, that I like it, for however necessary this confession may be, that feeling is not apt to sustain the amount of trouble the relation may require, or justify its taking me away from other interests and commitments in order to attend to it. Nor will it be enough to say that I do not like it, should that be required of me, for perhaps I am not very familiar with my likes and dislikes, having overcome them both too often.—If this is a good film, it ought to, if I let it, help teach me how to think about my relation to it.

Earlier, in registering the pace of this narrative as one in which a complete exposition is comically compressed into a stilted prologue, I described the hero as leaving to seek his fortune. His first name for this fortune is, conventionally enough, "a million dollars"; but the first thing he finds on his quest, the first of the nonaccidental accidents which punctuate quests, is a mix-up with an oddly isolated, athletic woman, suddenly appearing from the woods, who looks like a million dollars. (The camera's attraction to Katharine Hepburn's body—its interpretation of her physical sureness as intelligence self-possessed—is satisfied as fully in Cukor's comedies with her as in this of Hawks.) This hero's entanglements with this Artemis from the beginning, and throughout, threaten the award of his imagined fortune, both because she compromises him in the eyes of those who are to award it and because she herself seeks the same million. Yet when at the conclusion she confers it upon him, together with all other treasures, he seems unsatisfied. He gets the money, the lost bone, and the girl, yet he is not happy. What can he, do we think, be thinking of? Why is he still rigid; why is his monstrous erection still false? Do we think: He cannot accept these powers from her, as if these things are her dowry, for in accepting her right to confer them he must accept her authority, her fatherhood of herself? Or do we think: He still cannot think about money any more than he can (or because he cannot) think about sexuality? Or is it: The fate of sexuality and the fate of money are bound together; we will not be free for the one until we are free from the other? Perhaps we shall think, for Luther's reasons, or for Marx's, or Freud's, that money is excrement. I find that I think again, and I claim that such comedies invite us to think again, what it is Nietzsche sees when he speaks of our coming to doubt our right to happiness, to the pursuits of happiness. In the *Genealogy of Morals*, he draws a consequence of this repressed right as the construction of the ascetic ideal, our form of the thinker. He calls for us to have the courage of our sensuality, emblematized for him by Luther's wedding. For this priest to marry, the idea of marriage, as much as that of ordination, is brought into question. I do not say that the genre of remarriage thinks as deeply about the idea of marriage as does, say, the *Pagan Servitude of the Church*. Doubtless our public discourse is not as deep on these matters as it once was. I do say that a structure depicting people looking to remarry inevitably depicts people thinking about the idea of marriage. This is declared by a passage in each of these films in which one or both of the principals try a hand at an abstract theoretical formulation of their predicament. (Among the central members of our genre, *The Awful Truth* contains the most elaborated instance of this, with its concluding philosophical dialogue on sameness and difference, answering to its opening pronouncement about the necessity for faith in marriage.) It is why their conclusions have that special form of inconclusiveness I characterized as aphoristic. Nothing about our lives is more comic than the distance at which we think about them. As to unfinished business, the right to happiness, pictured as the legitimacy of marriage, is a topic that our nation wished to turn to as Hollywood learned to speak—as though our publicly declared right to pursue happiness was not self-evident after all.

About halfway through *Bringing Up Baby*, Grant/David provides himself with an explicit, if provisional, answer to the question how he got and why he stays in his relation with the woman, declaring to her that he will accept no more of her "suggestions" unless she holds a bright object in front of his eyes and twirls it. He is projecting upon her, blaming her for, his sense of entrancement. The conclusion of the film—Howard Hawks's twirling bright object—provides its hero with no better answer, but rather with a position from which to let the question go: in moving toward the closing embrace, he mumbles something like, "Oh my; oh dear; oh well," in other words, I am here, the relation is mine, what I make of it is now part of what I make of my life, I embrace it. But the conclusion of Hawks's object provides me, its spectator and subject, with a little something more, and less: with a declaration that if I am hypnotized by (his) film, rather than awakened, then I am the fool of an unfunny world, which is, and is not, a laughing and fascinating matter; and that the responsibility, either way, is mine.—I embrace it.

Bringing Up Baby

Gerald Mast

. . . *Bringing Up Baby* uses its two stars, Cary Grant and Katharine Hepburn, in what were, at the time, off-roles: Grant as the bumbling scientist, Hepburn as the bubbling nincompoop. Neither star felt comfortable with the role at first. But Hawks told Grant:

> You've seen Harold Lloyd in pictures haven't you? . . . Take his attitude— How he walks and how he moves, what he's doing, how he plays the scene.[1]

The reference to Lloyd (like his references to Chaplin) shows Hawks's awareness of the world of silent comedy and reveals that his own verbal comedy is deeply rooted in the physical and visual style of the silent comics. Even his dependence on highly communicative objects can be traced to those kinds of objects in that silent world. The parallel with Harold Lloyd also explains Grant's comic transformation of his star persona in the film, from the slick, suave, masculine charmer to the bumbling, bespectacled innocent. In *Monkey Business*, the silent comedy reference shifts from Lloyd to Laurel and Hardy—particularly in the scene in which husband and wife coolly, calmly, deliberately slop paint all over each other's bodies. For Hepburn, however, Hawks had other advice:

> We had a marvelous little guy on that picture. He was a great comedian for Ziegfeld—the fellow who played the sheriff, Walter Catlett. . . . One day I said to Katie, "For Christ's sake, can't I make it clear what I'm trying to tell you?" "I guess not, because I'm not getting it." . . . I said, "Go over and ask him how to do that scene." "Now I know what's wrong. Now I can do it." She told me, "You've got to keep that guy around." So I'd write scenes for him for about three weeks to keep him around. Hepburn was perfectly serious being completely zany. If she'd tried to be funny or cute, it wouldn't have been any good.[2]

From *Howard Hawks, Storyteller* (New York and London: Oxford University Press, 1982).

1. Howard Hawks, in an unpublished interview with Winston S. Sharples, July 27, 1977, in the papers of Howard Winchester Hawks, Harold B. Lee Library, Brigham Young University.
2. Howard Hawks, in an interview with Alex Ameripoor and Donald C. Willis, "Howard Hawks: An Interview," August 14, 1974, in Donald C. Willis, *The Films of Howard Hawks* (Metuchen, N.J.: Scarecrow Press, 1976).

The perfect seriousness of his actors' zaniness is one of the remarkable and essential qualities of *Bringing Up Baby* and the other major Hawks comedies.

That Hawks's characters are so seriously, so consistently, so perfectly "screwball" reveals his unique contribution to the "screwball comedy" genre and explains why he is, for many, its absolute master. In most of the major screwball comedies by other directors the leading character (particularly the leading *female* character) must at some point break down, reject her screwball attitudes, and expose them as a mask which covers her real, warm, and sincere feeling (Claudette Colbert in *It Happened One Night* and *The Palm Beach Story*, Irene Dunne in *The Awful Truth*, Jean Arthur in both *Mr. Deeds Goes to Town* and *Mr. Smith Goes to Washington*, Barbara Stanwyck in *Meet John Doe* and *The Lady Eve*). For Katharine Hepburn in *Bringing Up Baby*, being screwball is not a mask but an essence. She could no more reject her screwball manner than Geoff Carter could verbally ask Bonnie Lee to stay in *Only Angels Have Wings*. He expresses his feeling and maintains his psychological integrity by sharing a joke with her about coffee and a two-headed coin. Susan Vance-Hepburn expresses her feeling and maintains her psychological integrity by sharing her jokes and screwiness with another. Hawks himself wondered if he hadn't made *Bringing Up Baby* a bit too perfectly lunatic.[3] But that perfect lunacy redefines "normality" and remakes the world in its own image: the lunatic world itself becomes perfectly normal for those who are perfectly lunatic—more exciting, more vital, and more surprising than the "normal" world, with which these special people want nothing to do. The screwball character remakes the world according to her or his own law—precisely what Tony Camonte, Geoff Carter, Oscar Jaffe, and Walter Burns successfully accomplish in other Hawks films. This alternative private world for Hawks is always more exciting and more interesting than the normal public one where everyone else lives.

Hawks builds this alternative world of *Bringing Up Baby* by modifying the usual four parts of his construction to add a fifth that reaffirms the value of the separate, screwball world—a brief epilogue (or "tag") that returns the film visually and physically full circle to its beginning. . . . As the Chaplin films indicate, the circle is a particularly effective comic figure for sealing a special world off from the ordinary world surrounding it. Hawks's earlier comedy, *Twentieth Century*, also uses the epilogue to close a comic circle, enclosing the world of the theater upon itself, while the script of *His Girl Friday* originally devised such an enclosing epilogue which Hawks was able to eliminate by implying the circle's

3. See the interview with Peter Bogdanovich, in *Movie 5* (December 1962).

spiritual closing without its physical and visual return to the opening setting. With this five-act structure, the ending of these Hawks comedies is literally in their beginning (and literally parallel to Shakespeare's comic structure), whereas it is only figuratively so in the typical four-part construction of the noncomic films, which cannot separate themselves so perfectly from social reality. The reason for the perfect enclosure of Hawks's comic films is their exercising the traditional privilege comedies have enjoyed since Aristophanes: of rejecting all allegiance to normal, pragmatic social behavior.

As in *Only Angels Have Wings*, the careful narrative patterning of *Bringing Up Baby* emphasizes symmetries, and like *Only Angels, Bringing Up Baby* uses these symmetries to imbed a potentially improbable, wildly fanciful tale in the solid probabilities of narrative logic. There are two domesticated animals— Baby, the tame leopard, and George, the monster of a terrier. There are two leopards in Connecticut—Baby and the killer that escapes from the circus truck. There are two night scenes addressed to a second-story window of a proper suburban house—to Peabody's in Riverdale and to the psychiatrist's in Connecticut. There are two kinds of cages—the pen for Baby and the jail for humans, although the killer leopard will eventually be incarcerated in this human jail, while the humans and their domestic animals will use the cells not as cages but as places of refuge from the wild beast outside. Susan steals two cars—and the second one, belonging to the psychiatrist, she steals twice. Such patterning allows Hawks's narrative logic to refute the sheriff's sensible observation— everyone knows that there are no leopards in Connecticut—with the astounding yet probable revelation that there are in fact two.

This symmetrical patterning is accompanied by a temporal concentration that carefully alternates day and night sequences in perfect precision. The first section of the film, which establishes the essential conflict between the lives and values of scientist David Huxley and dizzy Susan Vance, uses a daytime sequence followed by a nighttime sequence. The second section, in which Susan carries David off to the Green World of Connecticut, occurs the next day. The third and fourth sequences recount the events of that night, first outdoors, then indoors. And the brief epilogue takes us back to the city, indoors, during the day. The only other Hawks comedy to use the same temporal compression of *Bringing Up Baby* and a similar succession of days and nights (other than *His Girl Friday*, in which there is a single, compressed day followed by night) is its companion film, *Monkey Business*, which almost exactly reverses the day-night succession of *Bringing Up Baby*.

The film's first section, establishing the clash between the scientific order of Dr. David Huxley and the vital disorder of Susan Vance, is itself a microcosm of the whole film's symmetry and balance. It divides nearly into two halves, day and night; and each of those halves divides into further halves, indoors and outdoors. The overwhelming impression of the indoor daytime scene, inside David Huxley's museum where his life is his work and his work his life, is of confined, calcified, and motionless deadness. Even the conventional establishing shots—a large, stolid, carefully framed brick building; a heavy metallic plaque, reading "Stuyvesant Museum of Natural History"—participate in this inert impression. The first indoor shot of the museum is filled with living things that have been petrified into dead things (which for Hawks means motionless things). There are statues of long-dead mammals and reptiles, glass cases filled with the inanimate parts of formerly whole moving animals, and the plaques of frozen, formerly swimming fish hang on the wall. A huge skeleton of a brontosaurus fills the center of the frame, another former living thing of beauty and power converted into a statue—a motionless artifact. The statuesque skeleton seems to press down and engulf the man who sits beneath it, frozen in the classic attitude of another statue—Rodin's *The Thinker* (for, after all, "Dr. Huxley is thinking"). Even the man has become a statue—motionless, inert.[4] And the platform, on which he sits and thinks, surrounds him with its metallic scaffolding, struts, and supports—a perfect visual cage.

Nothing lives in this room—quite ironic since its function is the study of forms of life. The room parallels that huge library in *Ball of Fire*, where the professors compile an encyclopedia that will contain the knowledge of all life in a room that contains no life—until Snow White invades this home of the seven experiential dwarfs. Dr. Huxley is himself under glass—behind those Harold Lloyd glasses. They will come off later in the film (just as they come off in *Monkey Business*). And Dr. Huxley is also imprisoned by his scientist's smock—tightly tied around his body. Similarly bound is his colleague Dr. La Touche, a shrivelled male whose lack of sexual vitality and identity is underscored by Huxley's mistakenly calling him Alice, the first name of his fiancée. That fiancée, Miss Swallow (Virginia Walker), is the ultimate sign of death in this room. Under glass, like Huxley and the exhibits in the display cases, tightly bound by her black clothing, the color of funerals and death, giving her a shape that parallels the constricted

---

4. For this reference to Rodin and for many other observations about the film's sexual puns and suggestions, I am indebted to Stanley Cavell's "Leopards in Connecticut," reprinted in this section.

rib cage of the brontosaurus itself, Alice Swallow is the ultimate attainment of a life yearning for death—like all the "life" in this room. Although the noun her name suggests is a delicate bird (not nearly as vital or powerful as a leopard or brontosaurus), even more significant is the verb it suggests—the devouring of another human being, just as Jonah was swallowed by that huge fish. For David Huxley, the brontosaurus seems destined to be his whale. As Swallow tells him, it will be their child, the product of their marriage, the result of their union.

But the scene also contains subtextual suggestions that Huxley knows something is missing from that room. His first utterance, as he stares at the fossilized bone he holds in his hand, is, "This one must belong in the tail." Although there is something very harmless about the surfaces of this line, the fact that "tail" is a familiar bit of sexual slang, that the bone sticks up into the frame in an erect position, and that Huxley grasps this erect bone firmly in his hand as he contemplates it, all suggest masturbation. . . . One might describe the whole narrative to follow as David's education about which bones go where.

Huxley is similarly disappointed when Swallow informs him there will be no honeymoon and that this skeleton will be their child. "You mean, no . . . ?" he begins to ask. No, their marriage will be based purely on their dedication to his work. There is also a hint of Huxley's discomfort in this house of death with his sudden use of slang, describing the impression he intends to make on Mr. Peabody, the lawyer who is supervising a gift to the museum of a million dollars. "I'll knock him for a loop." This use of slang also leads directly to *Ball of Fire*. Finally, there is a sense that David Huxley is himself painfully scattered and disordered in this room that is ordered to death. As he moves to its huge heavy door to make his exit, there is something both scattered and stuttering about his path and his movements—as opposed to the perfectly ordered lines and rectangles of the room. The remainder of the film will work on his subtextual potential for and delight in disorder.

With David Huxley and the brontosaurus Hawks has returned to his familiar concern with human vocation—this time in a comic and critical way. The vocation of David Huxley lacks life. Hawks's satiric disdain for the work of Professor Huxley (and for that of Professors Potts and Fulton in *Ball of Fire* and *Monkey Business*) may seem the typical cliché of Hollywood comic antagonism toward "absent-minded professor-types," an attitude of films that can be traced to the first decade of this century when professor-types were filled with both fear and trembling by the movies. The disdain, however, is also consistent with Hawks's preference for those occupations which put a person closest to life (which are also those which put one closest to death). The work of David Huxley, like his life as a whole (once again for Hawks, one's life is one's work), is too safe, too enclosed, too airless, too tidy. The irony that it is a work devoted to the study of life emphasizes that Huxley is a man who really knows nothing about what he claims to know (the psychiatrist in this film is another of those ignorant sages who presumes to know). In the remainder of the film David will discover what he does not know about life, and the series of madcap events to follow will be his new university.

The outdoor scene of the prologue's day sequence introduces us to the woman who will be the professor's professor. Out on the golf course, bathed in sunlight, surrounded by grass, sky, and trees, David Huxley encounters Susan Vance when she mistakes his golf ball for her own. The visual imagery, the quality of streaming light and shadow, and the evocations of the woman herself all contrast markedly with the strict rectangularity of objects, the stuffy evenness of light, and the restrictive clothing of the people in the previous indoor scene. Susan's hair is free and flowing, her dress white and loose (as opposed to Swallow's, which is black and binding), her walk spirited and sure—mirrored and transmitted by the traveling shot which moves with her in the active direction, from left to right, at her pace and in her rhythm, the typical Hawks method of conveying human spirit, power, and vitality. Susan's talk moves in the same rhythm, at the same pace, with the same energy and speed as her walk. This setting—visually, vocally, and spiritually—is Susan's world. Although she makes the mistake about the golf ball—and the later mistake when she takes David's car—she is the one who seems at ease and in harmony with her environment, while the bumbling David is obviously out of his milieu and his depth. Susan's naturalness in that visual setting is underscored by the shot in which she sinks a twenty-five-foot putt—in a very convincing Hawks long shot. There is no editing trickery here; she actually must sink a long putt in order for Hawks to film her sinking a putt—like filming airplanes in the air and cattle crossing a river.

David, however, plays the game indifferently, and he obtusely interferes with Mr. Peabody's concentration on golf by discussing the million-dollar grant. Peabody (George Irving) lectures the professor, "When I play golf, I only talk golf." There is also the clumsily comic repetitiveness of Huxley's refrain, diverted from his game with Peabody by Susan, "I'll be with you in a minute, Mr. Peabody," which, like many of the verbal assertions in the film (and Hawks in general), turns out to be the opposite of the truth. So does one of the final exchanges between Susan and David in this scene, after he angrily objects to her taking (and denting) his car. She retorts, "Your golf ball. Your car. Is there anything in the world that doesn't belong to you?" "Yes, thank Heaven," he answers, "you."

The night sequence of the prologue first moves back indoors, to a fancy restaurant where a top-hatted-and-tailed Huxley, meeting Peabody for an important dinner to discuss the grant, again makes a physical fool of himself. He clumsily drops his hat, then bumps heads with the hat-check girl when they both stoop to pick it up. The low-comic business again emphasizes both his social and spiritual clumsiness. His second meeting with Susan appropriately begins and ends with a pratfall (another perfect Hawks circle). As Susan plays the bizarre physical game of tossing olives into the air to catch with her mouth (conveying both her physical coordination and her spiritual eccentricity), she drops one of these olives on the floor—whereupon David slips on it and slides into the frame on his backside. "First you drop an olive, and then I sit on my hat. It fits perfectly."

A string of growing comic embarrassments will follow to make even more perfect sense. Susan will mistake another woman's handbag for her own (just as she mistook David's golf ball and car earlier). This mistake leads to the suspicion that David is a thief (he will be mistakenly suspected later of being both crazy and a Peeping Tom). She will rip the back seam of David's tailcoat (another possible reference to Harold Lloyd and his ripping clothes in *The Freshman*); this rip leads to one of Susan's many comic understatements that fails to fix herself as the cause of David's misery: "Oh, you tore your coat." But David gets even with her when he accidentally steps on the train of her gown, pulling it off without Susan's knowing it, and exposing her vented backside to the eyes of the world. David's series of spontaneous improvisations (covering her backside with his hat, pressing close to her with his entire body) attempts to protect her modesty and spare her embarrassment—the first time that David acts spontaneously and improvisationally in the film, and the beginning of his education which will teach him spontaneity and improvisation. The two of them, their bodies pressed together, make a sort of stage-exit from the elegant restaurant in perfect unison, two burlesque comics or tap dancers shuffling behind the music-hall's proscenium arch (like the exit of Laurel and Hardy, wearing the same huge pair of pants, in *Leave 'em Laughing*). The comic "stage-exit" will return at the end of *His Girl Friday* and *To Have and Have Not*.

Before her stage-exit, Susan discusses David with—appropriately enough—a psychiatrist she meets in the restaurant. The purse she mistakenly took belonged to his wife; she will later take the man's car (more symmetry). Twice. A brilliant piece of physical business deflates the doctor's pretentions to know (just as

Hawks deflated Dr. Huxley's), implying that his intellectual balloon is filled with hot air. As the psychiatrist (Fritz Feld) counsels Susan against referring to people as crazy, suggesting she realize that we all have our little oddities, he unconsciously squints his eyes and squeezes his mouth in a comic grimace of which he is totally unaware—unaware both that he is making the grimace and that it looks very silly. The psychiatrist, without knowing it, is an unwitting example of the very oddities he so calmly professes to understand. Ironically, Hawks himself feels similarly about unconscious human tics and the way they can make us all seem a little crazy.[5] But he puts this belief into the mouth of a man he finds ridiculous.

This ironic method also complicates the psychiatrist's explanation of David's relationship with Susan, which seems absurd on its surface but actually explains the underlying psychological basis of the love affair in this (and every other) Hawks film: "The love impulse in man very frequently expresses itself in terms of conflict." By putting this Freudian cliché into the mouth of a psychiatric clown, Hawks simultaneously ridicules the clown and his "science," establishes an essential piece of narrative and psychological information, and softens the blatancy of the information by making us suspect its declarer as a man who knows nothing, whom we know to be a fool. His psychiatric cliché turns out to be another of the film's verbal predictions which appears to be totally false but will prove to be perfectly true. In the same way, Susan keeps telling David, "Everything's gonna be all right," even when everything appears that it's not gonna be all right at all (for example, when Susan mistakenly clouts Peabody in the head with a rock). But, in another of the film's full-circle reversals, the verbal assertion that seems obviously false will turn out to be ironically true, just as their apparent conflict really is love (because it is potentially love from the beginning).

Susan must prove this potential to the man who is too blind to see it. When his glasses come off, he will see much better than he does. As in many amorous comedies, the hero's comic flaw in *Bringing Up Baby* (as in *Monkey Business*) is a defect in vision which the comic action will cure. The "blind" David has told Susan that he is going to be married the next day, at which point Hawks gives

5. In an interview with *Cahiers du Cinéma* 10, no. 56 (February 1956), translated into English in Andrew Sarris, ed., *Interviews with Film Directors* (New York: Avon Books, 1967), Hawks refers to his own nervous playing with his keychain (p. 237). He finds this mania both perfectly normal and quite idiosyncratic at the same time—depending upon how you look at the action. This consciousness of his playing with a material object implies how conscious that method is in his films.

Susan a very meaningful close-up—the very first close-up in a film that, as usual for Hawks, uses close-ups very sparingly. After pausing in this close-up to take in David's information with a slight catch of her breath, Susan's overt response is a tinkling laugh (she already sees more than he does). This verbal utterance of David's will also turn out other than as expected. David bids farewell to Susan for what he assumes will be the final time: "In moments of quiet I'm strangely drawn toward you. But there haven't been any quiet moments." After he makes this definitive farewell, he takes the pratfall out of the frame that closes the prologue. By the end of this prologue, the pratfall itself has become a comic physical symbol (like Chaplin's kicks in the pants)—the external sign of David's lack of knowledge and control. There will be more unquiet moments to come— for the quiet of Swallow is the quiet of death, and the noise of Susan is the noise of life, fun, and feeling.

The film's second section chronicles Susan's strategy to get David to her out- door world of spontaneous vitality, to get him to Connecticut, to do anything that comes into her head to keep David from being Swallowed on the morrow. The section begins with two phone calls for David—one from Swallow, the other from Susan. Hawks frequently relies on the telephone for significant narrative purposes: in *Scarface* with Angelo; in *His Girl Friday* as Hildy's link to the outside world in general and to Walter in particular; in *The Big Sleep* as part of Marlowe's and Vivian's strategies and counter-strategies; in *Monkey Business* as Edwina's appeals to Hank for help; and the radio in *Only Angels Have Wings* serves as its telephone. The perfect structural balance of these two phone calls not only establishes the two women as antagonists but, in effect, converts them into the two warring sides of David's own soul, the one luring him to a quiet hell that seems like heaven, the other to a spiritual heaven that seems like hell. Hawks intensifies the contrast of these "Good and Bad Angels" with contrasting visual imagery as each speaks on the phone: Swallow is pinched, cramped, and black; Susan free, flowing, and white.

Juxtaposed with each of these phone calls is a new arrival from the animal kingdom (further elegant patterning). While David talks to Swallow a package arrives containing the intercostal clavicle, the final bone needed to complete the brontosaurus. This dead reminder of David's vocation is also a reminder of Swal- low herself on the telephone. David will carry the bone with him to Connecticut, but he will lose it there. Susan's phone call is accompanied by the introduction of the tame leopard, Baby, a very much more living organism than that intercostal clavicle, which, in Susan's opinion, is "just an old bone." Baby becomes Susan's ally—and in Connecticut they find a third, another animal, the terrier George. These three musketeers manage to get rid of the bone and swallow Swallow. Susan first uses Baby to get David to her apartment, from which it is only a short step to Connecticut, claiming she needs his help since he is a zoologist and understands animals (an irony, since he most certainly does not). When David is incredulous, Susan takes a pratfall—and blames it on an attack by Baby. Hawks's camera drops to the floor with Susan, sympathizing with her energy and strategy, whereas in the opening shots of the film it stared upward at the distant David, disassociating itself from the man, his "thinking," and his world. David, the leopard tamer, then runs off to Susan's—taking his parallel pratfall first—carrying Swallow's bone with him.

When David meets Baby his initial response is fright. He climbs on a table to avoid the animal's advances, while Baby plays cunningly with his cuff. Late in the film David will use a chair to advance against and control a leopard, getting his chance to play leopard tamer after all. This Baby responds to a piece of music (as so many beings do in Hawks), "I Can't Give You Anything but Love, Baby," and he calmly and gracefully stalks toward the record player that utters his name and purrs in approval. There is an ambiguity about Baby's particular sex, which seems consistent for a film in which so many of the human characters are themselves sexually ambiguous. Although the pronoun "him" gets attached to the beast twice during the film, that diminutive "baby" is more frequently the slang term of endearment that a breezy or tough American male might reserve for his mate. Baby, who first appears in a frame beside Susan and almost seems to emanate from her, becomes the perfect sexual link between Susan and David, sharing the potential sexual characteristics of both or either.

Hawks's method of photographing the animal emphasizes it as such a link; he juxtaposes Baby and the humans in the frame as much as possible, leading to their visual interplay and physical coexistence within the same framed spaces. When Hawks later introduces the terrier George, he will photograph him in the same way—sharing the frame with the humans rather than separated from them by the use of editing. Hawks's composition of the ride in the car to Connecticut, which puts David, Baby, and Susan into an isosceles triangle . . . , is precisely mirrored by his composition at the supper table in Connecticut when Susan, George, and David sit in an identical isosceles triangle. Only in the nighttime sequences with Major Applegate (Charlie Ruggles) will Hawks resort to editing separate shots of the people and the leopard. Whether this other photographic method is intentional (implying that Applegate and the animal cannot share the same emotional space) or unintentional (either the leopard or Ruggles declined the other's company), these edited shots of the animals are far less effective than those which keep the beasts and the people in the same space.

The reason is not simply our belief in the authenticity of shared cinema space as opposed to our suspicion of trickery with montage—a point developed by André Bazin.[6] Shared cinema space in narrative cinema can be used to imply shared emotional space, a spiritual conversation between the beings enclosed by that framed boundary, a sharing which transmits itself not by explicit words but by the evocations of physical proximity. Such subtextual communication and implication is especially important to a director like Hawks who pushes so much of the film's thought and feeling below the surface of words. In *Bringing Up Baby*, people do attempt to converse with the animals who share those spaces—the song David and Susan sing to Baby is one familiar kind of Hawksian conversation. Later in the film, both Susan and David attempt to converse verbally with George; George and the humans talk at cross-purposes, however, as characters inevitably do in such comedies, for his shrill, irritating barks are his sole response to their articulate questions—barks that frequently invade the visual space from off-frame and drown out the human utterances altogether. By implication, these people are not only seeking a conversation with the animals who share the frame but also with the animal within themselves, particularly David's coming to know and express the Susan-Baby-George (as opposed to the Swallow-Bone-Brontosaurus) in himself. Baby, its name implying both conjugal life and conjugal love, must be brought up and brought out in David in order for him to be a whole, live, human animal.

Susan sends Baby to fetch David when he attempts to leave her apartment and go to Swallow. As David walks in the frame, holding the box with the bone under his right arm, Baby walks casually alongside him without his knowing it—a comic visual metaphor for his solid confidence in that dead bone and his conscious ignorance of the Baby in him. When he notices that Baby will not desert him, he knows that he has no choice but to go to Connecticut. When he gets there, the bone will come out of the box—as it lies on top of a bed—and be buried in the earth by the animal accomplice, George. David himself will be called "Mr. Bone" as a pseudonym, a name that is consistent with the film's clever verbal and visual sexual puns—for bone needs only an *r* to become a

6. Bazin articulates this point in his essay, "The Virtues and Limitations of Montage," in *What Is Cinema?* Vol. I (Berkeley and Los Angeles: University of California Press, 1967), pp. 41–52

familiar term of sexual slang, and the bone David held at the beginning of the film looked as if it had an *r*, and Applegate later makes the mistake of adding a letter, a *y* not an *r*, to the name of Bone.

The trip to Connecticut is another series of low-comic embarrassments and disasters, all of which are necessary elements of David's education about Baby and the bone. Most of the embarrassment arises from the fact that Baby, like all animals, must eat—and his healthy appetite contrasts markedly with the inability of humans to consume their supper in a later dinner scene. Baby helps himself to breakfast when Susan's car rams a poultry truck (the second time she rams another car), sending its occupants onto the road and into Baby's gullet. Hawks, of course, does not show Baby devouring any of these creatures—including two swans—since it would decrease our sympathy for him, just as viewing Tony's murders directly would do the same in *Scarface*. We merely watch and hear a befeathered David . . . total the contents of Baby's meal. Then David suffers the embarrassment of buying Baby thirty pounds of steak from the butcher in a small Connecticut town. When asked how he's going to cook it, David replies, "It's going to be eaten raw." "Do you grind this up before you eat it?" David answers, "This isn't for me. It's for Baby." The butcher and his customers, who share Hawks's frame with David, find him a very strange daddy. Meanwhile, Baby has leapt from Susan's car to another, like Susan preferring another's car to its own; so Susan takes a second car that is not her own, to avoid arrest. The small-town constable, Slocum (Walter Catlett), who is introduced in this scene, will get the chance to arrest her later. And she will escape that arrest as she does this one—by stealing this very car.

In Connecticut, Susan continues David's education by stripping him of his clothes. Having nothing else to wear, David grabs the first thing hanging in the bathroom—and Hawks uses David's shadow on the wall effectively to build suspense about what exactly he might be doing. When he emerges from the bathroom, he is wearing a woman's white, sheer, and fluffy negligee—exactly the kind of loose and free clothing the film has identified with Susan. David, disguised in Susan's clothes, unknowingly reveals a truth about himself; he has the potential to be a free and vital Susan. The false clothes reveal his true soul's apparel. His putting on those clothes has been a piece of spontaneous improvisation; from this moment forward, his life becomes a series of spontaneous improvisations. For in this embarrassing physical disguise (Cary Grant's first female impersonation in a Hawks film), he meets Susan's aunt, Mrs. Carleton Random (May Robson), the woman who intends to donate the million dollars to David's work. They talk at cross-purposes, for this is Mrs. Random's house (which David does not know), while he is a stranger wearing very strange clothes (and what is he doing in her house and in those clothes?). During this uninformative verbal interchange, Hawks and Grant underscore David's frustration with a spontaneously improvised line that seems so startling for 1938 today's audience might actually wonder if it really heard what it thinks it heard. "But why are you wearing these clothes?" Mrs. Random asks. David answers, as he leaps madly and devilishly in the air, "Because I just went gay all of a sudden!" The response, like his disguise, not only relates to the film's central issues of sexual fertility and exuberant improvisation; it is a reminder that certain seemingly contemporary terms have a long tradition (particularly among showpeople). Hawks could probably get this word past the censors because either they did not hear it or could not understand its sexual connotations.

The second section ends when David gets a new (but no less comic) suit of clothes—a ridiculously inappropriate and very binding riding habit. To get this at least masculine outfit, he has had to improvise again, convincing both Mrs. Random and her servant, Mrs. Gogarty, that he is a lunatic who will do something violent without it. Now David must use a disguised name in conversing with the woman who intends to give Dr. Huxley a million dollars, because, as Susan points out in another of those ridiculous understatements which exclude her contribution: "Oh, David, I'm afraid you've made a rather unfavorable impression on Aunt Elizabeth." Meanwhile, Susan has seen David without his glasses for the first time (when the clothes come off, the glasses do too), and likes what she sees. David not only looks better without his eyeglasses; there is a sense in which he sees better too. It is the same sense in which he is more alive, more truly his potential self, in Susan's clothes than in his own. George, who is far less polite than the supposedly wild leopard and whose yapping presence entered the house with the yapping Mrs. Random, has buried the "old bone," the reminder of David's former unspontaneous self. So Susan and David must follow George everywhere, playing with him, conversing with him, hoping he will lead them to the spot where he buried the thing. "Isn't this fun, David? Just like a game." Once Susan has transported David to her outdoor world, she can reintroduce him to the playful fun of childhood—the spontaneously energetic play that is so missing from his stiff and stilted adulthood.

The childish fun continues in the film's third section, that night, which takes the characters outdoors again—away from the proper, civilized dinner party and into the magical forest. Not coincidentally, the month is June (as Mrs. Random pointedly informs Horace), and the night may even be midsummer eve. In this section we meet the film's final character, Major Applegate, another sexless, lifeless, nonanimal bumbler and stutterer—the typical Ruggles persona. Applegate is so bumblingly ignorant of his own sexual identity that he later tells the constable, when asked who he is: "I'm the niece, er, I'm the aunt, er, I'm Major Horace Applegate." Applegate is also ignorant of animals, though he claims to be a big-game hunter, as ignorant of animal life as the zoologist David. He smugly and falsely identifies the leopard's cry as that of a loon, and then pedantically tells Mrs. Random, "That was a loon, Elizabeth. Loon. *L*, double *o*, *n*." For Applegate, animals are a matter of letters not of life, just as for David they are matters of skeletal frames, not of whole living, moving bodies. Applegate, like David's older colleague, La Touche, at the museum, is a visual reminder of where David's sexless, animal-less life with Swallow might lead.

Once outdoors, Susan and David have two apparent goals—recapturing Baby, whom a drunken servant, Gogarty (Barry Fitzgerald), has mistakenly let out of its cage; and following George so they can recapture the intercostal clavicle. Hawks is still using these two opposite suggestions of animal life in perfect balance. But beneath these apparent goals is the underlying spiritual union of Susan and David—spending this magical night of childish fun and games, and mistakes, and pratfalls, together. Susan and David are playing together—just as Baby and George play with one another in the sequence. Among the playful pranks is Susan's opening a cage to let a second leopard on the loose—this one a vicious killer on his way to the gas chamber. Like the people, even leopards wear disguises in this film. When Susan ducks beneath the branches that David inadvertently pushes in her face, he reprimands her, "Susan, this is no time to be playing squat-tag," another reference to a childhood game.

They take pratfalls down ravines, into a river, over the trunks of trees. As opposed to the earlier pratfalls, whose comic clumsiness mirrored the social discomfort and the spiritual blindness of the man who took the pratfalls, these spills, which the two of them take together, fit into their night of playful fun. So does Susan's hippity-hoppity walk, when she breaks the heel of a shoe, or her netting David's head, a comic image of capture, in the spill that separates him permanently from his glasses. When Susan confesses, "I do so like being with you," David is still unconquered; "You do? Well, I like peace and quiet." David's rejection produces Susan's most tearful moment (another childish ploy reminiscent of Stan Laurel), "After all the fun we had." Then Hawks snaps her tearful tenderness with a low-comic gag (a typical Chaplin touch) as Susan takes a pratfall over a tree branch and out of the frame (the film's second pratfall out of the frame). When David lifts her from this fall, the two share their ultimate emotional union with an almost kiss. They will not separate emotionally again.

Hawks celebrates this emotional union with a musical moment of spiritual communion; but this familiar use of music in Hawks fits uniquely into this film's playful ironies. Baby has gotten himself on the roof of a house—the one belonging to the psychiatrist—so Susan and David must improvise together to lure him off it. For the second time, they hold a nighttime conversation with a house. Baby's favorite song, "I Can't Give You Anything but Love," will be their text; Susan and David, holding George in his arms, begin their spontaneous serenade. After the first few bars, George joins in, followed shortly by Baby himself. The result is a very strange rendition of the song in close harmony—in fact, a Barber Shop Quartet arrangement for four voices, two human and two animal. (Hawks may be doing McCarey's duet for Cary Grant and the terrier, Mr. Smith, in *The Awful Truth* two better.) In this synthesis of song and "speech," human and animal, wild and tame, adult action and childhood game, the film reaches its ultimate spiritual synthesis and harmony as well.

But that discovery and its acceptance by David must be demonstrated in action and by action; the film's fourth section gives him the opportunity to demonstrate his new spiritual union with Susan rather than the old and dead one with Swallow (who returns to the film in this section). Because Susan appears to be crazy (singing to a leopard on a roof in Connecticut in the middle of the night!) and David appears to be a Peeping Tom, the constable and the psychiatrist take both of these suspicious persons to jail. All of the film's characters will eventually get to this jail and into its cells—Susan, David, the battling Gogarty, Mrs. Random and the flustered Applegate, Baby, George, the killer leopard, Peabody, Swallow, Slocum, the psychiatrist, even the two men transporting the killer leopard to the zoo (only Mrs. Gogarty remains at home to answer the telephone). Farce comedies typically end with this gathering of all the personages; the one way to eliminate the ignorance (the disguises, mistaken identities, and talking at cross-purposes) on which farce depends is to bring all the characters face to face to remove the disguises and reveal the mistakes. In indoor farces (like Jonson's *The Alchemist* or Feydeau's *A Flea in Her Ear*), this gathering is usually achieved by opening all the doors, bringing the characters out of the little cells where they have been confined, kept ignorant by their confinement, so they can all see one another. *Bringing Up Baby* ironically achieves this dispelling of ignorance by putting them back inside the separate cells—but because these cells permit their inhabitants to see beyond them, the cells both confine and illumine.

This visual and narrative use of the cells in the fourth section continues the film's paradoxical use of the cage motif—Susan's desire to get David out of one kind of cage (the glass display case for dead things) and into another (the cage for wild living animals). The fourth section also sustains the paradox by making it unclear whether the characters would prefer to get in or out of these cages, depending on whether the cage is perceived as a prison or a refuge. Susan gets out of her cage by improvising, pretending that she is a gangster's moll, that they are all members of "the Leopard Gang." She transforms herself into "Swingin'-Door Susie," and her exit from the cell, as she rides its swinging door, is a moment of both childish play and adult grace, another Hawks equation of life and motion. In one of those moments of self-reference in a Hawks film, David warns Slocum, "She's making all this up out of motion pictures." (Like, for example, *The Awful Truth*, in which his "sister" calls him "Jerry the Nipper." But then Susan's "society moniker," Vance, also comes from that film.) But David himself refers to movies when he names his associates as "Mickey-the-Mouse and Donald-the-Duck." Susan may also refer specifically to *Scarface* when she sniffs one of Slocum's cigars (just as Tony Camonte sniffed Johnny Lovo's cigars) and pronounces it a "two-fer"—"two fer a nickel." The male-like female that Susan impersonates in this scene parallels the female-like male that David impersonated earlier when wearing Susan's negligee, contributing to the film's collapse of apparent opposites—human life and animal life, adulthood and childhood, freedom and confinement, male and female, surfaces and essences.

After Susan's escape, David remains in the jailhouse for his own improvisations with the first leopard, Baby, whom he now approaches with familiarity and pets with fondness (as opposed to his initial fright and reticence in facing this beast). Then Susan returns to the jailhouse, dragging the killer leopard behind her at the end of a rope. Hawks again shows narrative cunning by deliberately omitting the scenes which show precisely how she snares this beast. Susan tells the recalcitrant leopard, "I'm just as determined as you are," . . . and she is just as determined with this leopard as she has been with David. David then takes over, improvising again, playing Susan's heroic animal tamer, spontaneously addressing the leopard with a chair (another form of human-animal conversation) and prodding him into an empty cell (even the fellow animals, George and Baby, have fled into a cell with the humans to escape this vicious beast). After David's moment of masculine assertion he faints dead away in Susan's arms. Caught and captured.

The fifth section, the film's brief epilogue, returns us to David's museum during the daylight. The black-clad Swallow dismisses David as a potential mate with more animal imagery, "You're just a butterfly." David has again seemingly returned to the calcified pose of Rodin's *Thinker* (and that pose precisely parallels the attitude of the dinosaur statue that sits in the frame beside him, whereas the living Baby previously had accompanied David without his knowing it). Just as David seems doomed to the world of puzzlement and death where he began, a black (but loosely) clad Susan enters that world (her dress perhaps a sign of deference to that world). Susan has both the million dollars for David and the intercostal clavicle. (See, everything *is* gonna be all right.) With Susan's entrance, a living force invades that mausoleum; David himself springs to life and into motion, spontaneously scampering up the scaffolding behind the huge brontosaurus. He puts that skeleton between Susan and himself, using its size, its age, and its deadness to protect him.

But to no avail. Susan improvises too—by scampering up the ladder on the other side of the brontosaurus. As they speak Susan begins to sway on that ladder. Her sway is the one way to bring motion (*i.e.,* life) to that room of motionless dead matter, which she fills with her vitality. The rhythm of her motion seems to elicit David's vitality as well, for he begins to sway with her, confessing that he just spent the best day of his life; he's never had so much fun (that all-important word of vitality for Hawks and this film). That immense edifice of deadness that separates them must come tumbling down, and down the brontosaurus comes when Susan starts to fall off her ladder and David must take some immediate spontaneous heroic action to save her. He grabs her arm as she dangles in midair, and the visual image to which their bodies refer is not a frozen Rodin sculpture but that familiar synthesis of human and animal life in the movies and American popular culture: he Tarzan, she Jane. As this Tarzan pulls his Jane to safety, he pulls her into the visual cage of his scaffolding, the exact same cage where he began the film alone, grasping his bone. Now, with the closing of another perfect Hawks circle, he will be caged with another—a living human-animal being, not an "old bone."

Bringing Up Baby translates the Evolution of Trust that underlies an adventure film like *Only Angels Have Wings* into comic terms—the evolution and expression of the calcified character's energy, vitality, and spontaneity. David Huxley discovers the value of living limbs (like the arm of Susan Vance that he pulls into his cage) rather than dead bones. This spiritual evolution, in the film's comic view, is every bit as vital to the human species as that Darwinian evolution which has guided the progress of biological life from the Age of the Brontosaurus to the Age of Tarzan. The film's breathless, breakneck pace reinforces and propels its comic evolution, for the driving rhythm of its talk and action is Susan-Hepburn's rhythm, with which David-Grant must keep pace if he wants to stay in the movie—just as he must keep up with her on the golf course if he wants to stay in Hawks's moving frame. While the pace of the opening scene in David's museum is slow and lumbering—in both speech and motion—once Susan strides across the fairway in the second scene the film hitches itself to her walk and talk—and David must grab hold to stay aboard. He can only do so by matching her instantaneous and spontaneous surprises with surprising improvisations of his own. His ability to improvise so quickly is both a sign of his underlying ability to improvise and of his successful development of that necessary talent.

Like so many "screwball comedies" (and so many romantic comedies from Plautus to Shaw) the underlying issues of *Bringing Up Baby* are human wholeness, spiritual vitality, and sexual energy. Unlike so many other "screwball comedies," however, the characters in *Bringing Up Baby* achieve that wholeness not in spite of their screwiness but because of it; to be screwball is itself to be exuberantly alive. Hawks anchors this screwball sequence of potentially wild impossibility (how do you get a leopard on a roof in Connecticut so you can sing, "I Can't Give You Anything but Love"?) in the perfectly probable logic of his carefully patterned, symmetrical fictional construction. The film's consistent verbal and visual motifs (animals, cages, bones), its pratfalls, its breathless pace complexly underscore its essential thematic issues—human spontaneity, animal vitality, sexual fertility, childhood fun. Like *A Midsummer Night's Dream*, the film's wildly fanciful and farcical action is the means to improve the amorous vision of its young lovers, so they can achieve a harmony both with nature and with themselves. . . .

Filmography and
Bibliography

Hawks Filmography, 1926–1970

This filmography lists only those finished films that Hawks directed or co-directed and on which his directorial contribution was either credited or publicly acknowledged. Hawks produced most of the films he directed, especially in the sound period, and he produced two films he did not direct: *Corvette K-225* (1943, directed by Richard Rossen) and *The Thing* (1951, directed by Christian Nyby). As producer of his films, Hawks exerted considerable control over the writing of his scripts, even if that contribution were uncredited. Indeed, credited attributions for screenwriting were determined by the Screen Writer's Guild, often on the basis of contractual agreements rather than actual contributions. The filmography below lists only credited screenwriters for each project, although many other writers, Hawks included, contributed to these screenplays.

1926   *The Road to Glory*
Screenplay by L. G. Rigby

Fig Leaves
Screenplay by Hope Loring and Louis D. Lighton

1927   *The Cradle Snatchers*
Screenplay by Sarah Y. Mason, based on a play by Russell Medcraft and Norma Mitchell

Paid to Love
Screenplay by William M. Counselman, Seton I. Miller, and Benjamin Glazer, based on a story by Harry Carr

1928   *A Girl in Every Port*
Screenplay by Seton I. Miller, Reginald Morris, and William Tommel

Fazil
Screenplay by Seton I. Miller and
    Philip Klein, based on a play by
    Pierre Frondaie

The Air Circus (directed with Lewis B.
    Seiler)
Screenplay by Seton I. Miller and
    Norman Z. McLeod, dialogue by
    Hugh Herbert

1929   *Trent's Last Case*
Screenplay by Scott Darling and
    Beulah Marie Dix, based on a
    novel by E. C. Bentley

1930   *The Dawn Patrol*
Screenplay by Hawks, Seton I.
    Miller, and Dan Totheroh, based
    on "The Flight Commander," by
    John Monk Saunders

1930–32   *Scarface*
Screenplay by Ben Hecht, Seton I.
    Miller, John Lee Mahin, and Wil-
    liam R. Burnett, based on "Scar-
    face," by Armitage Trail

1931   *The Criminal Code*
Screenplay by Seton I. Miller and
    Fred Niblo, Jr., based on a play
    by Martin Flavin

1932   *The Crowd Roars*
Screenplay by Hawks, Seton I.
    Miller, Kubec Glassman, John
    Bright, and Niven Busch

Tiger Shark
Screenplay by Wells Root, based on
    "Tuna," by Houston Branch

1933   *Today We Live*
Screenplay by Edith Fitzgerald,
    Dwight Taylor, and William
    Faulkner, based on "Turn About,"
    by William Faulkner

1934   *Viva Villa!* (directed with Jack
    Conway)
Screenplay by Hawks and Ben Hecht,
    based on a book by Edgcumb Pin-
    chon and O. B. Stade

Twentieth Century
Screenplay by Ben Hecht and Charles
    MacArthur, from their play,
    adapted from "Napoleon of
    Broadway," by Charles Bruce
    Mulholland

1935   *Barbary Coast*
Screenplay by Ben Hecht, Charles
    MacArthur, and Edward Chodorov

Ceiling Zero
Screenplay by Frank Wead, based on
    his play

1936   *The Road to Glory*
Screenplay by Joel Sayre and William
    Faulkner, based on a film, *Le Crois
    de bois*

Come and Get It (directed with
    William Wyler)
Screenplay by Jules Furthman, Jane
    Murfin, and Robert Wyler, based
    on a novel by Edna Ferber

1938   *Bringing Up Baby*
Screenplay by Dudley Nichols and
    Hagar Wilde, based on a story by
    Hagar Wilde

1939   *Only Angels Have Wings*
Screenplay by Hawks and Jules
  Furthman

1940   *His Girl Friday*
Screenplay by Charles Lederer, based
  on the play "The Front Page," by
  Ben Hecht and Charles MacArthur

1941   *The Outlaw* (directed with
  Howard Hughes)
Screenplay by Jules Furthman

Sergeant York
Screenplay by Abel Finkel, Harry
  Chandler, Howard Koch, and John
  Huston, based on *The War Diary
  of Sergeant York,* edited by Sam
  Cowan; *Sergeant York and His
  People,* by Sam Cowan; and *Ser-
  geant York, Last of the Long Hunt-
  ers,* by Tom Skeyhill

Ball of Fire
Screenplay by Billy Wilder and
  Charles Brackett, based on "From
  A to Z," by Billy Wilder and
  Thomas Monroe

1943   *Air Force*
Screenplay by Dudley Nichols

1944   *To Have and Have Not*
Screenplay by Jules Furthman and
  William Faulkner, based on a novel
  by Ernest Hemingway

1946   *The Big Sleep*
Screenplay by William Faulkner,
  Leigh Brackett, and Jules Furth-
  man, based on a novel by Raymond
  Chandler

1948   *Red River*
Screenplay by Borden Chase and
  Charles Schnee, based on "The
  Chisholm Trail," by Borden Chase

A Song Is Born
Screenplay by Harry Tugend, based
  on a film, *Ball of Fire*

1949   *I Was a Male War Bride*
Screenplay by Charles Lederer, Leon-
  ard Spigelgass, and Hagar Wilde,
  based on a novel by Henri Rochard

1952   *The Big Sky*
Screenplay by Dudley Nichols, based
  on a novel by A. B. Guthrie, Jr.

O'Henry's Full House—"The Ransom of Red Chief" episode
Screenplay by Nunnally Johnson,
  based on a story by O. Henry.

Monkey Business
Screenplay by Ben Hecht, I.A.L.
  Diamond, and Charles Lederer,
  based on a story by Harry Segall

1953   *Gentlemen Prefer Blondes*
Screenplay by Charles Lederer, based
  on a musical comedy by Anita
  Loos and Joseph Stein

1955   *Land of the Pharaohs*
Screenplay by William Faulkner,
  Harry Kurnitz, and Harold Jack
  Bloom

1959   *Rio Bravo*
Screenplay by Jules Furthman and
  Leigh Brackett, based on a story by
  B. H. Campbell

1962   *Hatari!*
Screenplay by Harry Kurnitz and
  Leigh Brackett

1964   *Man's Favorite Sport?*
Screenplay by John Fenton Murray
  and Steve McNeil, based on "The
  Girl Who Almost Got Away," by
  Pat Frank

1965   *Red Line 7000*
Screenplay by Hawks and George
  Kirgo

1967   *El Dorado*
Screenplay by Leigh Brackett, based
  on *The Stars in Their Courses,* by
  Harry Brown

1970   *Rio Lobo*
Screenplay by Leigh Brackett and
  Burton Wohl, based on a story by
  Burton Wohl

Selected
Bibliography

Belton, John. *The Hollywood Profes-sionals.* Vol. 3. New York: A. S. Barnes, 1974.

———. "Hawks and Co." In *Focus on Howard Hawks,* ed. Joseph McBride. Englewood Cliffs, N.J.: Prentice-Hall, 1972.

Bogdanovich, Peter. *The Cinema of Howard Hawks.* New York: Museum of Modern Art, 1962.

Branson, Clark. *Howard Hawks: A Jungian Study.* Foreword by Judith Harte, Ph.D. Santa Barbara, Calif.: Capra Press, 1987.

Britton, Andrew. *Katharine Hepburn: The Thirties and After.* Newcastle-upon-Tyne: Tyneside Cinema, 1984.

———. *Cary Grant: Comedy and Male Desire.* Newcastle-upon-Tyne: Tyneside Cinema, 1983.

Cavell, Stanley. *Pursuits of Happiness: The Hollywood Comedy of Remarriage.* Cambridge, Mass.: Harvard University Press, 1981.

Durgnat, Raymond. "Durgnat vs. Paul: Last Round in the Great Hawks Debate." *Film Comment* 14, no. 2 (March–April 1978).

———. "Hawks Isn't Good Enough." *Film Comment* 13, no. 3 (July–August 1977).

Dyer, Peter John. "Sling the Lamps Low." In *Focus on Howard Hawks,* ed. McBride.

Farber, Manny. "Howard Hawks." In *Focus on Howard Hawks,* ed. McBride.

Giannetti, Louis. "Howard Hawks." In *Masters of the American Cinema.* Englewood Cliffs, N.J.: Prentice-Hall, 1981.

Haskell, Molly. "Howard Hawks: Masculine Feminine." *Film Comment* 10, no. 2 (March–April 1974).

Jewell, Richard B. "How Howard Hawks Brought Baby Up." *Journal of Popular Film and Television* 11, no. 4 (Winter 1984).

Langlois, Henri. "The Modernity of Howard Hawks." In *Focus on Howard Hawks,* ed. McBride.

McBride, Joseph. "Introduction." In *Focus on Howard Hawks,* ed. McBride.

————. "Hawks." *Film Comment* 14, no. 2 (March–April 1978).

————, ed. *Hawks on Hawks.* Berkeley and Los Angeles: University of California Press, 1982.

Mast, Gerald. "Howard Hawks." In *The Comic Mind: Comedy and the Movies.* Rev. ed. Chicago: University of Chicago Press, 1979.

————. *Howard Hawks, Storyteller.* New York and London: Oxford University Press, 1982.

Obituary. *The New York Times,* 28 December 1977.

Paul, William. "Paul vs. Durgnat." *Film Comment* 14, no. 1 (January-February 1978).

Perkins, V. F. "Comedies." *Movie* 5 (December 1962).

Poague, Leland. *Howard Hawks.* Boston: G. K. Hall, 1982.

Rivette, Jacques. "The Genius of Howard Hawks." In *Focus on Howard Hawks,* ed. McBride.

Sarris, Andrew. "The World of Howard Hawks." In *Focus on Howard Hawks,* ed. McBride.

Willis, Donald C. *The Films of Howard Hawks.* Metuchen, N.J.: Scarecrow Press, 1976.

Wise, Naomi. "The Hawksian Woman." *Take One* 3, no. 3 (January–February 1971).

Wollen, Peter. "The Auteur Theory." In *Film Theory and Criticism: Introductory Readings,* ed. Gerald Mast and Marshall Cohen. 3rd ed. New York: Oxford University Press, 1985.

Wood, Robin. *Howard Hawks.* Rev. ed. New York: Praeger, 1982.

————. "Who the Hell Is Howard Hawks?" *Focus* 1 and 2 (1967).

————. "Responsibilities of the Gay Film Critic." *Film Comment* 14, no. 1 (January–February 1978).

9 780813 513416